D0860572

WHY THE U.S. MEN WILL NEVER WIN THE WORLD CUP

WHY THE U.S. MEN WILL NEVER WIN THE WORLD CUP

A Historical and Cultural Reality Check

Beau Dure

ROWMAN & LITTLEFIELD
Lanham • Boulder • New York • London

Published by Rowman & Littlefield
An imprint of The Rowman & Littlefield Publishing Group, Inc.
4501 Forbes Boulevard, Suite 200, Lanham, Maryland 20706
www.rowman.com

6 Tinworth Street, London SE11 5AL

British Library Cataloguing in Publication Information Available

Library of Congress Cataloging-in-Publication Data

Names: Dure, Beau, author.
Title: Why the U.S. men will never win the World Cup : a historical and cultural reality check / Beau Dure.
Description: Lanham : Rowman & Littlefield, [2019] | Includes bibliographical references and index. | Summary: "In this book, soccer journalist and historian Beau Dure traces the many issues holding back the U.S. men's soccer team, from failed leagues to the unique American sports culture. Yet, Dure argues that with the right long-term changes, the U.S. can build a soccer environment that spawns quality players and strong results on the national stage"— Provided by publisher.
Identifiers: LCCN 2019011042 (print) | LCCN 2019022218 (ebook) | ISBN 9781538127810 (cloth : alk. paper)
Subjects: LCSH: Soccer—United States—History. | Soccer—Social aspects—United States. | World Cup (Soccer) | Social structure—United States.
Classification: LCC GV944.U5 .D88 2019 (print) | LCC GV944.U5 (ebook) | DDC 796.3340973—dc23
LC record available at https://lccn.loc.gov/2019011042
LC ebook record available at https://lccn.loc.gov/2019022218

CONTENTS

ACKNOWLEDGMENTS

Or perhaps that should be "apologies."

I've met a lot of wonderful people through soccer. Hall of Fame soccer players have been generous with their time and put up with my stupid questions. Fans and fellow journalists have been like family. A dysfunctional family that fights over some of the silliest things, but a family nonetheless. They might not like hearing that the U.S. men are doomed to futility.

Perhaps they don't want to be named in this. Well, tough. This book is half reality check, half kick in the backside. If we want the U.S. men to be World Cup contenders, we can't keep pretending things are anything different than they are. A lot of these people realize that. I hope they enjoy this book.

So anyway—thanks to the people who have given me a chance to write over the nine years since I left *USA TODAY* to be a freelancer. That would include Tom Lutz (the *Guardian*), Mike Woitalla and Paul Kennedy (*Soccer America*), Jeff Kassouf (*FourFourTwo*), Chris Hummer (*SoccerWire*), Nate Wilcox (*Bloody Elbow*), and many more.

Thanks to the Society for American Soccer History and the many great historians of the game—Roger Allaway, David Litterer, Steve Holroyd, David Kilpatrick, Tom McCabe, Colin Jose, Jack Huckel, and David Wangerin, the last of whom is sorely missed.

Thanks to my fellow youth coaches and referees. I have to single out John Whelpley, who has served in the thankless job of age group commissioner and has always done his best to find players to make my teams competitive. I should've fired myself years ago.

Thanks to the folks at BigSoccer for pushing me into taking up refereeing, and thanks to Vienna Family Medicine for getting my Achilles back in shape after I overdid it.

Thanks to the wonderful staff at Starbucks for providing a nice place to work.

Thanks to Pearl drums, Vic Firth drum sticks, and Sabian cymbals for the stress relief.

Thanks to Rush, Metric, Angela Perley & the Howlin' Moons, Nicole Atkins, Belly, Blondie, Dropkick Murphys, the Joy Formidable, the Tragically Hip, Smashing Pumpkins, Stereolab, Enter the Haggis, Carbon Leaf, Throwing Muses, Liz Phair, the Stone Roses, Beastie Boys, Garbage, Yes, Ben Folds, PJ Harvey, Jonathan Coulton, the Sounds, and R.E.M. for providing the soundtrack while I worked.

Thanks to all *Ranting Soccer Dad* podcast guests: Alexi Lalas, Julie Foudy, Eric Wynalda, Kyle Martino, Steven Gans, Mike Winograd, Paul Lapointe, Mike Woitalla, Yael Averbuch, Gwendolyn Oxenham, Jen Cooper, Peter Wilt, Bobby Warshaw, Skye Eddy Bruce, Kris Ward, Travis Clark, Ronnie Woodard, Brian Dunseth, Chris Keem, Kevin Payne, Jef Thiffault, Neil Morris, Charles Boehm, Doug Wood, Mike Davitt, Leslie Hamer, Jason Longshore, Christian Lavers, Ian Plenderleith, Daryl Grove, Dennis Crowley, Lesle Gallimore, Nathan Richardson, and Kyle Williams.

Thanks to Jen Cooper (again), Jason Davis, and the SiriusXM FC staff for talking with me on their shows.

Thanks to Amanda Vandervort, Lynn Berling-Manuel, and everyone at United Soccer Coaches for putting on an amazing convention each year.

Thanks to Christen Karniski (former Washington Freedom player!) and everyone at Rowman & Littlefield who helped bring this book to life.

And thanks to my wonderful family.

INTRODUCTION

It's OK to Embrace a Lost Cause

I'd be perfectly happy to be wrong about this.

Maybe this book will inspire some kid somewhere to keep working to win the Cup and wave it in my face. Great. But get a move on. I'm getting older. If you're in elementary school now, you might have just enough time to win it all and tell me I'm wrong.

Just understand the message of this book: The odds are stacked against you.

In 20 years of covering soccer—not just on the field but behind the scenes, with countless hours of research (ask me about the United States Soccer Federation bylaws sometime!) and conversations with power brokers at all levels—I've seen a lot of progress. But I've also seen obstacles that are still in place.

And I've heard all the "quick fix" ideas. If only we hire this particular coach, or if we change our pro leagues to look more like Europe's, or if we stress dribbling—no, wait, passing!—at the earliest ages, the U.S. men will be the world power everyone says we're supposed to be.

That's not going to work. Ever. The United States is never going to be Germany. Or Spain. Or Brazil. Catching up to those countries is like running a marathon in which the finish line keeps getting farther away.

We've had plenty of small booms. With the American Soccer League of the 1920s and 1930s, the United States was arguably keeping pace with the rest of the world—a notion borne out by the U.S. team's third-place finish (admittedly out of only 13 teams) in the first World Cup in 1930. Forty-five years later, the North American Soccer League seemed to have taken root. But that league had little direct impact on the U.S. national team, and it was soon gone.

"Pro soccer seemed to have been a fad," wrote David Wangerin in the definitive U.S. soccer history book, *Soccer in a Football World.* "Attending a match had always carried a certain novelty appeal, particularly when tickets were cheap and the atmosphere was festive. While the NASL produced a clique of native fans who warmed to the game, and even embraced it, the result wasn't nearly enough to fill big-league stadiums."[1]

The game has at least, and at last, taken root in the twenty-first century. Youth soccer, which grew rapidly when the baby boomers signed up their kids for a safe activity, is now a booming business. Major League Soccer has far outlasted the other professional leagues in the United States. But growing from those roots to catch up with the redwoods of Europe and South America has been difficult. This book will argue that it's not going to happen.

Maybe we'll get lucky—even luckier than the 2002 U.S. team that caught many players at a career peak and got a few breaks to reach the World Cup quarterfinals. Maybe we'll have one of these mythical "golden generations" with a Messi and a Maldini born in the United States within five years of each other.

If you don't recognize the names Messi and Maldini, please Google them. Yes, that means you're part of the problem, but don't be too hard on yourself. It's not you. It's the United States.

It's not that the United States isn't a soccer nation. It is. It's just also a football (the National Football League/National Collegiate Athletic Association version) nation, a basketball nation, a baseball nation, an e-sports nation, and many other nations. And even within the soccer nation, we're divided. If you think "blue/red" is a divisive issue at your family dinner table, try talking "pro/rel" within a soccer community. (That's "promotion and relegation," a system in which the bottom teams in a league are sent to a lower league and the top lower-league teams move up. Most countries use it in soccer and other sports.) Or try devising a national curriculum that pleases thousands of coaches that have their own ways of doing things.

No one is saying we shouldn't try. I'm never going to play drums like Neil Peart of Rush, but I still go to the basement and thrash my way around. Lars Ulrich of Metallica is never going to play like Neil Peart, but he plays in front of sold-out crowds that tend to make someone forget about the haters. So instead of putting on airs and pretending we're going to be Neil, we should be like Lars. Embrace who we are and build from there.

Bill Murray's character in the film *Stripes* put it best: "We're Americans, with a capital A, huh? You know what that means? Do ya? That means that our forefathers were kicked out of every decent country in the world. We are the wretched refuse. We're the underdog. We're mutts! . . . But there's no animal that's more faithful, that's more loyal, more lovable than the mutt."

That's who we are. We're not the German soccer machine. We're not the Brazilian samba masters.

In women's soccer, we *are* the ones with the head start on the rest of the world. The rest of the world keeps getting better, but so does the United States—at least for now. The 2016 Olympic loss wasn't a fluke, and the youth national teams are no longer as dominant as they were. Eventually, some of the same issues we'll explore here may affect the U.S. women as well. The winning tradition, though, means the women's team will at least be a contender and often a favorite for the foreseeable future.

A word of warning: While we'd love to think of all sports as a respite from the sociopolitical issues of the day—in other words, we'd love to talk about all kinds of football without reflecting on the ridiculous things your grandparents share on Facebook—we really can't. We're going to see here that anti-elitism, nationalism, populism, and other -isms have all played a role in restraining soccer's growth here. The only hope is that postmodernism and globalism pave the way for greater soccerism.

We'll get into that right away in chapter 1. The obvious point here is that Americans play a lot of sports other than soccer, and you'll see plenty of statistics to back that up. But we'll dig a little deeper and talk about "American exceptionalism," a concept so controversial that academics can't even agree on what it means. We'll also take a peek at U.S. history to see how we wound up with other sports far ahead of soccer, but the full history will be found in chapter 6. Before that, we will see the way the U.S. melting pot makes us look in many directions in chapter 2, we will discuss our insecurities about our identities in chapter 3, and we will delve into our inability to agree on anything (chapter 4) and the ensuing parade of lawsuits (chapter 5).

Can we fix everything? We can try, but because we don't understand what we're up against, we look for quick and easy fixes (chapter 7). In doing so, we tend to take what should be a fun sport and make it too serious, scaring away many youth players and turning others into robots who are afraid to make the mistakes they need to make if they're going to learn anything (chapter 8).

But the women will keep winning, right? It's not so simple. The world is catching up, which is a good thing if you care about women's rights throughout the world. The less attractive aspect of things is that many problems that hinder men's soccer development are inevitably creeping into the women's side as well. That's discussed in chapter 9, the last before we try to wrap things up with a dose of optimism in the conclusion.

This book will be educational and informative. It will teach a lot of history. But it will also be fun, despite the depressing premise. Gallows humor is part of being a sports fan, especially in soccer. Some of the worst teams in the world have fans who create beautiful tifo displays (large, sometimes animated pieces of art in the crowd) and rock the stands with traditional songs. We can embrace being lovable losers, like the Chicago Cubs or Torquay United.

And maybe one day, we'll throw off the mantle of eternal futility, just as the Boston Red Sox shook off generations of frustration to win multiple World Series. We'll have home-field advantage in 2026, at least. Maybe the soccer guys will pull off their own version of the 1980 Miracle on Ice.

Or maybe not. But that's OK.

WE PLAY TOO MANY OTHER SPORTS

Are we ready for some . . . academic disputes about football?

Actually, we're not. We have some ground to cover before we get to the roots of all this, much of which we'll cover in chapter 6. Sociologists and historians have had a field day—do the English call it "pitch day"?—with the American preference for its domestic games over the global game. So we'll start with the obvious.

BY THE NUMBERS

Let's look at some numbers. Each of these metrics is insufficient in and of itself, but when we look at all of them, we get a clear contrast between the United States and most of the world.

Web Traffic

The website MostPopularSports[1] analyzed internet traffic for sports in countries around the world. The results: Soccer is the most popular sport in 57 countries with a total population of 2.3 billion. It's in the top three in another 18 countries, adding another 3 billion. (China and India are included.) It's in the top 10 in four more countries, including the United States and Canada. In the United States, soccer is *fifth* behind the traditional "Big Three and a Half"—American football, baseball, basketball, and ice hockey.

Revenue

A 2016 comparison of total revenue from sports leagues[2]—worldwide, not the amount of money made in the United States—gives us a bunch of soccer leagues and a bunch of American sports. The big American sports are first, second, fourth, and fifth. European soccer leagues are third, sixth, seventh, eighth, and ninth. After that, it's Japanese baseball, then many more soccer leagues, including Major League Soccer at 18th.

In other words, the United States has *four* sports leagues that pull in more revenue than the *top* league in every country except the United Kingdom, which has built the Premier League into the biggest non-American league in the world.

Attendance

We can give the caveat here that attendance figures aren't necessarily reliable, with some leagues including ticket holders who didn't show up and some leagues including tickets given away for free. All of the figures below are regular-season totals only, excluding playoffs.

Total attendance, which skews toward baseball and other sports that play from 80 to 162 games per year:

1. Major League Baseball (United States/Canada, 2018): 69,671,272[3]
2. Nippon Professional Baseball (Japan, 2018): 25,550,719[4]
3. National Hockey League, (United States/Canada, 2017–2018): 22,174,362[5]
4. National Basketball Association, (United States/Canada, 2017–2018): 22,124,559[6]
5. National Football League (American football, 2018): 17,177,581[7]
6. Premier League (soccer, England/Wales, 2017–2018): 14,552,748[8]

Major League Soccer clocked in at 8,552,503 in 2018, helped significantly by the stunning success of Atlanta United (average: 53,002).[9]

Average attendance, which skews toward various types of football played mostly on weekends and skews heavily against indoor sports with attendance limited by arena size:

1. NFL (2018): 67,100[10]
2. Bundesliga (Germany, 2017–2018): 43,879[11]

3. Premier League (2017–2018): 38,297[12]
4. Australian Football League (Australian football, 2018): 34,822[13]
5. Nippon Professional Baseball (2018): 29,779[14]
6. MLB (2018): 28,660[15]

The top soccer leagues in Spain (26,940), Italy (24,770), and France (22,520) weren't too far behind.[16] MLS averaged 21,873 in 2018.[17]

With these three measures, we're seeing that most countries put the overwhelming majority of their sports interest in one sport—soccer. In total attendance, as in revenue, the United States once again holds four of the top five spots.

The only major country similar to the United States is Australia, which spreads its support among several sports—Australian football, cricket, rugby, basketball, and soccer. Little wonder Australia's struggles, both in terms of creating a strong domestic league and a strong international team, parallel those of the United States.

Look at the United Kingdom at the other end of the scale. The two forms of rugby (union and league) and cricket have their constituencies. Second place actually goes to horse racing, which has a couple of big events as well as the regular races for benefit of bettors. But soccer accounted for well more than half of the overall sports attendance in 2017—47.6 million out of 74.5 million.[18]

A few other countries have strong leagues in other sports. New Zealand combines its rugby and soccer leagues with Australia and fares better in the former. South Africa's rugby strength is immortalized in the film *Invictus*. India and Bangladesh prefer cricket. Baseball rules in Japan, South Korea, Taiwan, and Venezuela, but it's virtually invisible elsewhere. Poland has a strange obsession with motorcycle speedway.

Everywhere else, it's soccer first. Sometimes second as well, depending on how much interest the second division of the domestic league draws.

And a quick reminder: We can't rely on any single metric. In some of the countries in which soccer is in second place in terms of attendance, the domestic soccer leagues struggle for attention in a new media landscape that beams the Premier League and other European giants around the globe. Fans are often watching or following the major global soccer leagues rather than going out and attending their local clubs.

So even in countries in which soccer is number two at the box office, it's never far from the population's heart.

Polls

In Gallup's annual survey of Americans' favorite sports, the good news for soccer in 2018 was that the sport was gaining on baseball for the number three spot.[19] The soccer community pounded on this measure as if to say "I told you so," because Gallup compiles fans of various leagues—MLS, the Premier League, Liga MX, and others—into one figure, while most other metrics (attendance, non–World Cup TV ratings, etc.) do not. At last, we had proof that soccer is big time! Right?

Not so fast. The number is still a lowly 7 percent. American football clocks in at 37 percent. And a 2017 *Washington Post*/University of Massachusetts Lowell survey[20] showed nearly the same results: American football at 37 percent, then basketball and baseball. Soccer was at 8 percent.

TV Ratings

Here, things get complicated. In baseball and hockey, the overwhelming portion of the viewing public is lined up behind one league. The American football audience may split somewhat between college football and professional football, but the NCAA and NFL carefully schedule around each other. In basketball, the college and the pro games inevitably coincide on TV.

No matter how they schedule things, the bulk of the action will be on the weekend. On a typical October weekend, with all five major league sports in session and a lot of other action, it's difficult to find a slot on the airwaves at all. Major League Soccer's critics say the league should switch from a spring-to-fall schedule to an academic-year schedule to avoid the conflicts between the MLS playoffs and American football, but the switch would just put the MLS playoffs at the same time as the playoffs in the NBA and NHL.

Let's look at October 27–28, 2018. We'll include only live events or significantly rated programming, or else you'll be reading all day. All times below are in the Eastern Time Zone; most ratings are from Show-BuzzDaily,[21] but some soccer ratings are from World Soccer Talk.[22]

Some ratings, including those for the broadcast featuring coverage of all MLS games running concurrently to give no team an advantage on the last day of the regular season, are not available.

Saturday, October 27, 2018

Morning: The early Premier League broadcast draws 459,000 viewers, mostly on NBCSN (416,000) but a few on Spanish-language NBC Universo. That broadcast for early risers easily takes in more viewers than other soccer (Bundesliga, La Liga), two tennis broadcasts, and three auto racing broadcasts (two of them merely *practice* sessions in NASCAR and Formula 1), but it won't compare to what we see later.

Early afternoon: Three college football games, led by ABC's Clemson-Florida State showdown (3.16 million), each draw more than 2 million viewers. The top broadcast aside from the college games was the Premier League broadcast of West Ham-Leicester on NBC (the main broadcast network), taking 710,000 on NBC and 50,000 on NBC Universo. Lucas Oil Off-Road auto racing on CBS gets 511,000. Further dividing the audience, we have more auto racing, more European soccer games, and more college football than we can count. A bigger matchup in the Premier League likely would have fared better.

Mid-afternoon: College football gets serious, with Florida-Georgia drawing 6.35 million on CBS. On ESPN, 3.27 million watch Iowa play Penn State. Another 2 million watch a variety of games, determined by region, on ABC. Nearly 2 million more watch a game on Fox. Away from the gridiron, 916,000 watch week-old figure skating highlights (Skate America) on NBC. Viewers can also watch a bit more auto racing and much more college football. This block is a frequent lull in soccer between European games and evening North American games.

Early evening: College football's mid-afternoon broadcasts continue, and a couple of games starting at dinner time on the East Coast break the 500,000 mark. Soccer kicks back up again with Liga MX (Necaxa-Atlas) on Univision Deportes getting 274,000 viewers, considerably smaller than some games to come from the Mexican league. Golf Channel and NHL Network are showing their sports as well.

Prime time: Time for the World Series, with game 4 of the Red Sox-Dodgers matchup pulling in 13.56 million on Fox and a few viewers on Fox Deportes. College football still picks off more than 7 million viewers, with Texas-Oklahoma State (ABC, 3.49 million) and Notre Dame-

Navy (CBS, 2.45 million) leading the way. Liga MX pulls in a solid share, with 904,000 watching Guadalajara-Morelia between Univision and Univision Deportes. The evening's UFC action starts on Fox Sports 2, and we have still more Liga MX and college football.

Late night (*prime time West Coast*): At last, soccer wins the time slot (for sports broadcasts, at least), with Cruz Azul-Club America drawing 1.23 million between Univision and Univision Deportes. A college football matchup out West (Oregon-Arizona) draws 1.19 million. More than 1 million people watch athletes beat each other up—543,000 for boxing on HBO, and 531,000 for UFC on Fox Sports 1. For those who aren't satisfied with those options, there's *still* more Mexican soccer, college football, and golf.[23]

Sunday, October 28, 2018

Morning: The NFL doesn't often have games this early, but the American football league plays the occasional game in London. This one, Philadelphia-Jacksonville, draws 3.59 million on NFL Network. That figure easily beats the combined viewing for one of the biggest soccer matchups in the world—Barcelona playing Real Madrid, which gets a combined total of 544,000,[24] though the two networks (beIN Sport and beIN Sports Español) aren't as prominent as the other networks we're checking here. The Premier League broadcast, Arsenal-Crystal Palace, draws 353,000 on NBCSN. Other soccer broadcasts split the audience.

Early afternoon: The NFL dominates. Games vary by region, with the aggregate audience on CBS taking in 15.52 million and the Fox games getting 10.38 million. A Premier League broadcast (Everton-Manchester United) takes in 779,000 on NBC and 243,000 on Telemundo for a total of 1.02 million. X Games highlights draw 349,000 on ABC. Soccer viewers have other options from Italy, Germany, Portugal, Mexico, and Spain.

Mid-afternoon: Fox has the NFL window to itself and reels in 21.88 million, the biggest sports audience of the weekend. Domestic auto racing, NASCAR's Sprint Cup, gets 2.15 million on NBCSN. Canned programming still draws viewers, with "Geico's 10 Greatest Golf Drivers" picking up 1.62 million on CBS and figure skating's Skate Canada, which wrapped up the day before, taking 880,000 on NBC. The international version of auto racing, Formula 1, picks up 776,000 on ABC.

Soccer broadcasts come from all over the globe, including a college game. The lack of reporting for the MLS broadcast, which focused on

Kansas City-Los Angeles FC but included live checks on many games as playoff berths were decided, is not a good sign for the league.

Evening: The final game of the World Series, with the Red Sox clinching another sports title for the overly successful New England region, gets 17.63 million on Fox and 577,000 on Fox Deportes. Even with that many viewers for baseball, the NFL's New Orleans-Minnesota matchup on NBC gets 14.09 million. Soccer struggles against that competition, with Leon-Puebla on Univision Deportes drawing 178,000, just behind the 179,000 for poker on ESPN.[25]

We're not counting horse racing on the specialty horse racing channel. Nor are we counting sporadically available networks like Eleven Sports, college conference–specific networks (SEC Network, Big 10 Network), or the Olympic Channel. Nor are we counting the myriad highlight and panel-discussion shows that fill time between games. Nor are we counting the hundred or so events on ESPN's streaming services or other pay services.

If we look at a weekend with no American football, we'll see how soccer struggles even in a less crowded time. In this case, with the European leagues off for the summer, we aren't even splitting the soccer audience among the various leagues—we only have four broadcasts, and none of those broadcasts coincided. Soccer fans could easily watch all four without having a laptop, a phone, and a TV all running at the same time as they might on a typical October day.

And the soccer games were marquee events—the semifinals of the Gold Cup (North America's attempt to mimic the European Championships or Copa America) and a pair of international club friendlies with four of the biggest clubs in the world.

These ratings are from July 22–23, 2017, combining data from Show-BuzzDaily and World Soccer Talk:[26]

1. Auto racing, NASCAR Sprint Cup race, NBC, 5.63 million
2. Golf, British Open final round, NBC, 4.91 million
3. Soccer, Mexico-Jamaica (Gold Cup), Univision/Fox Sports 1, 3.79 million (3 million of that on Univision)
4. Golf, British Open, third round, NBC, 3.07 million
5. Soccer, USA-Costa Rica (Gold Cup), UniMás/Fox Sports 1, 2.21 million (nearly an even split between the networks)
6. Baseball, Cardinals-Cubs (Sunday), ESPN, 2.12 million

7. MMA, UFC Fight Night, Fox, 2.05 million
8. Auto racing, NASCAR Xfinity (second division) race, NBCSN, 1.69 million
9. MMA, UFC Fight Night prelims, Fox, 1.14 million
10. Cycling, Tour de France highlights, NBC, 1.08 million
11. Auto racing, NASCAR Sprint Cup qualifying, NBCSN, 1.08 million
12. Auto racing, NHRA drag racing, Fox, 868,000
13. Soccer, Mexican league, Club America-Queretaro, combined Univisions, 829,000
14. Soccer, Mexican league, Tigres-Puebla, combined Univisions, 769,000
15. Soccer, Mexican league, Chivas-Toluca, combined Univisions, 767,000
16. Poker, World Series final table, ESPN, 741,000
17. CBS Sports Spectacular featuring Major League Fishing, 675,000
18. Basketball, WNBA All-Star Game, ABC, 606,000
19. Auto racing, NASCAR Sprint Cup *practice*, NBCSN, 580,000
20. Baseball, Cardinals-Cubs (Saturday), Fox Sports 1, 565,000
21. Soccer, Mexican league, Pumas-Pachuca, combined Univisions, 538,000
22. Tough Mudder, CBS, 534,000
23. Auto racing, NASCAR Xfinity qualifying, NBCSN, 518,000
24. Baseball, Rangers-Rays, Fox Sports 1, 479,000
25. Soccer, Real Madrid-Manchester United, ESPN, 443,000
26. Cycling, Tour de France final stage, NBCSN, 435,000
27. Soccer, Mexican league, Leon-Atlas, UniMás, 413,000
28. Soccer, Juventus-Barcelona, ESPN, 403,000
29. Cornhole, 2017 Championship of Bags, ESPN2, 359,000

I've omitted ancillary broadcasts around the British Open, some of which fared better than Juventus-Barcelona.

So *a meaningful U.S. men's national team game* was no match for NASCAR and a golf major. The English-language broadcast of that game lost out to one of the scores of baseball broadcasts for the week and UFC. Two big-time club friendlies lost out to poker, a long-distance obstacle course, and fishing. The two MLS broadcasts for the weekend farther down the list—with 222,000 and 155,000 viewers—were no match for cornhole, the backyard game of tossing bags into holes cut into boards.

Soccer broadcasts were a bit better during the week, when the competition from auto racing and fishing was gone. The USA-El Salvador game drew a combined 2.67 million, a bit higher than the weekend game, and Friday night's MLS broadcast drew 338,000.

Let's take a broader view. Here's how average U.S. TV ratings rank from a variety of sources:

1. NFL, 2017 regular season, 14.9 million[27]
2. NASCAR top tier, 2018 season (all networks), 3.3 million[28]
3. MLB on Fox, 2018 regular season, 2.23 million[29]
4. NBA, 2017–2018 regular season, 1.28 million[30]
5. MLB on ESPN, 2018 regular season, 978,000[31]
6. Premier League, 2017–2018 season, 449,000[32]
7. NHL, 2017–2018 regular season, 417,000[33]
8. MLB on Fox Sports 1, 2018 regular season, 410,000[34]
9. MLB on MLB Network, 2018 regular season, 239,000[35]

MLS numbers are difficult to compile, and some games aren't reported, but BigSoccer message board members crowd-sourced it and came up with an average of 276,000 for 2018.[36]

You get the point. It's a crowded table. Yes, soccer has carved out a greater place for itself. But it's a bit like getting a seat at Thanksgiving dinner with several generations of aunts, uncles, and cousins in town, and the turkey and stuffing can only get so much bigger.

Other countries have some big events and some stable leagues in basketball, ice hockey, and volleyball. Everyone loves the Olympics, and some people even pay attention to track and field when it's not an Olympic year.

Consider the United Kingdom, whose population of just under 67 million is several times smaller than the USA's 325 million. The track and field World Championships may crash the top 10. Same with Six Nations rugby, propelled by the fact that three of those nations are part of the United Kingdom—England, Scotland, and Wales. Wimbledon, the beloved tennis tournament, is also popular. But the rest is soccer.

Here are the Top 10 UK sports broadcasts of 2017:[37]

1. Arsenal-Chelsea (May 17), BBC1, 7.50 million

2. Athletics (track and field) World Championships, BBC1, 6.66 million

3. Six Nations rugby, Wales-England, BBC1, 6.51 million

4. FA Cup, Chelsea-Manchester United, BBC1, 6.43 million

5. England-Slovakia (World Cup qualifier), ITV, 5.71 million

6. England-Germany (friendly), ITV, 5.71 million

7. Six Nations rugby, England-Scotland, ITV, 5.63 million

8. BBC Sports Personality of the Year, BBC1, 5.48 million

9. Six Nations rugby, Wales-Ireland, BBC1, 5.40 million

10. Wimbledon, BBC1, 4.86 million

Weekly Premier League broadcasts actually don't compare favorably with the staples of British television—soap operas like *EastEnders* and *Coronation Street*, contests such as the awkwardly named *Strictly Come Dancing* (the U.S. version is *Dancing with the Stars*), and *Doctor Who*. But a typical week's top 10 sports will include several soccer broadcasts, even an occasional game from the second-tier Championship, alongside Formula 1, international rugby, and a crucial snooker showdown.[38] The big broadcast is the BBC's *Match of the Day*, which is actually a Saturday highlights package that, combined with Sunday's *Match of the Day 2*, might reach 7 million viewers a week.[39]

Why is the highlights package so popular? Simple. Britain does not allow live soccer broadcasts during the traditional 3 p.m. Saturday game time. (That tradition is being questioned.[40]) This is not unusual—on a trip to Spain, I tuned in to see a La Liga broadcast in which we saw players taking the field. They got in formation, the referee blew the whistle for the kickoff . . . and the camera cut back to two guys in a cheap-looking studio looking at a monitor to the left of the camera.

And we'll have to throw in the caveat that UK ratings don't even capture all of the football audience. A BBC survey found that 36 percent of Premier League fans—65 percent of fans ages 18 to 34—watch an illegal stream at least once a month.[41]

In the United States, seven of the top ten shows of 2018 were sports-related broadcasts.[42] Six were football—one college, five NFL. The seventh was the opening ceremony of the Olympics. The lowest of the top 10 was an NFL playoff game that drew 26.9 million viewers. The World Cup final drew 11.8 million (including those watching online), down from 17.3 million for the 2014 final.[43]

WHAT DO THE NUMBERS TELL US?

No matter how you measure it, the results are the same. In much of the world, it's soccer first and everything else second. In the United States, American football is dominant—not as much as soccer dominates elsewhere, but still the undisputed number one—with basketball and baseball maintaining loyal followings. We also have a couple million people who watch golf every week, a number that booms during the majors. Those of us who have worked at Southern newspapers can attest that we could never write enough about NASCAR. Soccer fandom is substantial, but the fervor elsewhere is exponentially higher.

To finish this point, let's look at Nielsen Sports' World Football Report 2018.[44] The company surveyed Australia, Canada, France, Germany, Italy, Japan, Malaysia, Poland, Spain, the United Kingdom, and the United States along with urban areas in Brazil, China, India, Russia, Singapore, South Korea, and the United Arab Emirates.

The results:

- Globally (including the United States), 43 percent of people are "very interested" or "interested" in soccer. Next on the list is basketball at 36 percent. Nothing else is above 30 percent.
- Soccer is the world's most popular sport among men (54 percent interested) *and* women (31 percent interested, with basketball again second at 28 percent).

Nielsen went on to add 12 more countries to compare interest across the world. In 19 of the 30 countries, the soccer interest was 50 percent or higher. In the United States, that number is 32 percent.

The good news is that the soccer numbers skew young. The interest level is a whopping 55 percent for ages 16–24, then a steady drop to 14 percent for ages 55–69.

The last statistic is a definitive statement of soccer's history here. Millennials and those after them have grown up as soccer fans. Previous generations did not. Period.

How did this happen? Why is the United States a late arrival to the global soccer party? That's a contentious subject.

POPULARITY OVER THE YEARS

Soccer has never been completely dead in the United States. Check chapter 6 to see how soccer clung to the continent, much like Irish monks
diligently copying manuscripts on island outposts in the Dark Ages. After
the successful American Soccer League of the 1920s collapsed, a low-key
American Soccer League continued on the East Coast for decades. ASL
exploits were even described in local newspapers, which some soccer
historians have cited as proof that soccer was always somewhat popular.

But newspapers in those days covered *everything*. That was the Gold-
en Age of American newspapers, which had a monopoly on advertising in
the days before television took the lion's share. The internet, which wiped
out newspapers' solid stream of classified advertising and provides free
content that used to require a newspaper subscription, was decades away
from existence.

Let's look at one particular example chosen mostly at random. Let's
make it a Monday, when the weekend sports action had wrapped up. And
let's make it the *Brooklyn Daily Eagle*, which covered soccer quite well
and had a distinguished soccer writer in Bill Graham.

Here's what the *Eagle* covered on Monday, October 23, 1950, when it
devoted 3 of its 24 pages to sports, one page more than the "What Wom-
en Are Doing" pages of weddings and needlepoint. (It was a different
time.)

Page 15: The top headlines went to baseball (the legendary Branch
Rickey was on his way out as Brooklyn Dodgers president/general manager, and the All-Star team included a couple of Dodgers), pro football
(41,734 fans watched the Giants win), college football, and boxing.

Page 16: A decent ASL roundup and local amateur soccer standings
shared space with more college football, ice hockey, tennis, multiple local
bowling roundups, multiple horse racing entries, multiple boxing briefs,
more baseball (including fretting over minor league attendance due to
rain and radio), fishing, and an NBA exhibition brief.

Also on the page, higher up than the soccer roundup, was a compelling
account of the Philadelphia Panthers defeating the New York Chiefs . . .
in roller derby.

And finally, two columns over from the ASL standings, ran a short
story about the Pi Phi Girls defeating the Alpha Xi team before a crowd
of 5,000 people ("many of them men") in the fourth annual Powder Bowl

football game at Ohio University. (This was a wire story. Shockingly, the *Eagle* neglected to send a correspondent to Athens to get the full story.)

The last of the three sports pages was mostly youth and high school football.

Such a juxtaposition was hardly unusual. Consider the 1950 World Cup coverage in the *St. Louis Post-Dispatch*, which boasted the lone U.S. reporter in Brazil, though the Soccer Hall of Fame says Dent McSkimming was there on vacation rather than on a *Post-Dispatch* assignment.[45] He also is surely the only U.S. soccer journalist ever portrayed on screen by Patrick Stewart.

A few generations before laptop computers and cell phones, most of McSkimming's accounts were published once everyone had arrived back in St. Louis. On game days, the *Post-Dispatch* relied on the wire services.

On June 26, after the U.S. men lost to Spain in the World Cup, the *Post-Dispatch* played the story on the third page of its sports section, after the Cardinals (baseball) and the semifinal round of the match-play PGA Championship (golf), just above the notice of a local man recording a hole-in-one on the 200-yard 12th hole at Forest Park, and the typical horse racing roundup.

On June 30, the momentous news that the USA had defeated mighty England was the top headline on the sports section's second page, though the headline also spanned across the top of a photo of a man bearing a faint resemblance to Babe Ruth showing off a 47-pound bass he caught in New England.

So it's safe to say soccer wasn't completely ignored, even in the relatively dark period between the high-profile ASL of the 1920s and the glitzy NASL of the 1970s and early 1980s. But neither was it a particularly big deal.

How soccer's small niche came to pass is the subject of a thornier academic debate. The definitive work here is *Offside: Soccer and American Exceptionalism* by Michigan professor Andrei Markovits and journalist Steven Hellerman. The tome was published in 2001 as part of the Princeton Studies in Cultural Sociology series, because we treat these things very seriously.

We have to discuss an academic term here, since academics love to redefine the language so no one knows what they're talking about. Academics define "American exceptionalism" not as "Yay, we're great!" but "Hey, we're not the same as European countries because we're a young melting pot with more than 300 million people and only two bordering nations!" Sometimes.

Franklin Foer, who drew a connecting line between American exceptionalism and soccer in *How Soccer Explains the World*, goes beyond "Hey, we're unique!" to "Hey, you can't tell us how to act." He defines American exceptionalism as "an idea that America's history and singular form of government has given the nation a unique role to play in the world; that the U.S. should be above submitting to international laws and bodies."[46]

Building on that definition, Ian Tyrrell, a scholar who has devoted significant study to the concept even though he happens to be Australian (he spent some of his student life at Duke, also your author's alma mater), puts it like this:

> American exceptionalism is not the same as saying the United States is "different" from other countries. It doesn't just mean that the U.S. is "unique." Countries, like people, are all different and unique, even if many share some underlying characteristics. Exceptionalism requires something far more: a belief that the U.S. follows a path of history different from the laws or norms that govern other countries. That's the essence of American exceptionalism: The U.S. is not just a bigger and more powerful country—but an exception.[47]

Which seems to be telling us what it's not rather than what it . . . never mind, let's jump out of this rabbit hole and agree that, for purposes of this discussion and with all due respect to Dr. Tyrrell, "American exceptionalism" means "different." Or, more precisely for a soccer discussion, if the rest of the world jumped off a cliff, we would not. If the rest of the world did *not* jump off a cliff, we just might.

Stefan Szymanski and Andrew Zimbalist, a pair of economists who wrote *National Pastime: How Americans Play Baseball and the Rest of the World Plays Soccer*, put it this way: "The American melting pot is a world unto itself. In the realm of culture, it is generally more concerned with its own comings and goings than with the wider world around it."[48]

In any case, the Markovits/Hellerman take seeped into soccer writing of the next decade, including my own. Well-traveled journalist Simon Kuper, who went on to write *Soccernomics* with Szymanski, sounded a similar theme in *Football against the Enemy* (called *Soccer against the Enemy* in its U.S. edition): "When immigrants from Europe landed in the

U.S., their children were teased on the street for their funny accents, clothes and parents. The last thing these children were going to do was play a funny European game on the streets and be teased, so they took up baseball. This is why Americans don't play soccer."[49]

This historical/sociological take is occasionally disputed. As we'll see in chapter 4, we're not likely to agree on much, and history is no different. Academic Steven Apostolov took issue with Markovits and Hellerman, particularly the claim that soccer was "crowded out" of the U.S. sports landscape even in its 1920s heyday.[50] The key to his argument: Soccer was actually ahead of the curve in putting together a pro league—the American Soccer League. However, the league, strong as it was, didn't have a national reach. The American Soccer League only covered the Philadelphia-to-Boston corridor. Another pocket of pro-ish soccer existed in St. Louis, and amateur teams from the Great Lakes entered the National Challenge Cup, now known as the U.S. Open Cup.

Meanwhile, baseball's National League and American League were thriving not just in the Northeast and in St. Louis, but also in Chicago, Cincinnati, Detroit, Pittsburgh, Cleveland, and occasionally Washington, DC. And while pro football was in its infancy, college football was dominant nationwide, with games from New York to Alabama drawing 10,000 fans on a bad day and upwards of 40,000 for rivalry games. Also, the National Hockey League expanded across the border from Canada to Boston, New York, Chicago, Pittsburgh, and Detroit, with attendance quickly breaking into a five-figure average in Boston.[51]

Apostolov raises an interesting argument that immigrants were less prone to assimilating to every aspect of American culture, but that's more a question of sociology than of soccer. Yes, soccer had a good foothold in the 1920s, and recent immigrants played a big role in that. Immigrants also helped to keep the sport alive through a long dry spell of professional soccer—the goal in the USA's 1950 World Cup upset of England was scored by Haitian American Joe Gaetjens. Not all immigrants succumbed to the pressures to assimilate by picking up the football and running with it. But we can't conclude soccer was ever close to being the country's dominant sport.

It's not so much that the sports landscape was completely fixed and *then* soccer was "crowded out." The U.S. sports landscape of the nineteenth century was wide open, and soccer—which was indeed played here in the pre-1900 days—simply fell by the wayside.

Consider another English sport—cricket. Szymanski and Zimbalist found reports of a USA-England cricket match in 1859 attended by 24,000 over three days at the Elysian Fields in Hoboken.[52] Over the next 150 years, cricket would fare far worse than soccer in this country.

And the United States is so protective of "its" sports that it has put up mythological stories about how baseball came into being. Rather than settling on a complex evolution of the sport from other batted-ball games such as rounders and cricket, which actually had a foothold in the USA in the early twentieth century but is now invisible in the American sports landscape, Americans invented the myth that a man named Abner Doubleday invented the game.

From the *New York Times*:

> The Doubleday myth arose in the early 1900s when the nation, relatively young and insecure over lack of pedigree, needed to possess the game as uniquely American. In 1905, Albert Spalding, a baseball executive and sporting goods magnate, organized a commission to study the origins of the game. After reviewing some dubious evidence, three years later the commission declared Doubleday the game's inventor.[53]

So we can't really argue with the idea that the United States, a fragile melting pot that had already shattered once with the Civil War of the 1860s, saw great value in propagating things that were uniquely "American." That concept seems foreign to those of us living in the twenty-first century, in which American culture is our greatest export. But the United States of the early twentieth century was not the dominant global power it is today. And we simply don't have as many things to unify us in comparison with other countries. The United Kingdom has soccer, Boxing Day, tea, *Doctor Who*, and complaining about trains even though their mass transit puts American trains to shame. We have *Star Wars* and the incessant din of Marvel movies, and even in those cases, we've seen a generational change in which comic-book fandom has evolved from the stereotypical "Comic Book Guy" from *The Simpsons* to Hollywood blockbusters.

Other countries have tried to ignore soccer in favor of other sports, including indigenous sports. Szymanski and Zimbalist traced efforts by fascists in Germany and Italy to emphasize domestic games, including a football-ish sport called *volata* in Italy, ahead of soccer.[54] Obviously, both efforts failed, but the word *calcio*, another variation of football once played in Italy, lives on in the name of the country's soccer federation: Federazione Italiana Giuoco del Calcio.

So Americans aren't alone in trying to use domestic sports to foment a national identity. They're just the most successful of anyone who's tried.

And now plenty of sports have American roots, even without the mythology of a Doubleday figure. College kids after the Civil War tinkered with soccer and rugby before developing what we now call American football. (A couple more decades would go by until the forward pass would be accepted, a development that certainly changed Tom Brady's life.) James Naismith's position as the inventor of basketball isn't in dispute. Ice hockey evolved in Canada and quickly spread across the border. Lacrosse was pioneered by indigenous North Americans.

We don't even race cars the way the rest of the world does. While some Formula 1 races draw global viewing audiences in excess of 100 million, U.S. racing fans watch NASCAR or, less likely, Indy car racing.

And we're not finished inventing. The United States pioneered many "extreme" sports such as skateboarding, snowboarding, and BMX, all of which are now in the Olympics. Ultimate, formerly known as Ultimate Frisbee before trademark issues came into play, started on college campus in the late 1960s and has a budding pro league.

You can bring international ideas into the United States—if nothing else, our palates thank you. You can connect Americans with the rest of the world via satellite TV and the internet. But you can't stop American ingenuity. And you can't stop American individualism. Some of us will choose to be soccer fans. Some of us won't.

2

WE WATCH TOO MANY OTHER SOCCER LEAGUES TO FOCUS ON OUR OWN

When I moved to the Washington, DC, suburbs in 1998, I was thrilled to be near a place called Summers. I had heard that the bar/restaurant, conveniently near a Metro station but with a good view of the sky for its satellite dishes, showed plenty of soccer. It didn't disappoint.

One week, I went twice for two games from different continents. Each time, the place was packed. Other than the wait staff, I was probably the only person in there for both games. Such diversity is great news for Summers, which gained some media attention by hosting large overnight crowds during the 2002 World Cup, played half a world away in Japan and South Korea; the place survived a couple of downturns and real-estate issues to remain a beacon of soccer in that prime location. But this shows how difficult it is to unite all of these soccer fans for anything other than a World Cup.

On a typical fall or spring Saturday (see previous chapter), a viewer in the United States can wake up at 7:30 a.m. Eastern time to catch the first Premier League match of the day. After that, it's a choice between the next Premier League game or perhaps a Bundesliga game. The lunch hour brings another Premier League game and perhaps some La Liga or more Bundesliga fare. In mid-afternoon, La Liga might have its best match of the day. There might be a lull when Europe finally settles down for the night, and we'd have to hope the typical American viewer uses that break for fresh air and exercise. By the evening hours, then the Spanish-language networks rev up their popular Liga MX (Mexico) broadcasts. All told, a viewer can easily watch five or six games on a Saturday without seeing a single U.S. team.

That's a threat to Major League Soccer or any professional league that tries to set up shop in the United States. (That's also a threat to Summers—if you can stay at home and watch everything, the pull of a sports bar is a little weaker, but Summers also shows a lot of games that are on the more expensive and obscure cable tiers. It also offers pay-per-view mixed martial arts and wrestling, the complete NFL package with several games airing at once, and karaoke.)

MLS's uphill battle is reflected in the TV ratings. One comparison, in which Stefan Szymanski compiled World Soccer Talk's numbers for 2017,[1] shows MLS flailing against the world's biggest leagues and the powerhouse just south of us in average viewership:

- 662,152 viewers: international games
- 584,769: Liga MX (Mexico)
- 383,480: Premier League (England)
- 298,725: Champions League (Europe)
- 285,285: MLS
- 186,938: La Liga (Spain)

The Bundesliga was far from cracking the six-figure mark, more of an indicator of the domination of NBC's excellent Premier League broadcasts than the quality of play in Germany. Szymanski also classified an "Other" group averaging 240,569.

Soccer fans are clearly spoiled by the choices they have today. In the 1990s, we might have the Mexican broadcasts on Spanish-language channels and one tape-delayed Premier League broadcast, along with some erratically aired highlight packages. In 2017, U.S. viewers enjoyed an average of 8.5 broadcasts per day.[2] That number obviously soars on weekends.

And that number only counts broadcasts. If you subscribe to ESPN's premium service, Fox Soccer Match Pass, NBC Sports Gold, fuboTV, and a few other online offerings, you can watch scores of games—often more than 100—on any Saturday or Sunday.

MLS's critics are quick to note that the league is getting only a small piece of the soccer-audience pie. MLS can counter that its audience has held steady through the years because that pie is getting so much bigger.

Ten percent of 5 million is bigger than 100 percent of 200,000. The league also has local broadcasts—Sporting KC on Fox Sports Kansas City, New England Revolution on NBC Sports Boston, and others that are available nationally through the ESPN+ subscription service.

So if you live in Des Moines but want to watch all games featuring the exciting Atlanta United team, you certainly can do so. The problem is that you can do the same for hundreds of other teams. So even if that pie continues to grow, which will surely be the premise of a Food Network competition before long, MLS is stuck defending its share.

It's a Golden Age for soccer fans, and those of us who suffered through the pre-internet days will never take it for granted. But MLS is the equivalent of a single stall in a crowded bazaar, trying to shout above the rest to make a few sales.

THE MLS STRATEGY

To keep up with the other leagues on TV, MLS has had to evolve.

From the outset, MLS knew it was competing in a global marketplace. At its 1996 launch, the competition on cable and the internet wasn't quite as fierce. But MLS was competing for players, a fact that helped it stave off a lawsuit by players claiming it was restraining trade. (We will most definitely get to that in chapter 5.)

So the league had to find that middle ground between being global cheapskates and spending themselves out of business. It settled on a clever business model called "single entity," in which the league's central office has considerably more power than it does in a typical league composed of wholly separate clubs. From a legal point of view, it's a novel defense against antitrust suits—again, something that was tested in the players' lawsuit. From an economic standpoint, the structure keeps clubs from trying to outspend each other in a financial arms race. MLS was anxious to avoid repeating the North American Soccer League's "keep up with the Cosmos" frenzy that was blamed, at least in part, for that league's demise.

At the outset, the MLS central office took care of everything. The league signed players and spread its biggest names throughout the 10 teams. The rest of the rosters were filled mostly by a player draft, familiar to fans of other U.S. sports but unheard of in global soccer. Players whose contracts ended were not "free agents" within the league—they were free to sign with another league at home or abroad, but MLS teams were not going to get in bidding wars with each other.

Other leagues took interest in the new model. The two rival women's basketball leagues, the American Basketball League (ABL) and the Women's National Basketball Association (WNBA), had some form of single-entity structure. So did the first U.S. women's soccer league, the Women's United Soccer Association (WUSA); and pro wrestling promoter Vince McMahon's football league, the XFL.

MLS also borrowed an innovation of U.S. leagues—the salary cap, restricting the total of each team's player salaries to a set number. When MLS launched in 1996, that number was a pittance of $1.2 million. Not $1.2 million per player—$1.2 million *per team*. A few marquee players found loopholes to get extra compensation, most notably Mexican goalkeeper/forward Jorge Campos's insistence that he be presented with a Ferrari, but the typical MLS player lived like a graduate student and couldn't do much about it.

Unless, of course, that player took one of two alternate paths. One was to play in the second-tier A-League in the summer and the indoor National Professional Soccer League (NPSL) in the winter. The other was to play in another country, an option that MLS lawyers hammered home in their successful defense against the players' lawsuit.

The money may not have been great when the league started, but the intrigue of building something new in the United States attracted most top American players and a handful of international stars. Carlos Valderrama and Roberto Donadoni were still viable international players when they signed with the new league, and the Bolivian tandem of Marco "El Diablo" Etcheverry and Jaime Moreno led the attack for D.C. United, the dominant MLS team of the 1990s. Americans John Harkes, Eric Wynalda, Alexi Lalas, Roy Wegerle, Brad Friedel, Thomas Dooley, and Tab Ramos all left top-division European teams to join MLS in the 1990s, while Marcelo Balboa and Cle Kooiman came up from Mexico.

But as the league went on, with attendance and interest dropping after the novelty of its first season, that allure faded. By the 2002 World Cup, more than half of the U.S. team that made a memorable run to the quarterfinals was based in Europe, a trend that repeated in 2006. It's one thing to lose a player like goalkeeper Tim Howard to Manchester United. It's another to lose defender Oguchi Onyewu to Belgian club Standard Liege.

The international talent also wasn't top-flight after the early stars retired or faded. Unheralded Central American players such as Carlos Ruiz, Amado Guevara, and Alex Pineda Chacon won the league's MVP award.

If MLS was going to produce games that would make a TV viewer take a look, something had to change. And it did. The league loosened the reins on its teams and invested much more money.

In 2007, according to an analysis by the *Philadelphia Inquirer*'s Jonathan Tannenwald, the league's median salary was $50,400. By 2015, the minimum for "senior" roster players was $60,000, and no one made less than $50,000. The median was a healthy $112,000. The mean had zoomed upwards from a little under $115,000 in 2007 to more than $290,000 in 2015.[3]

The catalyst for that spike in the mean salary was one of the most famous soccer players on the planet—David Beckham, a charismatic Englishman married to a Spice Girl. Long recognized as a great fan of the United States, even naming a son "Brooklyn," Beckham was often rumored to be seeking an MLS roster spot for his retirement years. He turned up sooner than expected, signing at age 31 while still committed to finishing a season with Real Madrid. Beckham's salary would be $6.5 million per year, and additional cash from various commercial deals would keep him rolling in money as long as he was in Los Angeles.

How did the Galaxy manage to pay one player more than most teams were paying their entire roster? The Beckham rule. Or, under its more formal name, the Designated Player rule, which gave each club the freedom to sign one player (later expanded to three) to any salary while counting only a small portion of it against the salary cap.

Teams tiptoed into these new waters at first. By 2018, nearly every team had at least two Designated Players.

But wait, there's more. MLS has since added mechanisms known as TAM and GAM. That's Targeted Allocation Money and General Allocated Money, two pools of money through which teams can qualify for extra salary-cap space for any number of reasons. These complex rules have brought about a few good quips from people wondering if JAM or BAM will follow, and they've made life difficult for the programmers of the popular computer game Football Manager, but they've helped MLS teams spend more and more on salaries.

The greater spending has coincided with a wave of managed but rapid expansion. In 2007, MLS added its 13th team, Toronto FC. In 2019, the league added its 24th, FC Cincinnati. (Yes, you could argue that MLS has run out of team names.) Miami, whose MLS rights are partially owned by Beckham himself, was scheduled to join in 2020 if it could sort out its stadium issues. Nashville also was set for 2020, with Austin coming aboard in 2021 after a complicated ownership square dance with Columbus.

Several expansion teams burst out of the gate with major signings. The Seattle Sounders brought in Premier League mainstay Freddie Ljungberg for their 2009 debut. The Montreal Impact debuted in 2012 with former Italian national team player Marco Di Vaio. Orlando City did even better in 2015 with Brazilian international Kaká, who had spent the previous 10 years with AC Milan and Real Madrid, while fellow 2015 debutant New York City FC had a trio of big names from Europe—David Villa, Frank Lampard, and Andrea Pirlo.

In 2017, Atlanta United set a new bar for an expansion team. The names may not have been as familiar as Beckham and David Villa, but Paraguayan Miguel Almiron and Venezuelan Josef Martinez immediately formed one of the most exciting attacks MLS has ever seen. Martinez shattered the single-season goal-scoring record in 2018, scoring 31 times in 34 games. Atlanta also signed a big-time coach in Gerardo "Tata" Martino, whose head coaching resume included Barcelona and the national teams of Argentina and Paraguay. Martino left after two seasons for another big gig—Mexico's national team.

The inaugural roster wasn't the end of Atlanta's spending. The club built a $60 million training facility for all its teams from MLS down to youth level. And it shelled out a $15 million transfer fee, unheard of in MLS, for young Argentine prospect Ezequiel Barco.

Also in 2018, Los Angeles FC debuted with three Designated Players all making more than $1 million, including Mexican star Carlos Vela, who made $4.5 million in base salary and more than that with bonuses.

Let's sum up the growth in player salaries. In 1996, a salary cap of $1.2 million × 10 teams = $12 million for the entire league. Adjust for inflation, and that number might exceed $20 million if you include Campos's Ferrari. But in 2018, Toronto FC alone spent more than $26.5 million. The Los Angeles Galaxy spent $17.5 million, followed by Chicago ($15.5 million), New York City FC ($14.8 million), and Los Angeles FC ($14.1 million).[4] Atlanta only spent $11.6 million, but that doesn't include the fee for Barco.

Other clubs are putting their investments elsewhere. FC Dallas, which still spent more than $9 million on its first team, has a thriving academy. In 2018, the club signed its 23rd "homegrown" player from its academy. In 2017, homegrown players accounted for 19 percent of the first team's playing time.[5] The club also sent Weston McKennie to Germany, but read on to see an issue with that signing.

A MORE AUTHENTIC MLS

The other change MLS made was an all-out quest to resemble the world's more successful leagues. Where the old NASL enticed the U.S. sports fan with Americanized rules (the league standings required a calculator), cheerleaders, and Bugs Bunny, MLS has done away with such novelties. The league did carry over the tiebreaking "shoot-out," not kicks from the penalty mark but a one-on-one live-ball showdown, but Commissioner Don Garber immediately removed the gimmick when he took office in 1999.

The next order of business, starting with the Columbus Crew in 1999, was to put teams in proper environments.

In the first season, every MLS team played in an American football stadium, where fans rattled around with a lot of empty seats around them. D.C. United has supporters groups that kept the stands bouncing at rickety RFK Stadium, which benefited from a partial canopy over the lower level, but other teams struggled to create any sort of atmosphere.

Through the 2000s, the league's clubs went on a building spree, seeking mid-sized grounds that would feel full with a crowd of 18,000 or 25,000. The Los Angeles Galaxy, Dallas, Chicago, Toronto, Colorado, Salt Lake, the New York Red Bulls, Philadelphia, Kansas City, Portland, Houston, Montreal, San Jose, Orlando, D.C. United, and Los Angeles FC all moved into or launched in mid-sized soccer stadiums by 2018. The term "soccer-specific" isn't quite accurate, because many of these stadiums are also used for some American football games and other events, but the soccer club is the primary tenant and, in many cases, the owner.

Seattle and Atlanta, meanwhile, have done the impossible, making NFL stadiums feel like home. In 2018, Atlanta averaged 53,000 fans. Seattle was second with more than 40,000.

In many of these cities, MLS is drawing young fans looking for a fun time. These teams now have a lively atmosphere with near-capacity crowds, coordinated chants, and tifo—the massive art displays that supporters manage to bring to life in the stands. The Portland Timbers experience was even immortalized in the TV show *Portlandia*, where Fred Armisen and Carrie Brownstein's characters fretted over finding the right sign to carry to a game, eventually settling on something cat-related that was accompanied by this memorable chant: "Please, please win, meow meow meow."

In short, MLS has become hip. Between the live experience and the improved talent pool, the league's attendance grew—from an average of under 14,000 in 2000 to more than 22,000 in 2017.

But live games are the easy part of the MLS sales pitch. As soccer grows in the United States, fans will want to see games in person. A fan can watch Manchester United or Club America play on TV in his boxer shorts, but he can only see those teams in person in the occasional exhibition on U.S. soil. (Also, the boxer shorts would be frowned upon in a soccer stadium. Maybe. Hard to tell with modern supporters groups.) Even if fans would pick a Premier League game over an MLS game, they might not be willing to wait until a European giant comes around like Halley's Comet, so they'll check out the local club—perhaps even at a lower level than MLS.

The bigger challenge is the TV audience. For all the spending MLS has done, the league is treading water in the intense race for viewers, as we detailed in the previous chapter.

MLS AND THE AMERICAN PLAYER

The race for talent can have unintended consequences. One way MLS can compete in the marketplace is with a better talent pool. The big-name European veterans get the most attention, but MLS teams have devoted a lot of energy and money to signing players from all over the Americas. MLS limits the number of international players on each team to eight, but those slots can be traded so that one team has ten and another has six, and so on. Also, the rule exempts players whom the U.S. government classifies as refugees, asylum grantees, or permanent residents (green-card holders). Then the league exempts international players who pass through an MLS academy.

Add it all up, and you may have a game with only one player on the field who's eligible for the U.S. national team. That happened on April 22, 2018, when Portland played New York City FC. That weekend, by the calculations of *Soccer America*'s Paul Kennedy, only 68 of the 242 players that started an MLS game were USA-eligible.[6]

So the league is in a catch-22 situation. MLS teams have managed to round up enough players to stock the rosters, even as the league expands, but despite one memorable interview when German star Bastian Schweinsteiger joined the Chicago Fire, MLS teams (or Premier League teams, or Bundesliga teams) cannot win the World Cup.[7] But the more MLS looks outside its borders for talented players, the fewer opportunities U.S. and Canadian players may get.

Either way, the U.S. national team is at least partially dependent on having a good league with domestic players. While a strong league is no guarantee of a strong national team, it's damn hard to have the latter without the former. Let's compare the world's top soccer leagues by revenue[8] and see how their national teams are doing:

- England (Premier League): World Cup champion on home soil in 1966, fourth place in 1990 and 2018, a couple more appearances in the quarterfinals. Two-time European semifinalist. Home fans may fret, but that's not bad.
- Germany (Bundesliga): Four-time World Cup champion, very rarely eliminated before the quarterfinals. Three-time European champion.
- Spain (La Liga): Shed its reputation for underachievement by winning the 2010 World Cup, sandwiched in between its second and third European championships.
- Italy (Serie A): Four-time World Cup champion.
- France (Ligue 1): Two-time World Cup champion and two-time European champion.
- Brazil (Campeonato Brasileiro): Five-time World Cup champion.

Let's choose another measure—the ranking of club teams around the world by FiveThirtyEight, the site that made data analysis cool in sports and politics. This is the site's median ranking of teams in each nation's league(s) as of November 27, 2018:[9]

1. Spain: 32
2. England: 63
3. Germany: 84
4. Italy: 95
5. France: 101
6. Brazil: 170
7. England (second tier): 209

A few notables: Mexico 12th, Argentina 14th, the USA 18th, the Netherlands 19th, Japan 20th. The Netherlands' ranking is deceiving. Ajax is 8th; PSV Eindhoven is 18th. The ranking is brought down by 12 teams outside the top 300. I'd also argue Argentina's ranking. I'm not sure how the top two teams in the league (River Plate, Boca Juniors) can be in the Copa Libertadores final and still rank lower than the fifth-ranked team in Brazil.

The reason to single out the Netherlands and Argentina is simple— along with outlier Croatia, they're the only countries to reach a men's World Cup final since 1966 aside from the Big Six of Spain, England, Germany, Italy, France, and Brazil. You get the picture. Where you have a big-time league, you have an international contender.

Among the Big Six leagues, the biggest disparity is between the Premier League and England's national team. In 2018, that disparity seems to be gone—England reached the World Cup semifinals but failed to hold on against Croatia, perhaps due to complacency after taking the lead in that game against an underdog.

The more general explanation for England underperforming is the lack of English players in the Premier League. A 2017 *New York Times* analysis put the percentage at 34 percent.[10] Italy was at 48 percent, Germany 49, and France 54. Spain was at a robust 59 percent. (By comparison, the percentage of U.S. players in MLS was 51 percent. That's not bad, but is 51 percent in MLS better than 49 percent in the Bundesliga?)[11]

But England still benefits from a healthy league because its clubs— most of them, anyway—plow some of their money back into youth academies. MLS clubs have jumped into this game with subsidized academies that play in U.S. Soccer's Development Academy (DA) program. The

DA has plenty of flaws (see chapter 8), but we can't really argue with the idea of pro clubs subsidizing youth development. England, like the other countries in the Big Six, is far ahead of the United States in that respect.

Worldwide, clubs can turn their academies into moneymakers. When a good young player transfers to a new club, his old club gets a transfer fee. The better the player, the higher the fee. The old club might get even more money when that player is sold again through the labyrinthian regulations on training compensation and solidarity pay. Ajax, the most successful club in the Netherlands, regularly cleans up on such payments.

So academies can help clubs in two ways. First, they develop players whom a club can sign from within, as FC Dallas does quite well. Second, they can sell some of those players to bigger clubs, turning that academy into a moneymaker in its own right.

Selling to the big clubs isn't necessarily a bad thing. Brazil's national team rarely has significant players who play at home, and yet that league is the best outside of Europe. Most of the top players in the Netherlands play elsewhere, and that revenue helps a nation of 17 million compete on the world stage. Croatia's World Cup finalists didn't play a single player based in Croatia at the time, but Dinamo Zagreb, Hajduk Split, and Rijeka are making tons of money on transfers, and that money is helping them slowly climb the ladder in European competitions. Unfortunately, U.S. clubs have an issue here. To see the problem, let's go back to FC Dallas and Weston McKennie.

First, a player has to sign a professional contract for the transfer fee to kick in. MLS clubs are signing plenty of teenagers these days, but some players hesitate to sign pro deals because they want to maintain their eligibility for a possible college soccer career. A player who signs a pro deal is basically going all in on a pro career rather than a college scholarship. McKennie, among others, did not. Second, the United States does not participate in the training compensation/solidarity pay system for reasons that can only be unraveled by lawyers and players' unions. (We'll *try* to explain in chapter 5. Temper your expectations.) All of which means FC Dallas watched McKennie move to German club Schalke . . . for nothing.[12]

Compounding the problem for MLS and any other U.S. professional clubs: These clubs don't have the monopoly on talent that such clubs have in other countries. Even with residential programs popping up at a few academies, the United States is simply too vast to have pro clubs everywhere, leaving scattered youth clubs to pick up the slack. In 2018–2019, the Development Academy league has nearly 100 clubs at the upper age groups and more than that at the lower age groups, with MLS taking up no more than 20 percent of the membership.

Feeding transfer money and solidarity pay to youth clubs scattered nationwide wouldn't be a bad thing for general development of U.S. players. Christian Pulisic didn't grow up near an MLS academy, and youth club PA Classics would surely benefit from training compensation as European clubs haggle over his services. (As of this writing, PA Classics seems unlikely to put in for payment for Pulisic's big-money move to Chelsea in 2019.) But until more youth clubs—the Richmond Kickers are an exception—enter adult teams in the pro leagues, that money will be staying away from professional clubs.

Some American prospects skip the U.S. system entirely, at least in their teen years. European clubs have found creative ways around regulations for bringing minors into their own academies. Ben Lederman went to Barcelona at age 11, moving his family to get around FIFA (Fédération Internationale de Football Association) rules—and still running into a bit of trouble when he was older. Mani Eftekhari and his family moved to Croatia so Mani could play for Dinamo Zagreb's academy at age eight. [13]

Moving overseas can certainly help individual players develop. Pulisic was the best U.S. player before his 20th birthday. Timothy Weah, son of 1995 Ballon d'Or (top player in the world) winner George Weah, left the New York Red Bulls academy for Paris Saint-Germain at age 14, and he moved onto the PSG first team and the U.S. national team by age 18.

But as the law currently stands, the Red Bulls won't get any money they can put back into their club, just as FC Dallas won't get money from McKennie's future moves.

Let's say, for sake of argument, that the United States solves this problem. We'll say the NCAA relents and allows a player to regain amateur status so that an athlete who signs a pro deal at age 15 still has the option of playing in college at age 19, giving clubs greater freedom to sign players to a pro deal and reap the transfer windfall. We'll say U.S. Soccer figures out a way to get solidarity pay and training compensation without angering lawyers and the MLS Players Association. We'll say these developments encourage more investors to buy or build soccer clubs and soccer stadiums.

MLS and any other U.S. league would still run into a glass ceiling.

THE GLOBAL REALITY

Big as they are, the big clubs aren't content with what they're making. The European powers have only consolidated their strength over the past two decades, thanks in part to a couple of developments.

First is greater freedom of player movement in what soccer writers call the "post-Bosman era." The era's namesake, Jean-Marc Bosman, is a Belgian player who had an offer to move to an unheralded French club after his contract with an equally unheralded Belgian club expired. The Belgian club said no. Bosman insisted. The case worked its way through the European judicial system. In 1995, the European Court of Justice dropped the hammer. Players were no longer tied to their original clubs once their contracts expired and could leave on a "free transfer." Also, European leagues could no longer impose restrictions on the number of European players each club signed.[14]

The impact is obvious from a glance at World Cup rosters. In 1990, most European national teams drew most of their players from their domestic leagues. By 2018, some European teams had players employed across 10 or more leagues, and the teams from elsewhere in the world were similarly scattered. England's leagues sent 124 players to the World Cup. Spain sent 81, Germany 67.[15] MLS sent a respectable 19 players despite the USA's failure to qualify. (Brexit, the United Kingdom's controversial move to break away from the European Union, might allow renewed restrictions on EU players trying to play for English clubs.)

The second factor is TV revenue. In England, the Premier League broke away from the rest of England's professional leagues (while maintaining promotion and relegation between itself and the next-highest tier) in 1992 with an eye toward capturing more money from TV. The move came just in time for a boom in satellite TV that opened the world to its games. By Ernst and Young's accounting, TV money has boomed from £11 million for the 1988–1989 season to £1.7 *billion* for 2013–2014, or nearly $2.5 billion in 2018 U.S. dollars.[16] The Premier League spread that money so that each club got at least £57.8 million. Across the biggest leagues—England, Spain, Germany, and Italy—every club earned at least £12.9 million from its own broadcasting revenue. The egalitarian Bundesliga only paid its top clubs the equivalent of around £25 million, while La Liga handed nearly £100 million to its top-finishing clubs.

Also in the early 1990s, the Union of European Football Associations (UEFA) revamped its Champions Cup competition, which had pulled together the champions of each league into a tournament that ran concurrently with the domestic league season. In 1992, this competition became the Champions League. At first, the change was mostly cosmetic, but in 1997 the Champions League expanded to give the big leagues more than one team in the competition. In the 1999–2000 competition, Spain was allowed three entries—all of whom made the semifinals. Today, some countries can qualify four teams for the competition.

As a result, clubs from smaller countries have to run a more difficult gauntlet of major opponents. With the exception of Portugal's Porto in 2003–2004, a run that set up manager Jose Mourinho for a lucrative career in the major leagues, Europe's top prize has been won by clubs from only four countries—Spain (nine), England (three), Italy (three), and Germany (two). The only other country to put a team in the final is France.

So the big clubs keep winning. And that means, of course, more money. In 2018–2019, Champions League clubs will split an estimated pot of 2.73 billion euros, or more than $3 billion.[17] The farther a team progresses, the more of that money it gets.

The rich get richer. And that's not going to change. The big clubs periodically threaten to break away to form a "Super League" in Europe, eventually getting concessions that ensure they get the lion's share of TV revenues, which in turn means they can keep buying the world's best players. (See chapter 7. Yes, American owners are part of it.) Even within each league, only a small number of teams have a legitimate chance of winning the championship, Leicester City's wonderful underdog run to the 2016 Premier League title being the big exception to the rule.

A club like Porto or Ajax (a European champion in 1995, before the dam burst) can reasonably hope only to make an occasional run. The Champions League revenue would then give that club a boost for a couple of years, but eventually, the lack of domestic TV money would force it to sell its best players and fall back. Players from the Porto club that won it all quickly dispersed across Europe.

Other former powers have dropped off the map entirely. Scottish club Celtic made a couple of Champions Cup runs in the past, winning it all in 1967. Romanian club Steaua Bucureşti won the Champions Cup in 1986 and was a finalist in 1989. Neither club has been a significant challenger in the big-money era.

So when a U.S. soccer fan sits down to watch a Premier League or Champions League game, he or she is contributing to the ever-tightening grip the world's best clubs have on the global game. The chasm between a young league like MLS and Europe's big leagues is even more difficult to bridge today than it was 1996.

That's not to pass judgment on anyone. As I write the first draft of this chapter, I have a Tottenham-Inter Champions League game playing on my phone while I seek updates on Liverpool, my favorite European club. (It's not going well. Thanks for asking.) Those of us who grew up in a soccer void can't take such opportunities for granted. MLS supporters can't ask people to turn off the TV, laptop, or phone when the world's best players are playing. They can only ask those people to tune into an MLS game as well.

The battle isn't hopeless. As MLS draws more fans through the gate, those fans develop loyalties that may entice them to watch their local clubs in addition to the Premier League. Investment has certainly soared, and some cities have embraced their local clubs.

Romantics may remember the glory days of the North American Soccer League (NASL), in which the New York Cosmos built an appropriately cosmopolitan roster and fared well in friendlies against major European visitors. But the Cosmos dollars went a lot further in those days than they would today. I analyzed the peak roster of the late 1970s for the *Guardian* and checked the team's value against that of the European giants. It's not close.[18] (In chapter 7, we'll get to the idea that a promotion/relegation system would open the floodgates to investment rivaling that of the Real Madrids and Liverpools of the world. It won't.)

The big leagues have that awesome combination of historical lore and modern money. The United States has neither. And that's one more obstacle in the way of building the soccer culture and development system the United States needs to compete.

3

WE'RE TOO INSECURE
IN OUR IDENTITIES

Other chapters in this book are supported by hundreds of articles and essays, all full of statistics and sources. This chapter isn't so easy to quantify. It's mostly the summary of observations as a soccer writer for the past 20 years, a dedicated fan for the past 30 years, and someone with at least a passing interest in what little soccer was available for the past 40 years. Coming up with stats to back up these observations would require some rather intrusive polling, possibly including the use of a polygraph or a psychic.

In other words, the depictions that follow aren't some drive-by observation of a snarky sports talk host sitting in a radio studio or staring into a TV camera. I've been immersed in soccer for a long time, and I've been fortunate to interact with people in all capacities of the sport—players, coaches, executives, and fans.

And let's be clear: The U.S. soccer community is justly proud of its inclusivity. Everyone is acutely aware that this is a global game. English-speaking soccer fans try to teach each other enough Spanish to follow broadcasts on Univision and Telemundo. Soccer is ahead of most sports in providing professional opportunities for women, and most of us recognize that we still have a long way to go. Soccer fans embrace the many lesbian players in the women's game, and it's no surprise that soccer was the first major U.S. sport with an openly gay player—Robbie Rogers, who came out after his release from English club Leeds United and figured his career was done,[1] only to be coaxed out of his brief retirement to play for the Los Angeles Galaxy, whose fans greeted his first appearance with a standing ovation.[2] We are a diverse bunch.

But among suburbanites and young urban hipsters, being a soccer fan used to carry a sort of outsider's cachet. This is a group that wants a wide selection of craft beers, and is more likely to argue the merits of recent Radiohead albums than dance to Taylor Swift. At the extreme, some soccer fans are the Goth kids from *South Park*—elitist nonconformists who frankly can be kind of obnoxious about it. Let the Great Unwashed watch brutal (football) or boring (baseball) sports.

So Major League Soccer's growth poses a problem. We want to keep up our soccer cred. But MLS isn't a microbrew. It's Budweiser, a former MLS sponsor. (The league has moved one rung up the beer snob's ladder, to Heineken.)

"We" are certainly divided. Young city dwellers are happy to partake of the MLS fan experience, especially in Portland and Seattle. But for many segments of this crowd, MLS is simply too pedestrian. And the world's biggest clubs are clearly better than any MLS club, even Atlanta United, so they can't support *that*.

We're that desperate to be hip. More precisely, we have to be snobs. In the parlance of the U.S. soccer community, Eurosnobs.

No one can cry foul if a U.S. soccer fan tunes in to NBC's outstanding Premier League broadcasts or revels in the occasional Barcelona appearance on a La Liga or Champions League broadcast. Soccer fans can't deny themselves the opportunity to watch a once-in-a-lifetime player like Lionel Messi. The question is whether they can bring themselves to watch a mid-table MLS game after watching Messi shred a hapless La Liga foe.

MLS is fully aware of the problem. The league realized many years ago that it didn't need to chase the general *sports* fan. The battle is to win the hearts of *soccer* fans. That's why the last vestiges of Americanized soccer, especially our insistence on breaking ties in the regular season, have gone away. MLS still has playoffs, but so do Mexico and some South American leagues.

The biggest difference between MLS and other leagues is the lack of promotion and relegation. Some fans are so insistent on implementing that system here that they follow lower-division leagues such as the National Premier Soccer League (NPSL) because they *want* to have pro/rel, even if they haven't actually implemented it.

Many of these fans are, in a word, hostile. Those of us who've been targeted by them, formerly on message boards but more recently and persistently on Twitter, can think of a few other words as well. In their minds, the MLS cost-containment strategy is part of some sinister conspiracy, and anyone who points out anything to the contrary is part of the cabal, most likely paid directly by MLS, its marketing arm Soccer United Marketing, and U.S. Soccer.

Or worse. Here's a tweet by Gary Kleiban, whose brother Brian is a well-regarded coach who, ironically, was working at an MLS academy as of 2018, four years after this was posted:

> It's about maintaining exclusivity.
> Of, by, & for "white culture."
> That's why they fight against pro/rel. [3]

That's right. In this world, people who argue against pro/rel aren't stating valid objections. (We'll cover those in chapter 7.) Nor are they simply wrong—they're racist.

I once wrote a piece for the *Guardian* directly inspired by my interactions with these accusers. The piece was about Flat Earthers. The echo chamber in which Neil deGrasse Tyson is said to believe in post-Copernicus astronomy only because he's a NASA shill is eerily similar to the echo chamber in which keeping pro/rel down is simply part of an anti-soccer conspiracy conveniently led by everyone in a position of power, including volunteer positions, in U.S. Soccer at large.

Like most political discussions, beliefs are on a spectrum. Not everyone who spurns MLS and preaches pro/rel believes race is a root cause of their opposition. Some pro/rel advocates are more hostile than others. And among the most dogmatic and accusatory MLS critics, the attacks may boost their indie cred, but it's not helping their cause.

"It is not enough just to have a good idea, which, as American soccer continues to grow, pro/rel increasingly appears to be," argues Canadian writer David Rudin. "But the 'ProRelForUSA' movement has nothing to offer here except sound and fury. After years of online activism with nothing to show for it beyond rancor, the promotion and relegation campaign has proven itself to be a remarkably ineffective political movement." [4]

So if you've ever wondered whatever happened to the guy in your college who insisted that the campus radio station had gone too commercial, now you know.

HYPERSENSITIVITY FOR ALL

We in the soccer community aren't just sensitive to each other's barbs. After generations of dismissive talk and outright verbal abuse from sports columnists and TV personalities, we have actually been united by our common enemy—the handful of sports pundits, less numerous than they used to be, who slam the global game.

But it's one thing to roll our eyes and write a long Twitter thread assailing the latest anti-soccer screed from some aging dude trying to provoke controversy. It's another to have no sense of humor.

The Simpsons, the long-running TV cartoon that has wonderfully satirized most aspects of life in the United States and elsewhere, has had fun with soccer over the years, dating back to a dismissive "Ugh, soccer" in the classic 1991 episode in which the Simpsons steal cable. Twenty-three years later, Homer becomes a referee and confronts diving and match-fixing controversies, concerns that any soccer supporter would share.

The most indelible *Simpsons* soccer segment was the opening act of a 1997 episode in which the Simpsons go to a soccer game, persuaded by an exuberant ad. A man resembling Hank Williams Jr., the country music star whose line, "Are you ready for some football?!" featured in television's *Monday Night Football* introductions for many years, is shown with a soccer ball on a charcoal grill. He yells, "Open wide for some soccer!" The ad hails all the joys of soccer such as low scoring and ties. "This match will determine once and for all which nation is the greatest on Earth—Mexico or Portugal!" (Some fans were rooting for that match-up in the 2018 World Cup final, but Mexico lost in the round of 16 for the seventh straight World Cup, and Portugal fell in the same round to Uruguay.)

In a packed Springfield Stadium, the pregame festivities include Pelé making a clumsy pitch for "Crestfield Wax Paper," for which he's handed a sack of money. A stadium vendor marches through the stands selling paella.

The game starts with a couple of players kicking back and forth. And continues with a couple of players kicking back and forth. The crowd goes quiet and sits down. Local news anchor Kent Brockman calls the action in a dull monotone and rolls his eyes, finishing with "Center holds it . . . holds it . . . (sigh) holds it." In the next booth, a Hispanic commentator repeats the same words with an accent and considerable enthusiasm: "Center holds it . . . holds it . . . HOLDS IT!"

A riot ensues when fans try to race for the exits. Groundskeeper Willie leads a band of Scottish hooligans into the fray.

Many U.S. soccer fans have embraced the satire. An insightful soccer blog named itself "Center Holds It." A group of Washington metro-area soccer writers launched the "Open Wide for Some Soccer" podcast. *Slate* commentator Alan Siegel found the *Simpsons* treatment both hilarious and affectionate, calling it "one inspired piece of U.S.-made satire that manages to mock soccer while also embracing the very thing it's laughing at."[5]

But the soccer community simply has to find fault somewhere. An essay in *Soccer Culture in America* includes the *Simpsons* treatment of soccer in a rundown of soccer slights on American television, with author Benjamin James Dettmar comparing the "Open Wide for Some Soccer" segment with an early baseball/softball episode that "focuses on the absurd" rather than commenting on the sport itself.[6]

If Dettmar's gripe, admittedly a minor one, was an isolated case of U.S. soccer fans being far too defensive, we could ignore it. But it's not. And the media—not just the knee-jerk, old-school, soccer-bashing grumps—have noticed.

In 2014, a couple of months before the World Cup, Deadspin held a vote—an NCAA tournament-style set of brackets in which the "winning" entity in the vote advanced to the next round—to find the "Bitchiest, Most Defensive Fans in America." The top seed in the sports-related bracket: Soccer fans. The explanation for that nomination was damning:

> American soccer fans believe that soccer ought to be the most popular sport in America, but is not because of stubborn, jingoistic assholes like you, who refuse to give soccer a chance. You probably complain about soccer without ever watching it, and therefore nothing you say holds any weight. Do you hate low scoring, dives, crypto-fascist fans, and/or grotesque oligarchs? Well, clearly you're just some mouth-breathing rube who has to be babysat at all times by made baskets and

cheap touchdown passes. And if you say one more thing about how you don't like the offsides rule, you can go to hell.
(juggles Adidas ball between knees)
(makes unintelligible rallying cry for some asshole EPL team)[7]

To give some perspective, Duke fans were seeded fourth in that bracket. Duke fans are not loved. (Trust me. I have two degrees from Duke. I've sometimes learned the results of basketball games only when people taunt me about it, even though I haven't bragged about Duke's basketball success since I was an undergraduate.)

In the *same bracket*, MLS Fanboys were broken out as a subset and seeded 12th: "Different from general soccer fans in that they are at constant war with both (a) soccer haters and (b) soccer fanboys who view MLS as an inferior product."[8]

The good news: Voters were less irritated with the soccer community, if only slightly. Soccer Fans and MLS Fans advanced past the first round but "lost" after that. Red Sox Fans, though only the eighth seed, knocked out Soccer Fans. MLS Fans were no match for Duke Fans. (Red Sox Fans then lost in the Final Four to Christian Conservatives, who advanced from a sociopolitical bracket.)

What's the harm in being easily offended snobs? Oh, there's plenty of harm . . .

THE BACKLASH

Whether it's watching soccer at all in 1993 or watching nothing but the Bundesliga in 2018, viewers are able to stake a claim as some sort of hipster elite. And Americans *hate* elites. Franklin Foer, who spends most of his time in the sociopolitical realm, writes with considerable understatement:

> Elites have never been especially well-liked in post-war American politics—or at least they have been easy to take swipes at. But the generation of elites that adopted soccer has been an especially ripe target. That's because they came through college in the sixties and seventies, at a time when the counterculture self-consciously turned against the stultifying conformity of what it perceived as traditional America. Even as this group shed its youthful radical politics, it kept

some of its old ideals, including its resolute cosmopolitanism and suspicions of middle America, "flyover country." When they adopted soccer, it gave the impression that they had turned their backs on the national pastime. This, naturally, produced even more disdain for them—and their sport.[9]

So we have a split between elites and anti-elites. Then we have a split within the elites, some of whom see soccer as just too foreign for their tastes. Foer catalogued one such elite—*Wall Street Journal* columnist Allen Barra, who asked in print whether other countries would embrace American sports if they could afford them, just as they'd eat something other than rice if they could afford it.[10] (No wonder people hate elites.)

Yes, "elite" sometimes translates to "American exceptionalism turned to xenophobia," which also explains why we have trouble winning everyone over. Older fans have had bitter arguments about the impact of clubs playing with ethnic names—the Philadelphia German-Americans, Kearny Scots, Ukrainian Nationals, and the awkwardly named Toronto Metros-Croatia of the NASL—in a country that often takes issue with any hyphen before "American." Such conversations have faded, and there's something charming about having teams like the Brooklyn Italians and Milwaukee Bavarians in the Open Cup. The debate is whether the Scots, Ukrainians, Irish, and other teams of the mid-twentieth century reinforced the notion that soccer is merely an activity for families who still maintain Old World loyalties.

Generally, fans will put aside their arguments and back the national team. Generally. Not always. U.S. Soccer finds myriad ways to exhaust fans' patience. Ticket prices, even for humdrum friendly matches, are giving fans sticker shock. The organization's coaching hires and stubbornness in sticking with them have driven some fans from "disgruntled" to "downright alienated."

Alexi Lalas, who went to a couple of World Cups for the U.S. men and now revels in provoking arguments with his commentary on Fox Sports and Twitter, is still optimistic that we can all come together when it counts.

> American soccer is a strange and wonderful animal. We will fight to defend its honor, but we love to eat our own. Our inferiority complex is legendary and we wear our insecurities on our sleeve. But in some ways it's understandable. It is borne of a country and culture that for

most of its history has looked askew at the sport of soccer and those who liked it. That creates a brotherhood/sisterhood with a proud tradition of antagonism and protectionism. It also creates incredible ownership. We know our soccer is different and far from perfect. But it's La Cosa Nostra. It's our thing. Oh, we'll fight amongst ourselves, often bitterly, but we also seem to unite when faced with an attack from outside. It's a family, and like all families it has plenty of dysfunction. [11]

Still, that dysfunction has ramifications all the way down to the grass roots.

THE YOUTH IDENTITY

In the youth game, our national lack of confidence can be more damaging. As a relatively new soccer nation, we have a lot of parents who don't know much about the game but eagerly sign up their kids and get weirdly competitive about it. And we have plenty of people who are happy to prey on their ignorance.

Consider a press release that made the rounds on behalf of a youth soccer coach who was in danger of losing his visa. You can't blame the guy for wanting to stay in the country, and we're living in a time in which a lot of Americans don't want to recognize the contributions of people who didn't come over here before the Revolution. But the gist of the press release wasn't a humanitarian appeal to keep a hard-working immigrant in the United States: "How do we save U.S. Soccer? With ubertalented coaches like [name and country redacted], struggling to get an O-1 Visa, but time is running out," read the subject line. The press release goes on to posit this coach as "that tiny bright light we need" who would be "bringing European soccer techniques to young US soccer players."

This press release wasn't sent in 1980. This was from 2018.

If you've spent any time at all in U.S. youth soccer, you know that hundreds of coaches have brought European soccer techniques to young American players for generations. But a lot of parents don't know that. This press release wouldn't have been sent if the coach and publicist thought the target audience of American parents understood that an accent does not a great coach make.

And we're still obsessed with TV commentators who have an accent. People who never watch soccer have heard Andres Cantor yell "GOOOOOOOOOOLL" for about 20 seconds or more. World Cup and Premier League broadcasts in the United States are filled with English accents.

Plenty of these coaches and commentators are excellent. Mark Parsons came over from Chelsea's academy to a small youth club in Virginia and quickly demonstrated enough aptitude to be a head coach for the Washington Spirit of the National Women's Soccer League before he turned 30. He was quickly snapped up by the biggest spending club in U.S. women's soccer, the Portland Thorns. Ian Darke and Arlo White back up their voices with professionalism and lively commentary. Rebecca Lowe is a welcome female voice on Premier League studio shows, which she moderates with skill that makes live television look easy. (It's not. Not at all.)

And we can't forget Ray Hudson, the former NASL player and MLS coach whose passion and capacity for extemporaneous analogy are unmatched. His highlights include "Like a vampire on a plate of liver," "He could follow you into a revolving door and come out first," and "Cool as a polar bear's backside."

So we can't argue that the United States has not benefited from the talented people who have come in and contributed soccer knowledge and brilliant wordplay. The problem comes with the *assumption* that the man with the accent is more knowledgeable than anyone from California or Ohio. And that assumption is shared by a lot of soccer parents and soccer fans.

In youth soccer, the quest for coaches with accents is just part of the identity crisis. By the time we started taking youth soccer seriously, we had a few differences about our soccer goals. (Figuratively.)

The AYSO (American Youth Soccer Organization, but like NASCAR, no one ever uses the full name) launched in the 1960s with a couple of revolutionary traits. If you signed up, you played—at least half of every game. Each season, team rosters would be shuffled in an effort to create parity.

The unintentional consequence was to "domesticate" a game that had been largely the province of ethnic groups, argues David Keyes in the essay "Making the Mainstream: The Domestication of American Soccer." And AYSO immediately felt backlash, Keyes says:

Not all were enthused by what AYSO was doing. Soccer officials in the ethnic communities were particularly unimpressed. Adolfo Miralles, a native of Argentina, had enrolled a team in AYSO in 1967. But he and a group of mostly foreign-born coaches became dismayed with AYSO's attempt to Americanize the game, in particular with some of the rule changes. As Miralles put it, they "wanted to play by FIFA rules, not AYSO rules." He continued: "We thought it would be good to be part of world soccer instead of just being part of AYSO." For these coaches, it was more important to be part of the world's game than it was to see the game Americanized in order to raise its profile in the United States. . . .

As Ric Fonseca, longtime soccer observer and former professor of history at Los Angeles City College, says, "AYSO tried to but was not successful in getting into the Latino community because of the philosophy that everyone plays." In particular, he said, Latinos were "more used to idea [sic] that you put a good team together and they stay together." [12]

By the time the kids of the 1960s were soccer parents, the notion of soccer as a safe activity had taken root, Franklin Foer says:

Soccer's appeal lay in its opposition to the other popular sports. For children of the sixties, there was something abhorrent about enrolling kids in American football, a game where violence wasn't just incidental but inherent. They didn't want to teach the acceptability of violence, let alone subject their precious children to the risk of physical maiming. . . .

But soccer represented something very different. It was a tabula rasa, a sport onto which a generation of parents could project their values. Quickly, soccer came to represent the fundamental tenets of yuppie parenting, the spirit of *Sesame Street* and Dr. Benjamin Spock. Unlike the other sports, it would foster self-esteem, minimize the pain of competition while still teaching life lessons. [13]

Today, some people are trying to tear down the notion of soccer as a recreational activity, perhaps too harshly. Do we want to have millions of kids happily playing the game, or do we want a Darwinian struggle to sort the future pros from the eight-year-olds with no future? Or can we have both? We'll get to that in chapter 8.

THE "NATIONAL" IDENTITY

So what are we doing here? Who are we? What are we? (Where, when, why, how, etc. Sorry. Recovering journalist here.)

We can't answer these questions as a society these days. We are progressive and we are conservative. We are immigrants, and we are anti-immigrant. We're diverse, and sometimes unhappy about it. We're well-educated, but academics aren't really represented in our mainstream media.

England is . . . English, united by a shared history of literary and scientific greatness despite horrible wars and cruelty. France has wine, the romance of Paris, and the incomparably beautiful countryside that makes the Tour de France a must-watch despite years of drug scandals. Brazil is a country of dancing and trying not to talk about the oppressive government that ruins any hope of dealing with the crippling poverty in so many areas. Germany is the land of chocolate, according to *The Simpsons*, and also the masters of machinery.

Many of these traits are reflected in the style of play of many national teams. Germany is methodical and efficient. Brazil's soccer carries the uninhibited joy of Carnival. Italy invented a stern defensive approach punctuated by breathtaking moments of skill. England is evolving but has a rugged mentality, no surprise for a country obsessed with hard work and character. The Scandinavian countries have an English-style "direct" approach of banging the ball around and running hard, mostly in an effort to avoid freezing. If Mexican teams ran that much, they'd collapse from the heat.

The American style is . . .?

We're trying, apparently. U.S. Soccer hired its first men's national team general manager in 2018, bestowing the job on 1994 World Cup hero Earnie Stewart, and one of his responsibilities is "ensuring that U.S. Soccer's style of play, team tactical principles, and key qualities are being implemented within the men's national team." Early in his tenure, he deflected the opportunity to define what that is. [14]

Tony Meola, also a standout on that 1994 World Cup team, seems skeptical that such a thing can be imposed from above:

> All of us who aspire to coach and analyze, we all have a style that we
> like, a style that we would want the team to look like. But I still think
> your style is a product of your players. We could have a Manchester

City style in mind but if we don't have the players, it's impossible to play that way. . . .

We've always talked about styles of play. For years, we talked about Tahuichi (an academy in Bolivia that developed early MLS stars Marco Etcheverry and Jaime Moreno). And then Portugal won a couple youth World Cups, and all of a sudden we were going to use that system. And then Brazil was winning World Cups and we figured we'll try that, and it didn't last long. Then it was the German system. [15]

For a while in the 2010s, the obsession was Barcelona, with its "tiki-taka" philosophy of short passes. This trend played into a sudden obsession with futsal, the indoor game (without the walls that American indoor soccer has) that puts a premium on short-range connections. Americans have failed to develop such skills, we were told, and so that became the focus on various curricula handed down from on high and usually ignored.

Americans also lacked the ability to dribble and beat defenders in a one-on-one situation, we were told. Those of us who coached the youngest players in recreational soccer were told to forget about passing for the first couple of years and just work on getting players comfortable with the ball at their feet. Some coaches took this to extremes, emphasizing individual efforts at older ages when the games expand from four-a-side to seven-a-side.

No one's going to argue against developing a good feel for the ball, both dribbling and passing at short range, at a young age. But that's not really a "style." That's simply teaching fundamental skills, like an elementary school teacher teaching multiplication or subject-verb agreement.

The worrying aspect of all this for many commentators is whether the American soccer community is doing enough to incorporate Hispanic influences. The question frequently reasserts itself. It came up when youth national team prospect Jonathan Gonzalez opted to switch his allegiance to Mexico. It came up when Hugo Perez, yet another 1994 World Cup player and now widely regarded as an innovative and inspirational coach, wasn't retained as a U.S. national youth team coach. It came up when U.S. Soccer named Gregg Berhalter as its men's head coach instead of any of the Hispanic or Spanish coaches who were available.

But the Berhalter kerfuffle may bring us back where we started.

Berhalter was raised the traditional American way. He played high school and college soccer. He finished his playing career in MLS with the Los Angeles Galaxy, and he coached the Columbus Crew until U.S. Soccer hired him. Further complicating public opinion, Berhalter's brother Jay is a U.S. Soccer executive.

Yet Berhalter is hardly unfamiliar with the rest of the world. With no top-flight pro options in the United States at the end of his college career, he went to the Netherlands. He had a brief spell in England, followed by many years in Germany. With the Crew, he took an underfunded team to several playoff appearances and an MLS Cup final.

Besides, the best modern World Cup run by a U.S. men's team was in 2002 under the guidance of former University of Virginia lacrosse coach Bruce Arena, who switched formations and tactics as needed as the USA team moved through the tournament. Little wonder Arena was dismissive of the concept of a national curriculum and a national style. "This country, I've always said, is too large, too different to have one style of play," Arena said just after Claudio Reyna, who played for him at Virginia and with the national team, unveiled a national curriculum. [16]

So do we really need a homogeneous national style? Were the complaints about Berhalter and the hiring process legitimate? Or are these questions simply manifestations of our belief that we Americans just aren't good enough? Do we, like so many youth soccer parents, need to find a coach from somewhere else?

WE CAN'T WIN

We can't please everybody. U.S. Soccer certainly can't. Go all in on a Barcelona-style passing game, and some good players developed by good coaches won't fit in. Go all in on MLS, and good players won't get opportunities with the big clubs in Europe. Go all in on sending players to Europe, and MLS will wither.

And the fan base can't win. Sit quietly on our hands, and we're accused of having no atmosphere. Come up with chants emanating from large supporters' sections, and we're accused of being mere imitators of the European game.

Simply put—if you hate soccer, you're ignorant. If you love European soccer and not MLS, you're a derivative glory hunter. If you love MLS more than European soccer, you're an idiot.

We can't even talk about soccer without offending someone. Call it "football," and you sound like a poser. Call it "soccer," and you're an ignorant American. *Wall Street Journal* columnist Jonathan Clegg, who has gone on to do groundbreaking work on the Premier League, gave American fans no way to proceed, ridiculing us for using words like "pitch" and "match" AND ridiculing us for *not* using such terms:

> These soccer snobs are so intent on maintaining an aura of authenticity that when they make a slip-up or use an incorrect or ill-advised term, I feel compelled to pounce on them with all the force of a Roy Keane challenge.
>
> There's no such position as outside back! (It is fullback.) The rest of the world doesn't call them PKs! (It is penalties. Just penalties.)
>
> Not to mention the fact that your fans happily refer to Team USA captain Clint Dempsey by the nickname "Deuce." Deuce?! This is international soccer, not "Top Gun."[17]

Clegg advises the United States to come up with its own identity. How are we supposed to do that when we can neither forge our own path nor come up with a hybrid of our European and Latin American influences?

Maybe we have every right to be defensive and insecure. How could we be otherwise?

4

WE CAN'T AGREE ON ANYTHING

The United States of America has many traits that distinguish it from other countries. Let's focus on two.

First: We're a melting pot. My family alone is French, English, Scottish, Irish, and Persian, and that hardly makes a ripple in the vast sea of cultures in a city like New York, where as many as 800 languages are spoken.[1] Then once we've all settled into this country, our experiences are shaped by the vastly different places in which we live—a northeastern urban center, a sprawling southern metropolis, a Rust Belt manufacturing city, a midwestern farm, a rugged Rocky Mountain resort, a coffee-fueled northwestern tech capital, or a sunny California traffic jam.

Second: We're stubborn individuals who don't take kindly to being told what to do. Yes, you could say that's a big part of why we're a politically divided country and can't come up with amenities such as national health care and half-decent mass transit that the rest of the developed world takes for granted.

And diversity is a difficult topic because if you say it makes American soccer difficult, you're going to face considerable backlash. Ask Alexi Lalas, who draws reactions like this from SB Nation's Parker Cleveland:

> Thinking about how these sentiments are misguided, confused, and exclusionary at best, and xenophobic and racist at worst is important. It does not seem like Lalas, Arena, or those discussing where the USMNT [U.S. Men's National Team] should play home games, in most cases, are racist. However, it is clear that they aren't considering

how what they are saying is exclusionary and how their statements are harmful to soccer in the U.S. as a whole.[2]

Underlying this discussion is a difficult problem that has been discussed for decades in U.S. soccer and not adequately addressed: We as a soccer community have not done enough to bring in people of color, whether they're African Americans who aren't exposed to the sport or immigrants from Central and South America who love soccer but don't have a pathway through the traditionally suburban (read: white) youth clubs.

That's a long, carefully worded sentence, and yet it's still too simple. This country has plenty of African Americans who love soccer, play soccer, and still aren't given a good pathway to elite levels. (And it has a few who have—think Freddy Adu, the Ghanaian-born player from the Maryland suburbs who didn't live up to his otherworldly expectations but still played for the national team.) Some organizations, such as the U.S. Soccer Foundation (led by a former *USA TODAY* coworker of mine, Ed Foster-Simeon), are getting into neglected urban areas and building soccer facilities, in one case even working to negotiate a truce among local gangs so people can find a safe space on the soccer field.[3] Some clubs *do* find players who aren't rich white folks and give them every opportunity. And some white people aren't rich suburbanites.

And even *that* doesn't capture the complexity. Our factions are easily defined by color or class. You can easily find an English-born coach teaching something different than a parent coach raised on baseball and gridiron football, or you can find a coach enamored of the Barcelona system who can't find common ground with the Scottish coach in the same club. African American comedian Dave Chappelle was talking about the United States, not soccer, but he may have put it best: "I saw two Irish dudes beating up an Italian guy. I said, now these people are *specific*." (On the TV show *Dr. Katz, Professional Therapist*, the joke is illustrated with an Italian guy with a soccer ball badge on his shirt.)

So we have culture clashes inherent in U.S. society writ large. Then add a sport that tends to start a lot of arguments even in homogeneous countries, and you have a good recipe for conflict.

The other issue in U.S. soccer, as we saw in the previous chapter, is that the sport has long been the province of outsiders, often self-defined outsiders trying to maintain their "indie cred." Twenty-five years ago, they had a superiority complex because they liked soccer. Now, they have to maintain that superiority complex by liking *only* European soccer. Or Mexican soccer. Somewhere, there's surely someone insisting on watching the Moroccan third division.

The good news: A lot of people like *some* form of soccer now. They'll all come together to watch the World Cup, even if some people insist that the American (or, more likely, imported English) commentators lack the tactical insight or passion of Spanish-language broadcasters and therefore watch only the Spanish networks.

The bad news: They can't agree on much else. And the U.S. Soccer Federation, either through a lack of infrastructure (throughout the twentieth century, it didn't have a lot of money at its disposal) or a reasonable aversion to lawsuits, usually doesn't step in to force peace. "If I were to be critical of the sport in our country in general, I think we have failed ourselves miserably because everyone is the smartest guy in the room and everyone is the biggest critic, inside the game and out," coach Jesse Marsch told the *New York Times* after he moved from the New York Red Bulls to Germany's Red Bull Leipzig. "And that will never be successful."[4]

A German federation official expressed it best at the National Soccer Coaches Association of America (later renamed United Soccer Coaches) convention. Sitting on stage in a packed lecture hall, he was asked to name the biggest difference between American and German soccer. He said the United States has a multitude of organizations that all have a say in how things are run. In Germany?

He held up one finger.

So with that in mind, let's jump into the issue long considered the "third rail" of American soccer discourse . . .

PROMOTION AND RELEGATION

For those who don't follow soccer (or basketball and several other sports) in other countries, here's a brief explanation of promotion and relegation: Put your teams in multiple tiers, with the bottom teams in a tier at the end of a season moving down while the top teams move up. England's Premier League sits atop a giant pyramid in which, in theory, a tiny club could win its way up from a local league all the way to the top. In practice, of course, that club would still need to build a stadium that meets the leagues' highest criteria, and it would need a ton of money to get the players and facilities to climb more than a division or two. But clubs move in and out of the Premier League every year, adding quite a bit of drama to the final weeks of each season. And in the lower tiers, moving up and down adds excitement that we don't see in American minor leagues in baseball and hockey. (Why pro/rel hasn't been attempted in the NBA, where the facilities already exist, is beyond me.)

So can we have it in the United States? Actually, we do—in many amateur leagues. The indoor soccer team on which I served as a goalkeeper was once promoted all the way to the Upper Division, where I spent most of each game watching unstoppable shots streak past me. But can we have it in the professional leagues? Let's go back to Stefan Szymanski and Andrew Zimbalist's *National Pastime* for more cultural history:

> [In the United States] the 1870s and 1880s were decades of concentrating economic power, which met with little resistance. Virtually any action to ruin one's competitors was acceptable as long as it did not egregiously transgress the boundaries of the law. Ruthlessness in the economic sphere became a virtue.
>
> Britain, by contrast, was already an industrialized nation approaching the peak of its imperial glory. Always a society in which distinctions of class and etiquette could be as influential as money, any innovation was required to fit into the social order, not least because that order was seen to be so successful.[5]

So it's little surprise that Britain eventually settled into a genteel cooperative effort in which the country's best clubs agree to move up and down based on results. Rival leagues didn't exist for long unless they were content to be much smaller.

American sports, on the other hand, have always been the Wild Wild West. The NFL has ruthlessly stamped out, or at least absorbed, all competition. And in all sports, including soccer, there's no sympathy for any team that can't keep up. You don't get to drop to a lower division and retrench—you fold up shop and write off your losses. The site *Fun while It Lasted*, a compendium of American sports teams that have gone under, will never run out of material.[6]

So historians haven't found much talk about the prospect of promotion and relegation through most of American soccer history. As far as we know, it wasn't an issue with any leagues of the sport's first century in this country, including the North American Soccer League (NASL), which expanded to 24 teams in the late 1970s. Around 1989 or 1990, someone at U.S. Soccer produced a fact sheet suggesting a three-tiered professional structure, "with a system of promotion and relegation that will be unique to American professional sports," but it offered no details, and historian Steve Holroyd's research of contemporaneous sources casts doubt on the prospect that a full-fledged, three-tier pro/rel system was ever seriously discussed.[7] And when Major League Soccer was one of three bidders for U.S. Soccer's blessing as the country's top pro league in 1993, promotion and relegation was hardly a major issue.

What changed? New media, mostly. While Gen Xers and baby boomers grew up with only the occasional glimpse of European soccer, younger generations have grown up with the ability to watch Liverpool and Barcelona (and relegation battles) every weekend of the academic year. And they've been able to go on message boards and Twitter to ask why we don't have such a system here. But if you point out the reasons why switching to pro/rel would be difficult for a variety of reasons, you're labeled as ignorant of the global game. Or worse, an MLS "shill."

The good news is that a few more reasonable voices have emerged in recent years. The bad news is that it's difficult for them to cut through all the noise. The conspiracy theorists were in full voice during the 2018 U.S. Soccer presidential election, where Twitter trolls were driving a lot of the conversation. (Not unlike U.S. politics as a whole in this era.)

In most countries, people who don't get their way have to roll with it. German clubs may have balked at the idea of setting up youth academies under federation orders, but what choice did they have?[8]

We'll get into more analysis of promotion and relegation in chapter 7, and delve into why it's not the quick fix claimed by some of its more strident advocates. The point here is that we're not in Germany or England or anywhere else. And in the United States . . .

YOU GET A LEAGUE! AND YOU GET A LEAGUE!

Chapter 6 will go into more detail about the tangled history of American soccer, but here's a brief glimpse at the major-ish leagues (including ambitious amateurs) we've had through the years, focusing on those that really tried to get beyond one metro area.

1894: The American League of Professional Football (ALPF) and the American Association of Professional Football (AAPF) spring up and immediately disappear. Even then, they were sometimes confused with each other.

1910: The Eastern Soccer League departs after one year.

1917: It's a bit arbitrary, but we'll promote the National Association Foot Ball League (NAFBL) from local to regional here, with the New York/New Jersey league expanding to Pennsylvania.

1921: The American Soccer League (ASL) is formed through the merger of the NAFBL and the Southern New England Soccer League (SNESL, not to be confused with the Sleestaks from *Land of the Lost*). In 1926, some ASL teams play a short season with Canadian teams and call it the International Soccer League (ISL).

1928: A new Eastern Soccer League is formed through belligerent mitosis from the ASL. Peace breaks out by 1930.

1933: The ASL folds, ending the run of the most successful league of the first several generations of U.S. soccer. A new ASL forms in obscurity.

1946: The North American Soccer Football League forms, then folds the next year.

1960: The International Soccer League, renting teams from overseas to play in the summer, sets up shop and runs through 1965.

1966: Three entities bid to become the next (first?) big U.S. soccer league. Two of them, the National Professional Soccer League (NPSL) and the United Soccer Association (USA), actually see the field in 1967.

1968: The NPSL and USA merge to form the North American Soccer League (NASL). At the same time, the ASL (kicking in the shadows since 1933) tries to expand beyond a few northeastern cities.

1978: The Major Indoor Soccer League (MISL) debuts.

1983: The ASL folds.

1984: The United Soccer League (USL, not to be confused with the USL that would spring up later) and American Indoor Soccer Association (AISA) debut.

1985: The NASL and USL fold, leaving just the two indoor leagues (MISL, AISA) and the new, small Western Soccer Alliance (WSA, briefly called WSL).

1988: A third ASL emerges on the East Coast, ranging from Boston to Miami.

1990: The ASL and WSA merge into the American Professional Soccer League (APSL). Indoors, the AISA changes its name to the National Professional Soccer League (NPSL, another abbreviation that would come into use by a totally different league later on), and the MISL counters by dropping the word "Indoor" (now MSL). We'll also need to add the indoor SISL (don't try to decode the abbreviation—it's going to change too often to count), which has expanded from its Texas roots to run from Georgia to New Mexico and will become much more important later in the decade.

1992: The indoor SISL continues its metamorphosis into a sprawling national outdoor/indoor league called the USISL. The MISL ceases to exist.

1993: The new Continental Indoor Soccer League (CISL) kicks off in the summer to fill arena dates for basketball and hockey teams.

1993: U.S. Soccer takes three bids for a league to be proclaimed "Division I." The USISL doesn't bid, but the APSL does. Another bid is League One America, which offers radical rule changes. The winner, though, is the league that would become Major League Soccer (MLS, not to be confused with MSL).

1995: The APSL changes its name to the A-League. The USISL splits into two tiers, then into three the next year. Don't ask about the names. The USISL also launches a women's league, the W-League.

1996: MLS debuts.

1997: The A-League folds itself into the USISL, which means the USISL's top tier is now called . . . the A-League.

1998: The CISL is dead. Long live the PSA, which stands not for Public Service Announcement but for Premier Soccer Alliance. In the women's game, still not professional, some western teams break away from the W-League to form the Women's Premier Soccer League (WPSL), which would start expanding nationally.

1999: The PSA becomes the World Indoor Soccer League (WISL), promising to include but never actually including European teams. And the USISL becomes the USL, no relation to the previous USL.

2001: In the wake of the 1999 Women's World Cup, a full-fledged women's professional league emerges—the Women's United Soccer Association (WUSA). Meanwhile, the WISL plays its final season, and the NPSL claims the old MISL name—a bit ironic, since the NPSL fiercely competed with the old MISL for years.

2003: The WUSA plays its final season.

2005: The NPSL is back—well, the letters, anyway. This time, it's the National Premier Soccer League, which plays outdoors in the summers for elite amateurs. It was originally the Men's Premier Soccer League when a handful of western teams split from the USL in 2003, but upon expanding to the Midwest, the "National" part made sense.

2008: After a few years of relative calm, indoor soccer—by now a shadow of its 1980s heyday—splits three ways as the MISL goes under again. The National Indoor Soccer League (NISL) takes a few teams, the Xtreme Soccer League (XSL) takes a few, and one goes to a new pro division of the Premier Arena Soccer League (PASL).

2009: Women's pro soccer returns with . . . Women's Professional Soccer (WPS). Indoors, the XSL disappears after one year, sending a couple of its teams back to the NISL, which again becomes the MISL.

2010: Time for outdoor soccer to get weird, as a few owners split from the USL to reclaim the old NASL brand, a peculiar claim for lower-division soccer. But not yet! Neither camp has enough teams to have a bona fide second-division league, so U.S. Soccer steps in and gets all parties to coexist as the USSF Division 2 Professional League for one year.

2011: WPS plays its final season, with a few clubs joining top WPSL clubs to form an ad hoc stopgap league in 2012. The new NASL plays its first season.

2013: Welcome the third—and so far, longest lasting—women's pro soccer league, the National Women's Soccer League (NWSL).

2014: The MISL, which had spent its last couple of seasons under USL management, disbands once again, with several teams fleeing to the PASL Pro division, which renames itself the Major Arena Soccer League (MASL).

2015: The long-running W-League, the second-tier women's league operated by the USL, disbands. United Women's Soccer (UWS) pops up to take its place alongside the WPSL.

2016: The MASL splits, with a couple of owners forming the Indoor Professional League (IPL). It never plays a game, and the owners go back to the MASL.

2017: Read the history chapter and the lawsuits chapter for the thrilling tales of NASL versus MLS and USL. Meanwhile, the California-based elite amateur United Premier Soccer League (UPSL) embarks on a rapid national expansion, mimicking either the Tribbles or the Borg, depending on which *Star Trek* you prefer or what you think of the league.

Bear in mind—these are *only* leagues with a national or large regional footprint. We're not counting various iterations of small but half-decent amateur/semipro leagues in St. Louis, New York, and elsewhere. Nor are we counting the Eastern Indoor Soccer League (1997–1998) or the Lone Star Soccer Alliance (1987–1992).

And still, we have three ASLs, two ESLs, two ISLs, three MISLs, two NASLs, two NPSLs, and two USLs. Depending on how you count the various sects and splinter groups, we've had between 30 and 40 soccer leagues in this country.[9]

That's on top of the various amateur leagues of varying quality and ambition. Those, at least, are generally reasonable. Your local metro area certainly should have a league that doesn't require much travel but caters to players of various ability levels up to the "best of the best of those who have day jobs" level. More than 25 leagues have teams that entered the qualifying rounds of the 2019 U.S. Open Cup. Some of these leagues are better organized than others. Some have ambitions of being part of a national umbrella like the UPSL, which has gobbled up everything from the Midwest regional Premier League of America to the Atlanta Caribbean Soccer League, which plays all its games at one soccer complex. Some are content being the best state or metro-area league they can be. Sure, these leagues have a few disagreements. A club might leave one league and join another. But there's a logical reason for all of these different leagues to exist, and the disagreements have no impact on developing players for the future.

On the other hand, let's dive into the biggest cesspool of the U.S. soccer community . . .

YOUTH SOCCER

For much of the last 50 years, U.S. youth soccer had a relatively simple structure. The American Youth Soccer Organization (AYSO) and Soccer Association for Youth (SAY Soccer) organized local recreational leagues that provided the first soccer experiences for some legendary players— including Landon Donovan, Julie Foudy, Eric Wynalda, and Alex Morgan. Then the appropriately named U.S. Youth Soccer and its state associations provided the umbrella for all youth clubs, most of which also ran their own recreational programs. Notwithstanding the cultural split we saw between AYSO and other Californians in Chapter 3, the scene was relatively simple.

Then it got interesting. U.S. Club Soccer started as the National Association of Competitive Soccer Clubs (NACSC) at the turn of the century, hoping to prod U.S. Youth Soccer into a few changes, such as easier movement of players between teams in the same club, easier scheduling of games outside a state association. Early in its history, U.S. Club decided to start its own leagues with its own player registrations.[10]

Within a few years, the Great Turf War was underway. It's mostly U.S. Club versus U.S. Youth, but it sometimes includes AYSO, SAY, the U.S. Specialty Sports Association, and the U.S. Soccer Federation itself:

2001: U.S. Youth Soccer adds the Under-15 and Under-14 age groups to its national championships.[11] The U19 boys group has been competing since 1935, predating the U.S. Youth Soccer organization itself (1974). Girls were added in 1980.

2002: U.S. Club Soccer launches the National Cup.

2004: U.S. Club Soccer forms the id2 National Identification and Development Program as supplement to or rival of the long-standing Olympic Development Program (ODP). Please note that id2 is *also* considered an Olympic development program, which is surely an important distinction to somebody, somewhere. The traditional ODP was invaluable for many generations of players trying to make their way to college soccer (until very recently, the highest level of soccer to which most players could aspire and the most common pathway for future pros), but it gets costly if you go on to regional camps.

2007: U.S. Soccer (the federation) forms the Development Academy for boys. All MLS clubs are expected to have teams involved.

2007: U.S. Youth Soccer forms something called the National League, though it's really a series of weekend showcases that top teams often play in addition to their local leagues. But there's no National League champion. The top teams earn their way into the National Championships.

2008: U.S. Soccer launches a Training Center program, sending national staff around the country to run training and talent identification sessions.

2009: U.S. Club Soccer sanctions the Elite Clubs National League (ECNL) for girls.

2011: U.S. Club Soccer establishes the National Premier League (NPL) framework, an umbrella of regional leagues all leading toward a national league championship. This league championship is *in addition to* the National Cup. The occasional team competed in both.

2017: U.S. Soccer launches a Development Academy for girls. U.S. Club Soccer launches an ECNL for boys, from which qualified teams move into the ENPL (Elite National Premier League), which is U.S. Club Soccer's national league trophy and also features winners from the various NPL-affiliated leagues.

Let's compare. In 2000, a travel soccer team would . . .

- Play in a U.S. Youth Soccer local league.
- Enter the state association's State Cup, from which it might qualify for regionals and then the National Championship.
- Have players participate in ODP, which was especially useful for players who were *not* on title-contending teams.
- Schedule around high school soccer.

In 2018, a travel soccer team would . . .

- Play in a U.S. Youth Soccer local league. Or a U.S. Youth Soccer regional league. Or a U.S. Club Soccer regional league. Or the ECNL. Or the Development Academy.
- Enter the state association's State Cup. Or a U.S. Club Soccer State Cup. Or neither, if they're a Development Academy club.
- Have players participate in ODP, but maybe not, because the club was so busy with everything else. Or have players participate in id2 or another U.S. Club program. Maybe they'll drop by a U.S. Soccer Training Center, which in 2019 was converted into the Youth National Teams Under-14 Talent Identification Program.
- Schedule around high school soccer, but maybe not. If the team is entered in the Development Academy, then no, because they're not allowed to play high school soccer except under special circumstances. (Also, because many regions now have far more travel soccer players than available roster spots on high school teams, a lot of travel teams don't have any players who make the varsity *or* the junior varsity, so they can keep right on playing through the high school season. You read that correctly—for all the talk that travel soccer parents are chasing college scholarships, many are just hoping their kids will make the high school team, and many will be disappointed.)

And this isn't just affecting superclubs with national ambitions. Here's how it trickles down to the local level, using Virginia and metro Washington, DC, as an example:

Pre-2009: The traditional leagues are the National Capital Soccer League (NCSL, only for boys at the time) and the Washington Area Girls Soccer (WAGS). Another traditional league, the Old Dominion Soccer League (ODSL), typically catered to clubs' lower-tiered teams, both boys and girls. They funnel the best teams to the top through promotion and relegation.

2018–2019: The NCSL and WAGS have merged. The ODSL still exists, but it's significantly smaller because many teams have merged to the NCSL to replace the teams that are in these leagues:

- The Development Academy, now for boys and girls.
- The ECNL, now for girls and boys.

- Club Champions League (CCL), which covers the southwestern and southeastern corners of Virginia and extends up to the DC area and just across the Potomac River into Maryland. It's affiliated with U.S. Youth Soccer, but it's a little different than a traditional league. It has "club-vs.-club" scheduling, in which Club A's top team in each age group plays Club B's top team in each age group. (Or each club's second-best team, if the top team is in the Development Academy.)
- Virginia Premier League (VPL), part of U.S. Club Soccer's NPL structure.[12] It mimics the CCL club-vs.-club model. Like the CCL, it stretches from the DC area down to Richmond and on to the Hampton Roads area.
- Elite Development Program (EDP), which now manages U.S. Youth Soccer's National League mid-Atlantic and northeastern regions but also has several tiers to accommodate a wide range of teams. It has some club-vs.-club scheduling.

The primary driver is FOMO (Fear of Missing Out). If Club A has teams in an "elite" league, Club B scrambles to join one as well.

To put this in perspective, I took the top 100 Under-14 boys teams in Maryland and the top 100 from Virginia listed at youthsocccerrankings.us—take all youth rankings with a grain of salt, but the data is interesting. I then eliminated all but the top team from each club, and I eliminated teams that weren't roughly located in the DC metro area. Here's what was left: five Development Academy teams, two ECNL teams, nine CCL teams (and one in the second-tier CCL2), nine VPL teams, twenty-one EDP teams, and fifteen NCSL teams.

If the "elite league" teams were clearly better than the rest, that would make sense. But it doesn't work that way. This isn't a neat and tidy English-style soccer ladder, where the top 20 teams have earned their places in the Premier League. It's closer to a comparison between Serie A and the Premier League—on the whole, the Premier League may be better, but the top Serie A teams would beat the lower half of the Premier League. (La Liga's better than both of them, anyway.)

By most rules of economics, competition would drive down costs. Not the case here. Yes, MLS Development Academy programs are generally free, as is id2 and the Program Formerly Known as the Training Centers. But other Development Academy programs are not. Neither are all the leagues and tournaments that have turned elite travel teams into airlines' and hotels' best friends.

The key word in travel soccer now is "more." More practices with paid coaches. More access to good fields. And the biggest one is the least conducive to developing good soccer players—more travel.

For one sample, I looked at the 2004 Richmond Strikers Elite in their Under-14 year. They were a bit lucky to be in a region that hosted a lot of tournaments. Three were specifically based in their metro area. Another, the U.S. Club Soccer State Cup, played its semifinals and final in town. But the Strikers, playing in the VPL, still had one league game about 120 miles away in Virginia Beach, plus six more in northern Virginia (100–110 miles). They combined two of those northern Virginia games into one weekend, reducing one trip but adding one hotel stay.

In the past, a team like the Strikers might play more games in and around Richmond, then go to northern Virginia or Virginia Beach for a tournament. But the Strikers' tournaments (aside from three in the Richmond area and a fortunate home draw in the U.S. Club Soccer State Cup), were much farther away—a weekend in Raleigh (160 miles away, likely requiring two nights in a hotel), the Dallas Cup (halfway across the country and at least four nights in a hotel), and a U.S. Club Soccer playoff in Lancaster, Massachusetts (532 miles, surely another four nights in a hotel).

Let's go a step further. These are the away *league* games for Braddock Road's 2004 team in its Under-14 year, the first year of the boys' ECNL (distances are from the team's usual home ground of Robinson Secondary School in Fairfax, Virginia.):

September 9: at Penn Fusion, West Chester, Pennsylvania (145 miles)
October 14: at PDA, Somerset, New Jersey (229 miles)
October 15: at Baltimore Celtic, Baltimore, Maryland (we'll assume they stayed in a hotel between New Jersey and Maryland, then played on the way home)
November 4: at Continental FC, Conshohocken, Pennsylvania (164 miles)
December 2: at FSA, Farmington, Connecticut (361 miles)
December 3: at CFC, Wallington, Connecticut (same trip)
December 9: at Maryland United, Crownsville, Maryland (54 miles)
April 7: at FC Bucks, Bryn Athyn, Pennsylvania (182 miles)
April 15: at Match Fit Academy, Hightstown, New Jersey (203 miles)

May 12: vs. FC Boston Bolts, Somerset, New Jersey (229 miles; neutral site)

May 13: vs. FC Stars, Morningside Farm (same trip)

Ready for the Development Academy? Here's the itinerary for Bethesda's Under-16 boys in 2016–2017 (distances from the Maryland SoccerPlex):

September 11: at PDA, Somerset, New Jersey (210 miles)

October 1: vs. D.C. United, Leesburg, Virginia (35 miles on the slow, scenic route; 47 miles on the faster Beltway route, traffic permitting)

October 15: at Baltimore Armour, Ellicott City, Maryland (30 miles)

October 22: at BW Gottschee, Hicksville, New York (270 miles)

October 23: at Everton FC Westchester, Dobbs Ferry, New York (another 40 miles from Hicksville)

October 29: at New York Red Bulls, East Hanover, New York (240 miles)

November 5: at Philadelphia Union, Chester, Pennsylvania (133 miles)

November 12: at Richmond United, Richmond, Virginia (138 miles)

December 2–5: three neutral-site games, in Bradenton, Florida (969 miles)

April 8: at Cedar Stars Academy–Monmouth, Tinton Falls, New Jersey (219 miles)

April 22: at Continental FC Delco, Conshohocken, Pennsylvania (153 miles)

May 13: at PA Classics, Manheim, Pennsylvania (100 miles)

Even if you're farther down the food chain, playing for one of those travel teams whose players aren't going to make their high school teams, let alone a college team, you may be asked to travel two hours each way on a regular basis, even if you're in a congested area like northern Virginia. That's what happens when the teams that were in the NCSL all move into other leagues, the teams that were in the ODSL all move into the NCSL, and the ODSL is left with teams traveling from Alexandria to Hagerstown, a tidy 90-minute drive if the interstates are clear and considerably worse if they aren't.

To some extent, U.S. soccer has benefited from all this money being poured into the sport. Local municipalities have built beautiful soccerplexes that serve local clubs while also hosting tournaments that bring the de rigueur "economic impact." Sounds great—until you're a travel soccer parent who realizes *you* are the "economic impact." So don't complain about how much you're paying for hotels, travel parent. Our economy depends on you.

"What's the big deal?" you might ask. "These parents are willing to pay for all of this, so what's the harm?" A couple of things:

First, even with all this traveling, the top teams in your region (and make no mistake, your region is as messed up as this one) aren't playing each other. That hinders player development. College players won't be as sharp, though they'll be used to buses and airplanes. Pro players won't be as sharp. And the national teams won't be as sharp. (The sales pitch is that clubs are traveling this far so they can play the best of the best. Outside the Development Academy, that's demonstrably false.)

Second, do you think the typical family making less than $100,000 a year can afford all this? And even with scholarships, do you think the typical family that has two working parents can figure out the time to spend so many weekends away from home? (Yes, a lot of people work on Saturdays and Sundays. They may be able to schedule around games in town, but multiple overnight trips?)

And generally speaking, they aren't doing this in the European youth systems we're striving to emulate. In Germany, home of the revered "Das Reboot" program to revitalize its youth development, the Under-17 Bundesliga is split into three regional divisions, leaving teams the occasional four-hour drive or five-hour ride in Germany's efficient railway system for the 42 teams at the top level. England has only recently launched an Under-16 Premier League Cup in which teams might have to make one or two trips along the length of the country, which is still considerably less than a trip from Bethesda to Bradenton. Clubs will occasionally take their youth teams overseas.

And those German or English teams are all part of pro clubs. If you're not part of a pro club, you may be in something like the M&S Water Services Chiltern Youth Football League, traveling from Luton to Lincroft School in Bedford—just past the Revolution Table Tennis Club, can't miss it. That's a 42-minute drive, depending on traffic. You'll find better bus service if you're traveling to a match in Leighton Buzzard.

How have coaches sold this chaos to parents?

In many cases, it's well intended. The clubs that broke away from the staid traditional leagues had valid reasons to do so, and once they're gone, it's difficult to put the genies back in the bottles. And the Development Academy and ECNL were at least intended to take the top 0.1 percent of players into a top-class environment. We can't blame them for the rush of every other club to say, "Hey, we're also elite!" (But maybe we can blame them for forming a girls' Development Academy and boys' ECNL instead of joining forces. The big issue, but not the only one, between those two leagues is the Development Academy's insistence that its players shouldn't play high school soccer.)

Then some of the sales pitches *sound* good to parents. Take the "club-centric" model. For parents who are used to driving their kids in different directions on a given game day, the idea of having all their kids in the same general area on the same day may be appealing. But that depends on having multiple kids all at the same level—the "A" team for clubs that have no Development Academy, ECNL, or other top-level teams; the "B" team for clubs that have national or other regional teams; the "C" team at clubs that enter every newfangled league they can find. And even if they are both on the same level in their respective age groups, you may be there from 8:00 a.m. for Maddie's game until 6:00 p.m. when Tanner finally finishes *his* game.

Who really benefits from the "club-centric" format? The technical directors. They can prop up a chair and watch all their "A" teams (or "B" or "C") in one place. And they don't need to bother with scouting any players at a lower level than that, so if you're on a B-team hoping to move up to an A-team, you may be out of luck.

HOW DO WE SOLVE ALL THIS?

Suppose we had a fully integrated model in the United States. A couple hundred clubs go pro in a coherent pyramid. Maybe we also have ODP/id2 programs in areas without a pro club, and those programs enter teams in the top-level competitions, giving us plenty of teams to have a legitimately "elite" competition without spending a lot of time in airports.

Below that, the amateur clubs have their own pyramids. They also have youth programs, and the youth pyramid extends all the way from the top-level competitions to the rec leagues. Amateur and youth leagues are designed to provide an appropriate level of competition and minimal travel for all. Can we all agree on that?

Of course not. Because we can't agree on anything.

5

WE CAN'T STOP SUING EACH OTHER

Ted Philipakos is an academic, a player agent, and a soccer executive. He's well-versed in the legal side of soccer, and wrote an essential book titled *On Level Terms: 10 Legal Battles That Tested and Shaped Soccer in the Modern Era*. Five of those legal battles took place in the United States. And the book didn't even reach back to anything that may have occurred in the first 100 years of American soccer history or any number of youth soccer spats.

Philipakos's book was published in 2015. Since then, the U.S. soccer-law scene has featured some legal actions from frustrated sports leagues, and a couple of labor actions. And the book doesn't include the years in which the U.S. Department of Justice shook the soccer world to its core. That wasn't a civil matter involving a lawsuit; it was a criminal matter, with arrests spanning the globe.

The central figure was Chuck Blazer, a colorful eccentric who was frequently compared with Falstaff, the corpulent power broker of several plays by Shakespeare. As a longtime FIFA executive committee member, CONCACAF (Confederation of North, Central American and Caribbean Association Football, the North American federation) general secretary, and behind-the-scenes dealmaker, Blazer was a powerful man in global soccer circles. He also lived extravagantly in Trump Tower in New York, and flew around the world living the high life.

That life, though, wasn't legally funded. In 2011, the FBI intercepted Blazer as he rode his motorized scooter toward yet another grand dinner in New York (several reports said he was headed for his usual VIP table at the gilded restaurant Elaine's, but alas, Elaine's had closed a few months earlier), presented him with evidence of several years of unpaid taxes, and offered him an ultimatum to become a whistleblower or else. A *Daily News* (New York) account of that incident and the years that followed started with the headline "Soccer Rat!"[1]

From that point on, Blazer was a dangerous man with whom to associate, wearing a microphone and gathering information that helped U.S. law enforcement officials bring down many a FIFA and CONCACAF executive. In 2015, Swiss police conducted two separate raids (May and December) and arrested FIFA officials.

The final tally of arrests and absurdities spawned many a stunning story:

- FIFA executives were arrested in a five-star Zurich hotel and escorted out a side entrance with sheets held high to hide their perp walks.[2]
- Sepp Blatter, elected to a fifth term as FIFA president in May 2015, was forced from office months later and banned from soccer for eight years, later reduced to six.
- In a heartbreaker for French football fans, legendary player turned FIFA executive Michel Platini also was banned for eight years, also later reduced to six.
- Jack Warner, the Tsar Nicholas to Blazer's Rasputin, cited a story from the *Onion* in a video blaming the United States' supposed jealousy over its failed 2022 World Cup for his downfall, not realizing the *Onion* was a satirical paper. The headline "FIFA Frantically Announces 2015 Summer World Cup in United States" should have tipped off the combative CONCACAF president and FIFA vice president who also held elected office in Trinidad and Tobago, given that no men's World Cup would be played that year (the Women's World Cup kicked off in Canada a couple of weeks later).[3]
- Jeffrey Webb, who replaced Warner as CONCACAF president, continued to live a life of luxury while under house arrest in his Loganville, Georgia, mansion, where he threw a rollicking birthday party for his wife.[4]

- U.S. attorney general Loretta Lynch triumphantly appeared on the *Late Show with Stephen Colbert* and referred to herself as the "FIFA slayer."[5]

Most of the matters in U.S. legal circles are a bit more mundane, but it's fair to say that these cases are a drain on productivity. Petty power struggles have been rampant for generations. Then there's the naming dispute of late 2018, when the U.S. Soccer Foundation was forced to sue the U.S. Soccer Federation, which had asked the charitable foundation to change its name. The overlap of a couple of board members between the foundation and federation didn't prevent the problem.

Some cases are important precedent-setting matters. The biggest of these actions threatened the existence of Major League Soccer, clarified what the U.S. Soccer Federation could and couldn't do (sort of), and gave professional players more of a say over their salaries and playing conditions.

Little wonder, then, that two of the most compelling voices in the bustling soccer Twitter community are Miki Turner (a lawyer) and Steven Bank (a law professor), both of whom are frequently interviewed on soccer radio shows. Neil Morris is both a journalist and a mediator whose two jobs sometimes overlap by necessity.

Many of the skirmishes over the years fall into two categories—labor disputes and interleague disputes, with the Byzantine realm of antitrust law spreading into both. We'll look at each of those categories, then a miscellaneous set of suits ranging from youth soccer to the foundation versus federation case.

LABOR VERSUS MANAGEMENT

Soccer players in the NASL and MLS have benefited from generations of legal battles in other sports that gave players greater freedom.

Consider Bill Radovich, an offensive lineman who played for the Detroit Lions before and after serving in World War II. He asked to be traded to the West Coast to be near his ailing father—perhaps more pay so he could fly home on occasion would suffice. Lions owner Fred Mandel Jr. said no, and he warned Radovich not to play in the leagues that had popped up as NFL competition. He did so anyway, signing with a team in the short-lived All-America Football Conference (AAFC). In 1948, he attempted to move to the San Francisco Clippers of the Pacific Coast League, which had an affiliation deal with the NFL. When that move fell through, he sued, claiming he had been blacklisted.[6]

The Radovich case encouraged other labor leaders to take up athletes' causes. In 1970, Curt Flood sued Major League Baseball and refused to go to the Philadelphia Phillies, to whom the St. Louis Cardinals had traded him. Flood was challenging the "reserve clause," in which baseball teams could essentially hold on to a player's rights as long as they wanted. He lost the case in the Supreme Court, but free agency—the right to let other teams bid on a player's services when that player's contract ran out—came to baseball a few years later.

Soccer has its own Curt Flood—Jean-Marc Bosman, who had finished his contract with Belgian club RFC Liège but was unable to move to French club Dunkerque because Dunkerque could not or would not pay the transfer fee Liège demanded. Bosman sued and won in 1995, forcing soccer clubs to change the way they did business. Players suddenly gained leverage—work out a contract with me now, sell me to a club I like now, or risk losing me for no transfer fee at all when my contract ends. (Some clubs still don't heed the message. Real Madrid watched in horror as David Beckham signed a contract with the Los Angeles Galaxy that would take effect at the end of his Real contract in the summer of 2007. Manager Fabio Capello proclaimed that Beckham, while still allowed to train with the club, would never be named in the gameday squad again. Capello's tantrum lasted only a few weeks, and Beckham returned to help Real win the La Liga championship before heading off to California.)

But U.S. soccer players still had a lot to argue—sometimes successfully, sometimes not.

NASL (the Old One)

From 1977 to 1980, the North American Soccer League reigned supreme. Soccer was drawing crowds that made the most hardened cynics take notice.

At the same time, the players were at odds with the league. In 1977, they started working with Ed Garvey of the NFL Players Association to form their own players association. The next year, the National Labor

Relations Board (NLRB) recognized the association. NASL owners weren't thrilled. "Two NASL owners, Lamar Hunt and Joe Robbie, were also NFL owners and had firsthand experience with Garvey," Philipakos writes. "Not surprisingly, Hunt and Robbie were among those NASL owners who most strongly opposed bargaining with the NASLPA."[7]

The league wouldn't budge. The players appealed to the NLRB. At the beginning of the 1979 season, the players voted to strike. Few of them actually did, in part because foreign players weren't particularly interested.

The players did at least force the league to deal with them, thanks to the NLRB. The league appealed (*North American Soccer League v. National Labor Relations Board*), saying players should bargain with teams, not with the league. In 1980, the Fifth Circuit Court of Appeals sided with the players, saying the league had substantial control over contracts.[8]

The NLRB also pushed the NASL into a corner with a second suit (*Morio v. North American Soccer League*), charging that "the NASL unilaterally changed the conditions of employment without negotiating with the players. The players union successfully won an injunction that rendered the charges voidable."[9]

So the players won. In December 1980, they reached a collective bargaining agreement with the league that ran through 1983. They signed a second agreement in early 1984, just in time for what would be the league's final season.

Fraser v. Major League Soccer

Fraser v. Major League Soccer easily could have wiped out MLS. And once again, the NFL Players Association played a role.

But the MLS players involved in this lawsuit can't be blamed for failing to be psychic. They filed the suit in 1997, when MLS was fresh from a debut season that exceeded most expectations. They certainly had no intention of putting the league out of business. Mark Semioli, one of the plaintiffs, spoke with me for the book *Long-Range Goals* and said the players simply wanted a better position at the bargaining table: "The idea was to win a verdict and then use that leverage, that hammer we didn't have, to create a system that would be mutually amenable to all the parties."[10]

By the time the case went to court in 2000, the league wasn't doing so well. Had the players pulled off the win in court, it's unlikely the league would've continued past the 2001–2002 crossroads in which Philip Anschutz, Lamar Hunt, and Robert Kraft decided to double down on their risky bet and kept the league going.

The target was the league's novel single-entity structure, the brainchild of sharp legal minds such as Mark Abbott, a lawyer at the firm of Latham & Watkins who answered a request from a partner in the firm— none other than U.S. Soccer president Alan Rothenberg—to draw up plans for a soccer league in 1993. Abbott wound up serving with MLS for more than 25 years.

By the time the case ran its course in 2002, no one looked like a winner. League management looked like a collection of ogres that cared little for players' wishes while managing to compile hundreds of millions of dollars in red ink. The players lost the case and several years of potential bargaining.

The case had five counts initially, but two were never argued. In retrospect, the second count—a challenge to FIFA's transfer fee policies—would have been interesting. In April 2000, Massachusetts district judge George O'Toole knocked out two more. MLS could not conspire with itself, he said, more or less taking out the first count. His dismissal of the fourth count contained harrowing words for the players' eventual fortunes: "Competition that does not exist cannot be decreased. The creation of MLS did not reduce the competition in the existing market because when the company was formed there was no market for professional soccer in the United States."[11]

The players persisted. Their lead attorney was Jeff Kessler, a powerful figure in sports law *and* antitrust law who surely inspired fear in NFL offices. But Kessler was left with some flimsy arguments. He tried to convince the jury that the low-profile APSL could have ramped up to be a big-time league, an argument soundly rejected by those who knew soccer, including *Soccer America* journalists Ridge Mahoney[12] and Paul Gardner,[13] the latter of whom also scoffed at "this totally fictitious exercise" in which sports economist Andrew Zimbalist (yes, the coauthor of a book with Stefan Szymanski, cited several times in this book) claimed salaries would have skyrocketed had U.S. Soccer approved two Division 1 leagues.

The notion of competing Division 1 leagues also led to the sheer absurdity of players on the stand dodging questions on whether any other country had two Division 1 leagues, professing ignorance of the concept of promotion and relegation. Kessler also pressed Sunil Gulati, later elected U.S. Soccer president but testifying in his capacity as the former deputy commissioner of MLS, on the same point, trying to catch Gulati misstating the complexities of the Premier League's breakaway from England's Football League and the resulting name changes. Any supporter of an English club would've been led away from the court screaming, as the exchanges mangled easily researched facts on English football.

More to the point, Gulati demonstrated that soccer players, as participants in a global sport, could play in leagues other than MLS. Some countries, England in particular, had work-permit regulations that limited U.S. players' options, but smaller European leagues were often able to pick off players who decided they could do better than play in the upstart MLS.

That argument swayed the jury. The official argument was that the market for soccer was not limited to the United States. In court, this point required considerable argument. In the soccer community, the proper response to this verdict was "Duh."

The players appealed, dragging the case out until March 20, 2002, when the First Circuit sided with the league. Everyone involved with MLS could exhale.

MLS players were finally free to unionize, forming the MLS Players Union (renamed MLS Players Association in December 2017) and negotiating collective bargaining agreements with the league. Players have made much more progress pushing for freedom of movement, better salaries, and better playing conditions since going the union route, even if the negotiations at the end of each agreement's prescribed time make fans a bit nervous about labor stoppages such as the ones that wiped out the 1994 World Series in baseball or the entire 2004–2005 National Hockey League season.

But the ramifications of *Fraser v. Major League Soccer* may linger for another couple of decades. Law students will refer to it when discussing single-entity structures, even though that wasn't really the focus of the decision. The appellate court left that question for future lawyers: "In all events, we conclude that the single entity problem need not be answered definitively in this case."[14] In the soccer realm, we're still finding after-effects that we didn't necessarily expect.

Solidarity Payments and Training Compensation

FIFA has a system of payments that sends some money back to clubs that developed professional players. When a player moves from club to club, some of the money is kicked back (legally—well, in most parts of the world) to the clubs that player frequented as a teenager, even before. Payments pegged to the transfer fee are called "solidarity payments"; other money transacted here is called "training compensation" and is more of a flat fee based on how much the purchasing club would have spent if it had trained the player on its own.

The United States does not abide by this system, at least as of 2019. The argument is threefold:

1. Child labor laws prevent such payments because those payments would mean youth soccer players are retroactively professional.
2. *Fraser v. Major League Soccer* included an agreement that U.S. Soccer would not enforce such payments. After keeping that agreement under wraps for years, the federation finally showed it to youth clubs in October 2015.[15] It's safe to say the fed was under pressure.
3. The MLS Players Association (formerly the MLS Players Union) will sue the crap out of us.

The first argument didn't hold up, for reasons Christian Hambleton (a former high school soccer coach) and Michael K. Wheeler made clear in a legal journal: "The Court made it clear that as long as the activity is voluntary, it cannot be considered work, even if there is a benefit to be gained in the process of the voluntary activity."[16] In other words, if a player willingly goes to play youth soccer, that's not "work," even if it helps him or her gain employment sometime later.

Miki Turner (see above)[17] and Terence D. Brennan[18] effectively squashed the second argument, pointing out that the language in the *Fraser* agreement wasn't really applicable to solidarity pay and training compensation, in part because FIFA set those rules in place *after* the *Fraser* agreement.

The third argument is more difficult to dismiss. It's fair to describe the union's stance on the matter as "hostile," prompting a 2016 lawsuit *against* the union, addressed below. But the union didn't sue when Bayern Munich bought Alphonso Davies from the Vancouver Whitecaps and kicked some money over to the Edmonton Strikers.[19] Canadian law might be more difficult to unravel for a union operating predominantly in the USA.

In the United States, well, we love our courts. Or the Court of Arbitration for Sport, based in Lausanne, Switzerland, with a court conveniently located in New York. Or FIFA's Dispute Resolution Chamber, which sounds like the place Spock and Kirk battled to the death on Vulcan in the original *Star Trek* series.

The last of these is where youth clubs Crossfire Premier, Dallas Texans, and Sockers FC (Chicago) filed complaints in 2015. Crossfire sought its share of the transfer of DeAndre Yedlin from the Seattle Sounders to Tottenham Hotspur. The Texans said they were due a fee when Clint Dempsey ironically made the reverse move from Tottenham to Seattle. The Sockers sought money on Michael Bradley's move from Roma to Toronto.

The U.S. Senate got involved with the case—which, if you've followed the legislators' ham-fisted questioning of U.S. Olympic Committee and other sports officials over the years, is never a good sign. Maria Cantwell, representing Crossfire's home state of Washington, sent four questions to U.S. Soccer. The federation's response leaned heavily on the *Fraser* agreement as well as some unsupported references to U.S. antitrust law and European court challenges to the solidarity/training system.

But another response to the Cantwell questions was overlooked at the time. "Historically, in the United States (as distinct from many countries elsewhere throughout the world), the cost of player training and development was typically borne by the families of young players," U.S. Soccer wrote.[20]

Guess who expanded a few years later on the argument that U.S. development is typically subsidized by parents, not clubs? MLS? No. U.S. Soccer? No. A random U.S. lawmaker? No. Tottenham Hotspur! ESPN's Jeff Carlisle reported:

> The source told ESPN FC that Tottenham are pushing back on three fronts. Tottenham allege that Crossfire is not a "training club" since its

business model—that of a non-profit in which team fees of other players helped subsidize those who couldn't afford to pay like Yedlin—doesn't involve investing its own resources and taking a financial risk in order to produce players. This is despite the fact that Crossfire has other sources of revenue including sponsorships and charitable donations.[21]

The Spurs stance was a change from the club's previous "Hey, we paid everything to MLS, so it's up to them" argument, which it sent to Crossfire in May 2015.[22]

The youth clubs also sued the MLS Players Union in 2016 in a preemptive strike against the union potentially suing *them*. The case was dismissed because a Texas court decided it had no jurisdiction over the matter, but not before MLSPU executive director Bob Foose lobbed this angry attack at the clubs:

> The FIFA system that these clubs are seeking to exploit would be immensely damaging to the development of soccer in the United States. By filing this lawsuit against all players even before FIFA or U.S. Soccer has acted, these youth clubs have revealed their true colors. Their focus appears not to be on the development of players, but instead on ensuring themselves a piece of the action when a player makes it professionally. Parents should take notice.[23]

The solidarity/training argument rose up anew in 2019 with the news of Christian Pulisic's big-money transfer from Borussia Dortmund to Chelsea, even though Pulisic's old youth club, PA Classics, said it wouldn't be asking for any money. Alexi Lalas asked Foose if the union still felt the same way on the issue. The answer was an emphatic yes, including these points:

- These mechanisms "operate as taxes on players when signing and both inhibit players ability to move freely."
- Training compensation in particular is a tax on signing out-of-contract players that "would make it more difficult for our players to sign contracts abroad."
- Pay-to-play clubs have already been compensated and will use a big-name signing to market themselves.
- The system doesn't reward clubs that develop good domestic pros. It rewards a club that brings a player through its club, perhaps for a

short time, who then goes on to be transferred several times over-seas.[24]

Foose isn't out on a limb of American exceptionalism here. FIFPro, which represents players worldwide, put out a study by the peripatetic Stefan Szymanski in 2015 that casts a dim view on the training/solidarity system:

> The requirement to provide compensation for training imposes a particular burden in the case of younger players. This acts like an additional tax on the mobility of younger players. It pushes down the amount buying clubs will be willing to offer and limits freedom of movement. To the extent that compensation payments are incorporated even when a player moves to a second or third club limits mobility yet further.[25]

National Teams

Some disputes between U.S. Soccer and its national team players are relatively minor. In 2016, the Seventh Circuit Court of Appeals overruled an arbitrator who said players could deny the federation the rights to use a picture of six or more players in a tequila ad.[26]

Other cases broke more ground. Modern national-team labor history goes back to 1995, when the men and women independently and coincidentally took on the federation.

Late that year, after the women took third in the 1995 World Cup, the federation locked out nine players—eight of whom started a few months later when the U.S. women won Olympic gold in Athens, Georgia. (The ninth, Carin Gabarra, appeared as a substitute.) The dispute, which brought lawyers to the table, was quickly resolved.

The U.S. men, having just played at home in the high-profile 1994 World Cup, were at their peak visibility. The South American federation invited the team to play in its continental championship, the Copa America. On the flight down to South America—literally, on that flight—the players reviewed the federation's contract offer and decided to strike. After a couple of awkward days of not practicing in South America, the situation was resolved, and the U.S. men had one of the best tournaments in the country's history, smashing Argentina on their way to the semifinals. The next year, the U.S. men unionized, though one game against Peru was played with replacement players.

"The Players Association was founded in 1996 by the members of the US National Team to represent them in collective bargaining with the United States Soccer Federation," the Players Association site reports. "Until that time, individual players negotiated their own appearance fees and contracts with the Federation, and payment varied widely."[27] A year later, the NLRB ordered the federation to bargain with the players union.

The women took that step a couple of years later after a short strike early in 2000, just a few months after the 1999 World Cup win landed them on magazine covers and talk shows. The federation sent replacement players to a minor tournament in Australia before reaching a new deal and working with a new players' union.

The men went to the brink just before the final round of World Cup qualifiers in 2005, fighting with the federation over mediation terms just a couple of weeks before the first game. Coach Bruce Arena called in a team of replacement players from lower-tier U.S. leagues, which proved to be a great opportunity for the unheralded Clyde Simms, who went on to a long career in MLS. The regular team was back in camp in time for the first qualifier, and duly qualified.

But the highest profile national team labor dispute happened in 2016. At the urging of combative goalkeeper Hope Solo, the women's team's players association had replaced longtime lawyer John Langel with Rich Nichols, a prominent sports attorney who had spent years on the difficult task of representing former Olympic gold medalist Marion Jones in her ultimately unsuccessful quest to defeat persistent doping allegations. For extra assistance, the union brought in Jeff Kessler, the same lawyer who had represented MLS players in *Fraser v. Major League Soccer* and was once again poised to spar with Sunil Gulati, now U.S. Soccer's lightning-rod president.

A full-fledged collective bargaining agreement was surely overdue. The federation and the union had signed a deal in 2005 that ran through 2012. In 2013, with U.S. Soccer also setting up the new pro league (the National Women's Soccer League) and agreeing to subsidize national team players' club salaries, the federation and union scratched out a Memorandum of Understanding (MOU) that would run through 2016.

Not so fast, Nichols said just before Christmas 2015. The players can cancel that MOU at will, and if we don't have a new deal within 60 days, we will. A couple of weeks before that deadline, not wanting to see its 2015 World Cup champions walk away before the Olympics, U.S. Soccer sued its own players.[28]

It wasn't just the money. Players were aggravated over the playing conditions in their post-Cup Victory Tour, which ended with a match being canceled in Hawaii in a fight over the suitability of Aloha Stadium's artificial turf. On the same trip, Megan Rapinoe tore an ACL—on a grass practice field, but one whose quality was also questioned.

The players countered by filing a wage discrimination complaint with the Equal Employment Opportunity Commission in the spring of 2016. Surely that would push things along before the Olympics. It didn't. As of January 1, 2019, the EEOC had not acted. In June, a district court judge ruled that the MOU did indeed carry over a no-strike clause from the previous CBA. The players' leverage was gone.

But the players had plenty of sympathy, especially from media that didn't typically delve into the complexities of the soccer world. The mantra "equal pay for equal play" fed the prevailing narrative that the federation was coddling the men's team and robbing the women. The two teams, though, can't really be compared.

On the "equal play" front, the women's team does not have to deal with the laborious process of traveling several times to Central America and the Caribbean for World Cup qualifying. Comparing an exhibition in Houston to a qualifying game in the cauldron of Mexico City's Azteca Stadium isn't easy. (Conversely, nor is it easy to quantify the intangible benefit of the women's team's success on the U.S. soccer community as a whole, or on the inspiration the team gives to young women in search of role models.)

The "equal pay" part of the slogan also didn't lend itself to apples-to-apples comparisons. The women, unlike the men, had long received a salary simply for being on the team—at least if they're part of the "core players" in the pool. The women don't receive massive salaries from their club teams, so the national team salaries provide a bit of stability. Add in bonuses for World Cup wins, something the U.S. men certainly weren't getting in 2018, and some women could easily out-earn their male counterparts. In theory, the U.S. women could have invoked an equal-pay trigger in their existing deal, which Julie Foudy dug up and confirmed was still in existence. The clause reads:

If in any calendar year, the ratio of aggregate compensation of wom-
en's national team players to the aggregate revenue from all women's
national team games (including all games in U.S. Soccer promoted
women's tournaments) is less than the ratio of the aggregate compensation of the men's national team players compensation to the aggregate
revenue from all men's national team games (including all games in
U.S. Soccer promoted men's tournaments), then U.S. Soccer will make
a lump sum payment to the women's national team player pool to make
the ratios equal.

Foudy asked players why they hadn't invoked the clause.[29] She didn't
really get an answer.

By the end of 2016, after a shocking loss in the Olympic quarterfinals,
U.S. Soccer had effectively washed its hands of Hope Solo. The union
also parted with Nichols, the lawyer she had brought into the fold. In the
spring of 2017, the women reached a new deal with the federation, running through 2021.

In 2018, Solo ran for U.S. Soccer president, falling far short in a
crowded field of eight candidates. In August 2018, she sued the federation.

Imagine what the men will do if they ever win anything.

Other Labor Suits

Sometimes, labor issues are safety issues. Such was the case with Bryan
Namoff, one of several MLS players whose careers were cut short due to
concussions. In 2012, Namoff sued D.C. United and former coach Tom
Soehn over the handling of his 2009 concussion, claiming he was improp-
erly rushed back into action without proper diagnosis. More parties—a
trainer, a doctor, and the doctor's practice—were added as defendants.
The case was dismissed. Namoff later sued his lawyers for malpractice,
eventually settling.

Peter Nowak was a distinguished MLS player, arriving from the Bundesliga in 1998 to lead the Chicago Fire to the MLS championship in the
club's first year. He later coached D.C. United to an MLS championship
and coached the U.S. team in the 2008 Olympics. Things went sour when
he took over as coach of the Philadelphia Union, where he was fired in
2012. He sued for wrongful termination and wound up appealing an
arbitration decision to a federal judge, only to see embarrassing details

emerge of spankings, withholding water, and not following MLS policy on concussions.[30] The judge dismissed his appeal.

LEAGUE (OR TEAM) VERSUS LEAGUE

As difficult as the labor disputes have been, they're minor slapfights compared to the bare-knuckle boxing that takes place when people want to start their own leagues.

Antitrust disputes are part of American sports lore. Baseball has an exemption to antitrust law that was upheld in court multiple times in the twentieth century. Other leagues have had to fight a bit more. The NFL has fought lawsuits from the AFL and USFL. A merger between the NBA and ABA was delayed when players brought an antitrust suit, leading to a settlement that established free agency. Even the laid-back sport of beach volleyball has had some turbulence spilling into the judicial system. So why should soccer be any different?

NASL (Still the Old One) versus NFL

The National Football League is a powerful organization that isn't afraid to flex its muscles. Plenty of factors have made it the biggest sports league in the United States and, by revenue, the biggest in the world, but a willingness to beat down its rivals hasn't hurt.

For years, the idea that NFL owners could own teams in other sports was frowned upon. "Cross-ownership had long been a contentious issue between NFL owners, who had an informal policy in place prohibiting NFL owners from owning controlling interest in franchises in other professional sports leagues," wrote Glenn M. Wong in his comprehensive book, *Essentials of Sports Law.*[31]

In 1978, the NFL made it official by levying fines on owners who put any of their money elsewhere, a direct shot at owners such as Lamar Hunt, who had diverse sports business interests and would later be one of the pillars of Major League Soccer. The NASL fired back and saw the case through to the bitter end, losing in district court but winning in the Second Circuit Court of Appeals: "The court found that there was a submarket for sports capital and the cross-ownership ban had an anticompetitive purpose and effect in that market. Defendants failed to prove that the proposed ban was the least restrictive way to achieve their purpose. Defendants' counterclaim was held to be meritless."[32]

One note on the case that would prove important later—the final appellate court ruling denied the NFL's "single entity" defense, which argued that the league was a single corporation. The NFL argued that violating the Sherman Antitrust Act requires an agreement between multiple entities, and the NFL is only one. That argument worked in district court, but the appeals court found otherwise. MLS later made more of an effort to be a single entity. See the discussion of *Fraser v. Major League Soccer* above to see how that turned out.

The NFL asked the Supreme Court to review the case. The Supremes declined, though future chief justice William Rehnquist dissented. "Justice Rehnquist's dissent would provide some hope for the single entity argument in professional sports in the future," Philipakos wrote.[33] The court then spent a considerable amount of time working out the damages. As in the USFL case, the final verdict was for $1. The NASL was already collapsing at that point, anyway.

At least future generations of sports owners could take heart from the verdict. MLS has had several NFL owners in its ranks. Microsoft mogul Paul Allen owned the NFL's Seattle Seahawks, the NBA's Portland Trail Blazers, and part of the Seattle Sounders when the club set up shop in MLS. Stan Kroenke has owned, wholly or partially, teams in the NFL, MLS, Arena Football League, NBA, NHL, National Lacrosse League, and video gaming. (And the English Premier League.)

But in the twenty-first century, the disputes have turned U.S. pro soccer into something with the complexity and unlistenability of a Dream Theater epic. Some of it is ego; some of it is legitimate discussion of business models; and some of it is our old friend, promotion and relegation. And they often end with one league going under.

Borislow versus Women's Professional Soccer

Discovery Communications founder John Hendricks is one of the biggest boosters professional women's soccer has ever known. He helped found the first U.S. pro league, the WUSA, and served as its chairman. When that league's three-year run ended in 2003, he continued to own the Washington Freedom, keeping coach Jim Gabarra employed and running a team that played some exhibitions and some amateur league seasons while keeping up ties to the area youth community. When Women's Professional Soccer launched in 2009, Hendricks and Gabarra were right back in place with the Freedom in the thick of it.

In late 2010, Hendricks finally let the Freedom go. (Gabarra, husband of women's team legend and Naval Academy head coach Carin Gabarra, had already gone.) He sold the Freedom to Dan Borislow, a then-mysterious South Florida tech mogul whose neighbors included one Donald Trump. For a few months, the team was shrouded in secrecy—even after word filtered out in women's soccer circles that a whole bunch of big-time players were headed to South Florida, the team did little to no marketing, and at least one major newspaper was tipped off to the team's arrival by an outside reporter (me). Some of the world's best soccer players played to crowds of fewer than 1,000 people.

Then details emerged. The team would be renamed "magicJack" after one of Borislow's tech products. With scant parity protections in place in WPS, Borislow assembled a team of giants, including Abby Wambach, Christie Rampone, Shannon Boxx, Becky Sauerbrunn, and Australian Lisa de Vanna. All five would be on 2011 World Cup rosters, as would *both* of the team's top two goalkeepers, Hope Solo and Jill Loyden.

Then the fun began.

Through their lone year (2011) of coexistence, Borislow and WPS feuded over everything. Signage boards and sponsor obligations. The size of the team's home field. Media availability. Borislow's decision to name himself coach (with Rampone) after the original coach left three games into the season. (He later passed those duties to Wambach.)

Legal maneuvering started in the summer. The league wanted a hearing to decide whether to terminate Borislow's ownership rights. Borislow countered in court.[34] The team managed to finish its uneasy season, shrugging off a players' grievance along the way.

In October, the league dropped the hammer. Borislow and magicJack were out. That spawned the first of several biting headlines over the next few months at irreverent sports website Deadspin: "How Boca Raton Lost Its All-Star Pro Soccer Team without Even Trying." Another Deadspin headline was taken directly from one of Borislow's emails to the league that became public in court filings: "'I Expected Nothing Less from a Bunch of Blithering Idiots': The Angry Emails That Helped Cost Boca Raton Its All-Star Pro Soccer Team."

Borislow certainly wasn't going quietly. He filed suit in Palm Beach County, Florida, and somehow convinced Florida circuit judge Meenu Sasser to deny WPS's request for a change of venue, even though the documents clearly seemed to point elsewhere to this layman.

Under pressure, having already scrambled to convince U.S. Soccer to sanction the league for a fourth season with only five teams, WPS made a deal with Borislow to allow him to play an exhibition schedule, like a Harlem Globetrotters team of women's soccer stars, in 2012 and 2013. That deal quickly fell apart. So did WPS.

Borislow passed away in 2014. Having dealt with him so much over the course of that tempestuous year, I was moved to write a remembrance: "Dan Borislow's larger-than-life reputation was so great that, upon hearing of his death this morning, I immediately thought I needed to get his side of the story. I was sorely tempted to text him, thinking I might get an entertaining response about a bunch of idiots declaring him dead when he had every right to be alive."[35] The remembrance certainly didn't gloss over the many incidents of his WPS tenure, but members of his family loved it.

In retrospect, Borislow may have done professional women's soccer a favor by finishing off Women's Professional Soccer. Out of those ashes rose the National Women's Soccer League, which easily outlasted both WPS and the WUSA. The league certainly doesn't pay players as well as Borislow did, but the courts have been much quieter. For now.

Promotion and Relegation

People have pleaded for promotion and relegation in U.S. soccer. They've run for U.S. Soccer office pledging to institute it. They've even offered to pay for it—see chapter 7, where Riccardo Silva's dubious offer to MLS is discussed.

And they've asked the world's top sports court to make U.S. Soccer do it.

In the summer of 2017, soon after Silva's implausible offer to buy media rights at MLS if the league would institute promotion and relegation, he and Dennis Crowley, the amiable open-books owner of the amateur Kingston Stockade club, filed a request for arbitration with the Court of Arbitration for Sport.

Silva and Crowley base their argument on Article 9 of FIFA's Regulations Governing the Application of the Statutes (yes, FIFA is a bureaucratic entity that rivals the Central Bureaucracy in *Futurama*), paragraph 1, which says a club's participation in a domestic league "shall depend principally on sporting merit."[36] Unfortunately for their claim, paragraph 2 of that same article reads, "In addition to sporting merit . . . " Also, FIFA took care to mention when implementing this rule in 2008 that it was targeting clubs that "achieve promotion artificially by buying or moving a club," and it made a nonjudgmental reference to the "closed leagues" of the United States and Australia.[37]

Lawyers have spent considerable time parsing this language even without being hired by the parties involved. Terence D. Brennan, writing before the Silva/Crowley filing (as if eerily anticipating it), left the interpretation open: "While there are arguments to be made on both sides, the U.S. system does not fit neatly into Article 9's regime. From one perspective, it conflicts with the rule's plain language. Nonetheless, when it implemented Article 9, FIFA was not trying to overturn the 'closed' league set-up that prevails in this country."[38]

The ubiquitous Steven Bank is skeptical of the Silva/Crowley claim:

> Will CAS rule that U.S. Soccer must adopt a promotion and relegation system under FIFA regulations? This essay concludes that the odds are against it. There are at least three possible obstacles to the Claimants' case, although some are more formidable obstacles than others. First, it is not clear that CAS will accept jurisdiction in this case or conclude that it is ripe for arbitration. Second, even if it does decide to rule on the merits, there is legislative history that suggests that FIFA's adoption of Article 9 was intended to regulate existing promotion and relegation systems rather than force nations with closed leagues to convert to open ones. Finally, the Claimants' request for declaratory relief may have trouble satisfying the narrow conditions under which CAS jurisprudence and Swiss law permit the issuance of a declaratory judgment.[39]

The amusing part will be if CAS decides Article 9 means pro/rel must be implemented everywhere, which would cause a flood of injunction requests—not just in the United States, but in every country that has a wall between its professional and amateur leagues. But that's not the only legal battle Silva and company are fighting.

NASL (the New One) versus Everybody

The new NASL actually started from strife that veered toward court. Through a long history described elsewhere, the United Soccer Leagues (later to drop the "s" at the end) had been operating at the three levels of soccer below MLS, topped by the league formerly known as the A-League but now the USL First Division—an odd name for the *second* tier of pro soccer, but England used these names for a while, so in a weird way it seemed authentic. Disgruntled USL clubs sought to break away from the league and form something new, grabbing onto the long-discarded NASL name.[40] With neither league maintaining a critical mass of clubs, U.S. Soccer stepped in with a novel solution, running a Division 2 league on its own and getting all the clubs to play nice for one year (2010).

After that, the NASL eagerly claimed the Division 2 sanction that had been beefed up with new stringent U.S. Soccer Federation standards, though they first had to clean up the mess when the St. Louis organization—run by one of the breakaway's leaders, Jeff Cooper—folded up shop, having closed its women's pro team a third of the way into the 2010 WPS season. The USL retrenched as a Division 3 league and continued to operate an amateur league, the PDL.

In 2012, the NASL came close to an affiliation agreement with MLS, the result of talks that weren't reported until Neil Morris (the journalist/mediator mentioned above) reported them in 2015.[41] In June 2012, the NASL abruptly shut down the talks, then announced that the New York Cosmos were in.

The Cosmos had a tenuous intellectual-property connection to the glory days of Pelé and company. When the old team disintegrated, the team's name wound up in the hands of Peppe Pinton, a longtime confidant of Cosmos striker Giorgio Chinaglia, who earned a few battlefield promotions to become the team's general manager as everything collapsed around him. Jay Emmett, one of the Warner Communications executives who worked with the Cosmos, memorably summed up Pinton's holdings in the 2006 documentary, *Once in a Lifetime: The Extraordinary Story of the New York Cosmos*: "Let's be very clear. Peppe owns the Cosmos. The Cosmos are nothing today. So Peppe owns nothing!"[42]

But Pinton sold the name to English businessman Paul Kemsley, who didn't do much with the name before selling it again to a group that included sports businessman Seamus O'Brien and Saudi Arabia's Sela Sport. The reborn Cosmos flirted with MLS, but opted to go elsewhere.

Over time, the NASL established itself as a quirky but stable second division even as the FIFA/CONCACAF scandal that started this chapter ensnared Traffic Sports, which had a heavy ownership stake in the league. By 2015, though, the league was bristling at its place in U.S. Soccer's league hierarchy. The league hired, you guessed it, Jeff Kessler.

The NASL had made some noise about, but taken no action toward, setting a pyramid with promotion and relegation. To speed things along, the NASL prepared a push to be recognized as a second Division 1 league alongside MLS.

The league's timing wasn't great. Some teams were angling to follow previous second-division teams (Seattle, Portland, and Montreal among them) up to MLS. Others were moving to the USL, which expressed interest in having a Division 2 league again. Expansion teams were falling through. And worst of all, the mighty Cosmos were folding again and selling off its trademark again, this time to MLS-affiliated Soccer United Marketing, before being rescued at the last minute by the colorful Rocco Commisso, who was prone to being as combative in press availabilities as Dan Borislow was in emails.

Instead of pushing for Division 1, the NASL was fighting to remain at Division 2. U.S. Soccer's board of directors overruled its Pro League Task Force to grant that D2 sanction for 2017.[43] By September 2017, U.S. Soccer had run out of patience, informing the NASL it wouldn't get renewed for 2018, but it was welcome to apply for Division 3. And off to court we went.

The NASL sought an injunction to play Division 2 in 2018. That was denied. Two teams moved to the USL, one moved to the Canadian Premier League, one went on hiatus, and one folded, leaving three teams— Commisso's Cosmos, Silva's Miami FC, and the Jacksonville Armada, owned since the summer of 2017 by Robert Palmer (not the late singer).

But the larger court case—*North American Soccer League v. United States Soccer Federation, Inc.* (MLS is also a defendant)—was just getting started. It was filed in September 2017. Near the end of 2018, both parties agreed to extend the discovery period from April 30, 2019, to November 11, 2019. By the time you read this, we may have seen a Halloween with hundreds of skeletons liberated from various closets.

Other League/Team Suits

This list is most definitely *not* a complete accounting of every soccer-related suit in the United States. It doesn't include Major League Soccer's aggressive defenses of its trademarks. It's just a sampling.

In 1991, Hector Marinaro sued the MISL over a suspension stemming from an allegation of match-fixing in Singapore. Even before then, Marinaro claimed to have spent $30,000 in legal fees.[44] For its part, the Canadian courts claimed they had no jurisdiction over the case.

In 2006, the Carolina Dynamo sued MLS and Anschutz Entertainment Group when an MLS team moved from San Jose to Houston and named itself the Dynamo. The case was settled a year later. Five years prior, the Miami Breakers sued the then new Boston Breakers of the WUSA.

In 2007, the Long Island Rough Riders sued United Soccer Leagues (USL) over territorial rights for the USL's youth operation, the Super-Y League. The Eastern District of New York court ruled that the Rough Riders hadn't exhausted their internal grievance process, nor did other clubs' tryouts and practices violate an agreement that specifically stated the Rough Riders had exclusive rights for *competitions*.[45]

In 2012, the USL faced another suit, this time from former team owner Dmitry Piterman. A Ukrainian Californian, Piterman had held ownership stakes in multiple Spanish clubs and once installed himself as manager of Racing Santander. When asked in 2003 about managing a club without a coaching license, he replied, "There's a dork running the most powerful country in the world without a qualification to his name. And you ask me for a diploma to run a football team?"[46] Piterman's next club, Alaves, started a USISL team called the California Victory. When Alaves pulled out, Piterman alleged, the USISL leaned on him to support the team personally and then failed to live up to its obligations. After an amusing legal skirmish over whether the USL was the same entity as the old USISL, the case was settled.[47]

EVERYONE VERSUS EVERYONE

Youth soccer is prime hunting ground for lawyers.

Sometimes, the disputes are mere ego clashes or buck-passing. Organization X says Organization Y won't accept its registration cards and insurance for Tournament Z, Organization Y has some counterclaim, and the whole thing winds up in front of U.S. Soccer or a judge.

Sometimes, they're issues of greater import. Title IX, the same legislation that has boosted women's sports in the United States, is the rationale for some of these suits. In many of them, you would think the defendants simply should've known better. In *McCormick v. School District of Mamaroneck* (2004), a few schools scheduled their girls' soccer season in the spring, which was a bit unfortunate because the state of New York has its state championship in the fall. McCormick won.

Youth soccer has also seen a few lawsuits over concussions, one of which named FIFA as one of the defendants. Concussion awareness is now part of coaching education, and in 2015, U.S. Soccer unveiled new rules limiting heading in younger age groups.

And while soccer hasn't had the systematic negligence that forced USA Gymnastics into a drastic reorganization, youth soccer has seen a few heartbreaking suits over sexual abuse by coaches. As with concussions, U.S. Soccer and other organizations now require coaches to watch awareness videos.

But the last two cases on our docket bring us back to money, egos, and dubious judgment.

ChampionsWorld v. U.S. Soccer Federation

Can a country's soccer federation demand a fee from a third party that puts on a soccer game within that country's borders? FIFA says yes. U.S. law also says yes, but it took a while.

In 2003 and 2004, ChampionsWorld put on summer exhibitions between several big-name European clubs in the United States. MLS had brought over a few clubs over the years—in 2001, the MetroStars beat an exhausted (some would say hungover) Bayern Munich a few days after the German club won the Champions League—but ChampionsWorld revved up the marquee value and the hype.

The games were successful, but ChampionsWorld couldn't keep up the spending. The company shut down in 2005, but managed to sue U.S. Soccer (and MLS) the next year, following in the footsteps of a similar lawsuit (later settled) by the Los Angeles Memorial Coliseum Commission in 2001.

Ted Philipakos has a detailed account of the case in *On Level Terms*. The short version: Both parties appealed to FIFA, which more or less sided with U.S. Soccer in February 2010. The parties then went back to Illinois district court to argue about the definition of "amateur" and whether the Ted Stevens Olympic and Amateur Act—clumsily rewritten in 1998 to account for the fact that the Olympics had allowed professionals to take part—allowed U.S. Soccer to do as it pleases with professional teams. Judge Harry D. Leinenweber said ChampionsWorld had made enough of a case to proceed, but that was as far as the plaintiff's good fortunes would go. "Clearly, there was a tension between FIFA's view and Judge Leinenweber's view on the scope of U.S. Soccer's authority," Philipakos wrote. "That tension was resolved by the Court of Arbitration for Sport."[48] Indeed, CAS ruled in U.S. Soccer's favor. U.S. Soccer was able to convince the U.S. judge to go along, and the case ended in 2012.

ChampionsWorld CEO and founder Charlie Stillitano, in addition to his hosting duties on a SiriusXM soccer show, went on to be the chairman of Relevent Sports, once again bringing famous European clubs to the United States but this time with smoother relationships with the federation and MLS. *Der Spiegel* also identified him as one of the power-brokers talking with European megaclubs about breaking away to form their own Super League, in which many clubs would be exempt from relegation.[49]

United States Soccer Foundation v. United States Soccer Federation

In 1994, the World Cup came to the United States. And the United States took some of the profit from that smashing success and made a bigger investment in underserved communities, launching the U.S. Soccer Foundation.[50] The organization offers afterschool programs and works with other groups to get soccer in the cities in particular, trying to put small soccer fields wherever it can. The Foundation even helped a Los Angeles neighborhood start a soccer program that bridged gaps between gangs.[51]

And for close to a quarter-century, the Foundation was on perfectly good terms with the U.S. Soccer Federation (U.S. Soccer). The boards between the two organizations tend to have overlapping members. The Foundation's name in legal documents is "United States Soccer Federation Foundation, Inc."

So how did it come to this, according to the Foundation's pre-emptive lawsuit?[52] At a meeting on or about November 12, 2018, between representatives of the Foundation and the U.S. Soccer Federation, the USSF represented that: (i) the USSF is the owner of the name "U.S. Soccer Foundation"; (ii) the USSF had an interest in using the name "U.S. Soccer Foundation" for its own services in the future; (iii) the Foundation's use of the Foundation Marks purportedly had caused and will cause customer confusion; (iv) the USSF expects the Foundation to stop identifying itself as the "U.S. Soccer Foundation" and must cease use of the name; and (v) unless the Foundation signs an agreement to change its name, the USSF would initiate legal action.

This is internecine conflict between organizations that, by any reasonable account, should be on the same page.

WHAT CAN YOU DO WITHOUT LAWYERS?

In other countries, the federation can generally run things without legal entanglement. Germany had little trouble imposing the sweeping changes known as "Das Reboot." English clubs grumble, as the English tend to do, but such grumbling is generally contained within the FA.

The idea of U.S. Soccer imposing the perfect league structure and the perfect youth system, even if the best possible people were elected and hired, without a host of lawsuits is pure fantasy. Change the pro leagues, and the pro leagues will sue. Change the youth leagues, and the youth leagues will sue. Change the labor conditions, and players will sue. You will see Swindon Town win the Premier League/Champions League double before everyone agrees to everything without going to court.

The ultimate power in American soccer does not lie with the U.S. Soccer president or CEO. It lies in a judge's gavel.

6

WE FELL BEHIND BY 100 YEARS

"**W**hen I started here, all there was, was swamp. All the kings said it was daft to build a castle on a swamp, but I built it all the same, just to show 'em. It sank into the swamp. So I built a second one. That sank into the swamp. So I built a third one. That burned down, fell over, then sank into the swamp. But the FOURTH one stayed up. And that's what you're going to get, lad, the strongest castle in these isles." So said the ruler of Swamp Castle, played with gusto by the great Michael Palin, to his son Herbert (Terry Jones) in *Monty Python and the Holy Grail*.[1]

For purposes of this book, we're not talking about the inheritance of the reluctant prince, who'd rather just sing. We're talking about U.S. soccer history. And for a century and change, U.S. professional soccer was the swamp.

The first castle in this scenario would be the stunted efforts to start a professional league in the nineteenth century, most notably the American League of Professional Football (ALPF), formed by baseball owners to get more use out of their ballparks, staff, and even the occasional player. See the 1894 entry below for more on what historian David Wangerin called "the spectacularly ill-fated venture."[2]

The second castle had a bit more potential. The American Soccer League started in 1921 with a merger between smaller leagues in New England and the New York/New Jersey region. Powerful clubs such as the Fall River Marksmen and Bethlehem Steel signed players from Scotland and England, along with a considerable number of local guys, and games sometimes drew the five-figure crowds that were far from guaranteed at baseball games of the era. The league provided the bulk of the players—some naturalized, some native—for an American entry in the first World Cup in 1930, where they reached the semifinals. (Yes, really. Only 13 teams entered, but twin 3–0 wins over Belgium and Paraguay aren't bad by any measure, and perhaps they could've gone even farther if Argentina hadn't broken U.S. player Raphael Tracy's leg early in the semifinal.)[3] But a complex and nasty political battle known to historians as the "Soccer War," coupled with the Depression, killed off the league in the early 1930s.

The third castle was the North American Soccer League (NASL), which started in the late 1960s and caught fire when Pelé, Franz Becken-bauer, and other big names signed with the New York Cosmos, lighting up Giants Stadium and Studio 54 for a few years. But that fire eventually burned down the castle, and it fell over and sank into the swamp. (Giants Stadium is indeed in the midst of New Jersey swampland.)

The fourth castle is Major League Soccer. It stayed up, even through its near-collapse in 2001–2002. But just as Prince Herbert wasn't sure he wanted to inherit Swamp Castle, the next generation of soccer fans isn't sure it wants to devote energy toward MLS. (U.S. professional women's soccer is on its third castle in a more compressed time frame. The WUSA ran from 2001 to 2003, followed by Women's Professional Soccer from 2009 to 2011, then the National Women's Soccer League from 2013 to present. It's not perfect, gaining stability through salaries that require players to take second jobs or get creative with their expenses, but it's not on the verge of burning down.)

A big-time pro league isn't necessarily correlated with World Cup success. Brazil won World Cups before it managed a full-fledged profes-sional league. Like its South American neighbors and rivals, Brazil still sends most of its best players to richer leagues in Europe today.

But Brazil and Argentina still have a few big clubs with fanatical support, supplemented by hundreds of smaller clubs. These clubs are part of a thriving soccer culture and an intricate talent-scouting and develop-ment network. Young players dream of starting with their hometown clubs, then going to the bigger ones, then overseas.

Smaller European nations such as Belgium and the Netherlands also send many players to countries with bigger economies. But their leagues are about as good as they can be given their limited population, and they are similarly able to maintain a sturdy fan base and a talent pipeline.

In any case, the leagues are more of a symptom of a thriving soccer culture than a cause. Sure, we can always wonder what would have happened if the ASL hadn't bungled its promising start. But if the United States had a thriving soccer culture, the ASL might have weathered the storm. Or maybe we wouldn't have needed more than a decade to launch another full-fledged pro league after the NASL's collapse.

It's not that soccer ever disappeared entirely. The sport's hold on the imagination of immigrants who have populated this country is more stubborn than soccer's naysayers will ever understand. From Kearny, New Jersey, to St. Louis and on west to California, a few leagues and clubs can trace their history back generations before television and the internet made European and Mexican soccer hip.

If you compare where the United States has stood with the rest of the world, year by year, it's less of a "tortoise and hare" tale and more of a "dog chasing hare but occasionally getting distracted by squirrels" story. The hare, on the other hand, is focused and steadied by fresh infusions of billions of dollars.

Here's how the soccer world and the U.S. sports world have unfolded over the past 150 years and change.

1862–1884

In the United States, as in the rest of the world, various forms of "football" are played throughout the early nineteenth century. The Oneida Foot Ball Club of Boston is possibly the first soccer club outside England, but we're not really sure whether the game they played qualified as "soccer."[4]

Colleges continue to play a variety of "football" games after the Civil War, eventually settling not on soccer but on rugby and then the gridiron version of football that would come to dominate fall in the United States, spurred along by innovator Walter Camp.[5] Meanwhile . . .

. . . in England, the Football Association is founded and the first "Laws of the Game" are drawn up in London in 1863, officially separating the sport we now call soccer (or football, in countries where soccer is the dominant sport—or association football if we're being technical) from other versions of football such as rugby football, which splits off on its own. Blackheath FC withdraws, angry that the other clubs won't allow "hacking"—or kicking other players in the shins. Blackheath instead opts to play rugby, which itself bans hacking a few years later.[6]

. . . in Britain, an "English" team plays a "Scottish" team derived from Scottish players in London in 1870. Two years later, England and Scotland contest the first official international match. It ends 0–0. People continue to enjoy the game anyway, and the FA Cup is played for the first time in 1871–1872.[7]

. . . in Europe, a few clubs form outside the British Isles.

1884–1893

Despite losing out in the college "football" scramble, the American Football Association (AFA) forms in 1884 and organizes the first American Cup in 1884–1885, won by Clark O.N.T. "O.N.T." stands for "Our New Thread," in homage to patron Clark Thread Company. Its home field is in East Newark, New Jersey, a small area that would officially secede a decade later from the U.S. soccer epicenter of Kearny.[8]

A sort-of U.S. team plays for the first time. Clark O.N.T., the Kearny Rangers, and a couple of neighbors join forces to form an unofficial U.S. team that loses 1–0 to a Canadian side in "one of the best contested games ever seen in this neighborhood," the *New York Times* reported, despite very rough play and the odd fistfight.[9] The Americans would, however, win the rematch.[10]

The O.N.T. team goes on to win the next two American Cups, but it appears to have diverted more of its attention to cricket before professional soccer took root. The next five Cups go to teams from Fall River, Massachusetts, a town that would become one of the most important places in American soccer's early history.

So in terms of launching a Cup competition, the United States is merely 13 years behind England, but still several decades away from playing an international game. Meanwhile . . .

. . . in the United States, college football (the gridiron version) spreads from coast to coast.

. . . in England, the International Football Association Board (IFAB) meets for the first time and takes charge of the Laws of the Game, and so much soccer is in progress that English clubs finally get on board with the "league" concept in 1888, having conceded a few years earlier that professional soccer is OK. That league continues in the twenty-first century, something no American top-tier league that started play before 1996 would manage.

Some English clubs opt instead to form something called the Football Alliance. In 1892, the leagues merge, with the Football League introducing a system of promoting and relegating clubs between two divisions. The Northern Football League, founded in 1889, has no such merger and continues as an amateur league, eventually eclipsed by many other amateur and semipro leagues but still running in the twenty-first century. England's national team also gets three international games a year with the official formation of the British Home Championship in 1884, contested between England, Scotland, Wales, and Ireland. Scotland wins.

. . . in Argentina, the game has attracted to enough clubs to form the Primera Division.

. . . in India, the Durand Cup launches in 1888, initially for British military units but taken over by domestic clubs in the twentieth and twenty-first centuries.

1894

Catch ALPF fever! Or don't. Baseball league owners try to get a league up and running in ballparks from Washington to Boston, with little success and without the support of the AFA, which resolved to ban any league players from AFA competitions.[11] Historian Steve Holroyd summed up the short-lived endeavor: "In many ways, the United States' first professional league presented a blueprint for all those that would follow—absentee ownership with interests other than the development of the sport, domination by foreign players, in-fighting within the soccer community, outside factors detrimental to the sport's development, and lack of fan interest."[12]

Also this year, the American Association of Professional Football (AAPF) forms, debuting with an 11–1 Philadelphia win over Trenton. The league rolls out four teams—Philadelphia and three New Jersey teams—and apparently plays only a handful of games. Only the dogged efforts of historians such as Philadelphia's Ed Farnsworth 120 years later would save the league's records from disappearing into the ether.[13]

1895–1903

The National Association Foot Ball League (NAFBL) sets up shop a little more locally than the ALPF, with most teams based within a few miles of Kearny. It would've been called the New York State league if not for the objections of the New Jersey clubs.[14] The league runs through 1899 and is revived in 1906, eventually merging with the Southern New England Soccer League to form the powerful American Soccer League of the 1920s. "There are quite a number of clubs in the vicinity which follow the game, and it is rapidly gaining in popularity, although the unfortunate professional scheme started in the Autumn threw a damper upon it for the time being," the *New York Times* said of talks to start the league in late 1894.[15]

The league's membership varies widely from season to season, especially after its reboot in 1906, with clubs frequently coming and going, sometimes in mid-season. Meanwhile . . .

. . . in the United States, professional baseball teams are dipping their toes into football again. But it's gridiron football, which does not yet have a full-fledged professional league.

. . . in western Europe and Scandinavia, more national club competitions are being organized, most notably the forerunner of Italy's Serie A league in 1898 and Spain's Copa del Rey in 1902.

. . . in central Europe, Austria and Hungary launch the first European national teams outside the British Isles in 1902 and start playing each other. England and Germany would finally visit in 1908.

. . . in South America, Argentina and Uruguay start national teams and play each other in the start of an intense rivalry. Both countries have national leagues, and São Paulo is the first Brazilian state to form a regional league, an important competition to this day.

1904

The soccer hotbed of St. Louis hosts the Olympics, and yes, soccer is included, though these are clubs rather than full-fledged national teams for the second straight time. The vast majority of the athletes in the Games and two of the three clubs are from the United States, and yet they manage to lose the Olympic soccer gold to a Canadian side.

By this time, organized amateur soccer officially exists from coast to coast, with the Southern California Foot Ball League (later to be renamed the Greater Los Angeles League)[16] and the California State Football Association (overseeing multiple leagues in the Bay Area) providing a firm foothold on the Pacific coast.[17] Meanwhile . . .

. . . in Europe, FIFA (Fédération Internationale de Football Association) launches as soccer's international governing body, at first with just western European nations.[18] Belgium is now playing internationally, as is Bohemia (modern-day Czech Republic).

1905–1912

Enter the English evangelists. The Pilgrims, a team of top English amateur players, pops up in 1905 and 1909 for tours. They win most of their games—in 1909, the only U.S. teams to win in 22 tries are the New England League champion Fall River Rovers and Football Association of Pennsylvania champion Philadelphia Hibernians,[19] but the publicity is more important than the scores. The Corinthians, a globe-trotting team from England, also plows through Canada and the United States in 1906, losing only near the end of the tour to Fall River, and returns in 1911.[20]

The rebooted NAFBL and the sometimes fractured St. Louis Soccer League make it through the years prior to World War I. The Eastern Soccer League, with teams in Rhode Island, New Jersey, and Philadelphia, does not. It folds after one season—1909–1910. But an ex-ESL team, Howard & Bullough, wins the American Cup in 1911. Meanwhile . . .

. . . in the United States, President Theodore Roosevelt hosts a meeting at the White House to address a rash of serious, even fatal, injuries in college gridiron football. The sport goes on.[21]

. . . in England, the national team finally ventures outside the British Isles, traveling to play Austria, Hungary, and Bohemia. England wins rather easily. A Great Britain team also wins two straight Olympic tournaments (1908 and 1912), followed each time by Denmark and the Netherlands.

. . . in Europe, Germany launches a national team in 1908, along with Sweden and Denmark. Two years later, Italy joins in. League competition is also underway in many European countries.

. . . in the Caribbean, Trinidad and Tobago plays British Guyana in 1905. Yes, Trinidad and Tobago (see 1989 and 2017 for major roles that country would play in U.S. national team history) played before the United States, though it wouldn't play outside the Caribbean for many decades.

. . . in Africa, a South African selection travels to Argentina for an unofficial match.

1913–1915

The American Amateur Football Association, formed two years prior, morphs into the U.S. Football Association, the forerunner of today's U.S. Soccer Federation, and wins recognition from international governing body FIFA.[22] Only three other non-European nations—South Africa, Argentina, and Chile—had been accepted into FIFA.[23]

The new association launches the National Challenge Cup, now known as the U.S. Open Cup, and also affiliates with the powerful Amateur Athletic Union (AAU).[24] That spells doom for the AFA, though its American Cup would linger for a few years. Another league, the Southern New England Soccer League, joins the NAFBL and the St. Louis league in keeping higher-level play alive.

And the Bethlehem Steel club sets up a grandstand on its field and starts winning Cup trophies. Meanwhile . . .

. . . in Europe, the progression of the sport grinds to a halt due to World War I. But to demonstrate how firmly football was rooted on the continent, British and German troops play the game together when a truce is declared for Christmas Day.

. . . in the United States, Yale opens the Yale Bowl for college gridiron football, debuting with a crowd of 68,117 people.[25] Would that have been a soccer crowd if the English game had won the battle for "football" supremacy on campus a few decades earlier?

1916

The U.S. men's national team (hereafter called USMNT) officially debuts with a 3–2 win in Sweden and a 1-1 tie in Norway. It wouldn't play again until the 1924 Olympics. Meanwhile . . .

. . . in South America, four countries (Uruguay, Brazil, Argentina, Chile) play the first continental championship, later called the Copa America.

1917–1920

As everyone settles back to normal life at the end of World War I, Ben Miller FC of the St. Louis Soccer League is the first team outside the Philly-to-Fall-River circuit to win the Challenge Cup.[26] Bethlehem Steel and a St. Louis team tour Scandinavia.[27] Meanwhile . . .

. . . in England, the Football League takes the top teams from the Southern League to form a Third Division. The next year, northern clubs are added to form a Third Division North, giving England 86 clubs in a professional pyramid.

. . . in Europe, most countries restart league competitions that were suspended during the war.

1921–1924

Behold the American Soccer League (ASL), a rough merger of the NAFBL and SNESL. For the better part of the next decade, clubs such as the Fall River Marksmen and Bethlehem Steel would attract decent talent from Scotland and England, even elsewhere at times.

The USMNT returns to action in the 1924 Olympics, beating Estonia and losing to Uruguay, the small South American country that was already a global power and would remain one. The team goes on to win in Poland and lose in Ireland.

More touring teams visit. The Third Lanark Rifle Volunteers of Scotland win 24 straight games before finishing up with a draw against everpesky Fall River. The next year, the English women's team Dick Kerr Ladies would tour the United States and post a strong record in a series of games against ASL teams and others. One reason for the tour: England had just effectively banned women's soccer, at least in front of spectators.[28]

And in some respects, the United States is now ahead of other countries. The British countries withdraw from FIFA rather than associate with World War I enemies, and the 1921 FIFA meeting has only 20 countries. But other competitions here and abroad are either way ahead or gearing up to pass U.S. soccer. Meanwhile . . .

. . . in England, the FA Cup moves to iconic Wembley Stadium, where the game is in danger of being called off until a lone policeman on a white horse slowly but surely moves the overflow crowd off the pitch. The stadium—capacity roughly 125,000, though with an official attendance of 127,000—can't hold the crowd estimated at twice that number.[29] Safe to say the United States has no crowds close to that.

. . . in the United States, gridiron football is finally getting organized on the pro level after some fits and starts with disorganized teams coalescing into the National Football League. The college game is already staggeringly popular.

. . . in Central America, Costa Rica forms a national league, now approaching its 100th year.

1925

The Challenge Cup winner is the Shawsheen Indians of Massachusetts. The ASL and the St. Louis Soccer League sit out the competition over a dispute with the USFA, a harbinger of trouble ahead. The two pro leagues do manage to stage an American Professional Championship, in which the ASL's Boston Wonder Workers prevail over the Ben Millers. Shawsheen then briefly joined the ASL.

The USMNT plays its first game on home soil, a 6–1 win over Canada that avenged a 1–0 loss in Montreal earlier in the year. Meanwhile . . .

. . . in the United States, NFL crowds grow to 36,000, then 75,000.[30] And basketball follows football's path by adding a professional league atop a popular college game. The American Basketball League (ABL) would follow a similar path to the ASL over the next few decades, declining for a while and then being eclipsed by a more ambitious league.

1926–1927

The Challenge Cup returns to normal, and ASL teams join Canadian teams for a loosely organized International Soccer League (ISL) that was more of a mini-tournament than a league.

More international teams visit. The Hakoah All-Stars (Vienna) and Sparta FC (Prague) win most, but not all, of their games. A Hakoah game at New York's Polo Grounds draws a reported 46,000 fans, which the *New York Times* reported as a record crowd in the United States. Historian Steve Holroyd says the record lasted for more than 40 years.[31]

The ASL experiments with rules changes, some of which took root in later years (substitutions) and some of which didn't (a penalty box).

On November 6, 1926, the USMNT beats Canada 6–2 in Brooklyn. The game draws 2,500 fans, down from 8,000 the year before. It's the second official home game for the team, but it would be the last for more than two decades. (Read 1934–1935 and 1947–1948 below to see why this isn't a simple question.)

1928

The "Soccer War" sees the ASL in open rebellion against the USFA. Historian Roger Allaway sums up the problem:

> Although the issue over which those two organizations locked horns centered on participation by ASL teams in the National Challenge Cup (now called the U.S. Open Cup), the battle really was over the question of which of them was to be the controlling organization of soccer in the United States.
>
> The ASL had been upset for several years by the schedule difficulties the National Challenge Cup caused, and had boycotted the 1924–25 tournament. Then, in 1927, the United States got into hot water with FIFA over the signing by ASL teams of players who were under contract to European teams. USFA president Andrew M. Brown made an emergency trip to the 1927 FIFA Congress in Finland and reached a compromise that fended off moves sought by Austria and Hungary, the countries from which players had been poached, to penalize the United States. However, the USFA's bowing to foreign authority inspired in some ASL owners a desire to free themselves from

the limitations imposed on them by the USFA and FIFA's European leaders. This was particularly true of New York Nationals owner Charles Stoneham, who also owned the New York Giants baseball team and wanted to see American soccer run more like baseball was (and without European interference). [32]

The ASL decides to skip the Challenge Cup again, but three teams dissent and enter anyway. The ASL kicks them out. They form the Eastern Soccer League instead, with Bethlehem Steel winning.

On the bright side, the USMNT plays in the Olympics but loses 11–2 to Argentina. They hang around in Europe and tie Poland 3–3.

1929

The Great Depression hits.

Peace is declared between the ASL and other parties, and they get back together for a short spell as the Atlantic Coast League before resuming play as the ASL. The league never really recovers, descending into a spiral of relocated and shuttered clubs. Even with a World Cup coming the next year, the USMNT stands idle. Meanwhile . . .

. . . in Spain, the home national team is the first from outside the British Isles to defeat mighty England. [33]

1930–1932

The first World Cup! The USMNT, composed mostly of ASL players with a couple from the St. Louis league, reaches the semifinals. Only 13 teams entered, but two 3–0 wins over teams that had been ranked 15th and 25th in the retrospective world Elo ratings of 1929[34] isn't bad. (Argentina, which knocked out the USA, was ranked number 1.) The U.S. team is nicknamed "the shot-putters," emblematic of the athletic style the Americans had developed (and, according to many critics looking for something more skillful, maintained well into the twenty-first century). The World Cup also fills the void in the Olympics, which proceeds in 1932 without soccer due to a dispute over amateurism. [35]

International exchanges are all the rage, with European clubs coming over to play a few games and some U.S. teams going in the other direction.

1933

The ASL officially collapses after a couple of seasons of chaos. A new ASL immediately pops up and carries on for 50 years, but spends most of that time in obscurity.

Though the ASL had a good run by most standards, and drew the occasional crowd of more than 10,000 fans, it was never stable. Teams came and went, often in mid-season. For every Fall River Marksmen or Bethlehem Steel, there was a one-year wonder like Fleisher Yarn, Todd Shipyards, or Paterson Silk Sox.[36] David Wangerin notes that the league never completed a season in which every team played all its games.[37] One thing that didn't help—the ASL insisted on playing a fall-to-spring schedule, as they do in England and Scotland. It's rather chilly in the northeastern United States in the winter.

The St. Louis Soccer League continues, usually with just four teams each season. The USMNT doesn't play for the third straight year, idled since tacking on some friendlies after the 1930 World Cup.

1934–1935

The USMNT attends the second World Cup in Italy and beats Mexico in a qualifier to reach the round of 16, but is swiftly beaten 7–1 by the host nation. The win over Mexico would be the USMNT's last victory until 1949, though 10 of those years were idle, thanks in large part to the war.

Did the USMNT play in 1935? Sort of. A Scottish side, apparently not consisting of full Scottish internationals (at least one was actually Irish) visits the United States and Canada to play various clubs and All-Star teams.[38] The games against the ASL All-Stars, who would indeed compose the bulk of a USMNT at the time, are counted in the USA's Elo ratings.[39] Other historians refer to the games as unofficial, and the Scottish FA site lists the first USA-Scotland game in 1952.[40]

The National Junior Challenge Cup, later renamed the James P. McGuire Cup, is contested for the first time in 1935, won by Reliable Stores FC of New Bedford, Massachusetts.[41]

1936–1938

With World War II on the horizon, the United States decides to skip the 1938 World Cup.[42] Italy wins again, just as it did in 1934 and in the 1936 Olympics (beating the United States again in that tournament, though by just one goal this time). The USMNT, which lost three games to Mexico in 1937, is idle and doesn't play again until 1947. Meanwhile . . .

. . . in Scotland, a home game against England draws more than 149,000 fans.[43]

1939–1945

Soccer is the least of anyone's concerns. The second ASL continues its low-key existence in the mid-Atlantic metropolises, and its teams win most of the Challenge Cups. At the end of the war, the USFA changes its name to the more cumbersome U.S. Soccer Football Association (USS-FA).

But the sports world still sees a few milestones. Meanwhile . . .

. . . in the United States, a National League baseball game is broadcast on TV.

. . . in Mexico, various regional leagues unite into a national league.[44]

1946–1949

The U.S. men return to action, sort of, in 1947 with U.S. Open Cup and U.S. Amateur Cup champion Ponta Delgada of Fall River playing as the U.S. team and losing two North American Cup games to Mexico and Cuba. All sources, though, consider these games official.

The full-fledged national team plays in the 1948 Olympics, but exits immediately with a 9–0 loss to Italy. A follow-up game in Norway is worse—11–0. Northern Ireland also beats up on the U.S. team, winning

5–0 in a game that may or may not have been a full international. The *Belfast News-Letter*, which referred to the team as "U.S. Olympic XI," kindly called the U.S. performance "creditable" and said they too often had "one pass too many."[45]

When would the losing streak end? Depends on how you're counting. A team from the new nation of Israel visits the United States in fall 1948 and drops three games to the U.S. team. David Litterer lists the games in his 1948 recap,[46] but they're not in the 2012 U.S. men's soccer media guide, and the *Blizzard*, a football quarterly, recaps the tour while mentioning FIFA does not recognize the games as official internationals.[47] The Elo ratings, which include the decidedly unofficial 1935 games against Scotland, do not mention these games. So, officially, the U.S. men host their first home game since 1926—and only their third home game *ever*—on June 19, 1949, losing 4–0 to Scotland before a crowd of 17,000 in New York.

Or *was* it official? David Litterer includes it.[48] It's in the Elo ratings. But it's not in the Scottish FA archive.

Better news comes in a North American championship that doubles as a World Cup qualifier, with spots available for two teams out of the three contestants—USA, Mexico, and Cuba. The losing streak ends September 14 with a 1–1 draw against Cuba. Finally, one week later, the USMNT wins for the first time since 1934, beating Cuba 5–2. That's enough for the team to qualify for the World Cup, which would prove quite important.

The neo-ASL continues. The North American Soccer Football League, spanning from Pittsburgh to St. Louis with a detour up to Toronto, does not, collapsing in its second year.

ASL teams no longer routinely win the Challenge Cup (eventually called the U.S. Open Cup), with reborn semipro clubs in St. Louis and strong amateur teams in Pittsburgh, New York, and Chicago taking control for a few years. Meanwhile . . .

. . . in the United States, the Basketball Association of America (BAA) and National Basketball League (NBL) merge to become the National Basketball Association (NBA).

1950–1953

June 29, 1950: The U.S. men shock the world, beating England 1–0 in the World Cup. Joe Gaetjens of the ASL's New York Brookhattan scores on a header, and goalkeeper Frank Borghi of St. Louis Simpkins Ford keeps the soccer superpower at bay. But they lose their other two group games and bow out.

That would be the last U.S. appearance in a World Cup for 40 years. The funny thing—the USMNT at this point officially has more wins in the World Cup (3) than it has on home soil (2).

The United States capitalizes on this momentum by doing absolutely nothing of interest. The USMNT plays no other games in 1950 or 1951, returning to action in 1952 to be drubbed in a friendly in Scotland and in the Olympics by Italy (again!). Then in 1953, England exacts revenge with a 6–3 win in New York, a game witnessed by only 7,271 fans in Yankee Stadium after a one-day delay that forced the cancellation of a ceremony paying homage to Queen Elizabeth's coronation.[49]

The good news is that the second ASL is carrying on with relative stability, as are substantial city leagues in New York, St. Louis, Chicago, and Pittsburgh. A Manchester United tour before the World Cup is lengthy and draws the occasional crowd of more than 10,000. And the game is growing in U.S. colleges. Meanwhile . . .

. . . in the United States, pro American football is unified again as the NFL absorbs the All-America Football Conference (AAFC), and the league's games are becoming fixtures on this new thing called television.[50] The NBA also is on television, getting a broadcast deal with the Dumont network, a big deal at the time.

. . . in Brazil, the World Cup final draws roughly 200,000 fans, most of them heartbroken when Uruguay beats the hosts.[51]

. . . in England, the game's inventors suffer an earth-shattering defeat, losing 6–3 at home to Hungary, removing any lingering idea—which probably should've gone away after 1950—that England was the world's dominant power.

1954–1956

Having played only once since the 1952 Olympics, the USMNT convenes for World Cup qualifying and duly drops out of contention with two losses to Mexico. But in April, in a couple of irrelevant qualifiers between two eliminated teams, the USMNT wins for the first time since the 1950 World Cup, beating Haiti twice. They would next win an official international game in 1965. That's not a bit of dyslexia striking. It wasn't 1956. It was 1965.

Not that they're playing a lot. The lone game in 1955 is a friendly away to Iceland, which they lose 3–2. In 1956, the team plays some unofficial games in Asia on their way to the Melbourne Olympics, winning a few, but they get swamped 9–1 by Yugoslavia at the Games. (These Olympics would be the last in which U.S. Soccer considers the games to be full internationals, given the growing gulf between the pro and amateur ranks. The Olympics insisted on amateurs for another couple of decades, then allowed pros, but with a multitude of caveats so that it wouldn't be a second World Cup.)

The ASL continues, but the 1954 New York Americans are the only team from the league to win the Open Cup in a 14-year span, reflecting the strength of the local leagues in St. Louis, Pittsburgh, Chicago and, most disturbingly for the New York–centric ASL, New York's German-American Soccer League. Meanwhile . . .

. . . around the world, FIFA is up to 85 members. [52]

. . . in Europe, the first European Cup is held in 1955–1956, with Real Madrid beating Stade de Reims in the final.

1957–1959

Having played just twice since the 1954 Haiti games, the USMNT tries again to qualify for the World Cup through a series of games in 1957. In their semifinal group with Mexico and Canada, they lose all four games by a combined score of 21–5. By the end, the federation doesn't even bother to put together a full team and just sends St. Louis side Kutis to a game conveniently held in St. Louis. They actually come close, losing 3–2 to Canada. Kutis did win the Open Cup and Amateur Cup that year, so they weren't a bunch of people rounded up off the street.

And the amateur leagues are still interesting. In 1958, the Los Angeles Kickers are the first West Coast team to claim the Open Cup.

But the U.S. amateurs fall flat in Olympic qualifying. The full national team plays England in Los Angeles and loses 8–1. Meanwhile . . .

. . . in Africa, the CAF (Confederation of African Football) is formed to put the continent's teams on the global stage and hold the first African Cup of Nations in 1957.[53]

1960

Having played just once since the World Cup qualifiers in 1957, the USMNT tries again to qualify for the World Cup, getting a promising 3–3 draw against Mexico in Los Angeles but then losing 3–0 in Mexico City, ignominiously eliminated 18 months before the Cup itself.

In pro soccer, if you can't beat 'em, rent 'em. The International Soccer League lives up to its name by bringing in 11 foreign teams (the 12th was called the New York Americans, though it was not the former ASL club) for a handful of games. It was merely a summer invitational for teams in their off seasons, but it was something.[54] The founder is Bill Cox, who briefly owned the Philadelphia Phillies before being banned from baseball. Meanwhile . . .

. . . in Europe, the first European Championship is a bit of a mess, with England, West Germany, and Italy among the absentees. Then Spain withdraws rather than travel to the Soviet Union, which goes on to win the whole thing.[55] But it would continue on a quadrennial basis under the snazzy name "Euro (insert year here)."

. . . in South America, club football takes a step forward. Inspired by the success of the European Champions Cup, the continent's leagues band together for the first Copa Libertadores.[56]

1961–1964

The USMNT loses 2–0 in Colombia in 1961, takes a couple of years off, then loses 10–0 to England before a middling crowd of 5,062 in New York. "It was Valley Forge all over again," reported Wes Gaffer in the

Daily News (New York).[57] With that 10–0 loss, the USMNT's Elo rating drops to 82nd in the world.

The Olympics proceed without a U.S. team once again. But at least the ISL grows its average attendance to the five-figure mark.[58] European teams are still traveling to the United States in the summer, and some are going in the other direction. But 50 years into the official existence of U.S. Soccer (dating back to the federation's launch), pro soccer in the United States is still being played by people who are only here for a brief summer tour.

And the continent finally gets its own full-fledged confederation. The North American Football Confederation and the Football Confederation of Central America and the Caribbean merge into the Confederation of North, Central America and Caribbean Association Football . . . just say "CONCACAF."[59]

The confederation immediately launches a Champions Cup competition for club teams. The 1962 debut edition goes forward without a U.S. representative, but New York Hungaria represents the country in 1963 and wins its first series against Mexico's Deportivo Oro.[60] CONCACAF also launches a championship for national teams in 1963. The USMNT is not involved.

In 1964, a couple of Californians launch the American Youth Soccer Organization (AYSO) with nine teams. The guiding philosophies are "Everyone Plays" (players must play at least half of every game) and "Balanced Teams." Meanwhile . . .

. . . in the United States, CBS buys two years of NFL broadcast rights for $28.2 million, or $14.1 million a year.[61] That's $115 million a year in 2018 dollars.

. . . in Europe, West Germany finally forms a national professional league, the Bundesliga, which quickly becomes one of the world's best.

1965

Having played just twice since the World Cup qualifiers in 1960, the USMNT tries again to qualify for the World Cup and . . . breaks the 11-year winless streak with a win over Honduras! Unfortunately, they had already been mathematically eliminated.

Several teams from the ASL and New York's German-American League join forces for the short-run Eastern Professional Soccer Conference. It goes nowhere.[62]

But an American team wins something! The New York Americans return to the ISL, this time drawn from German-American League teams, and they win their section over teams from Brazil (Portugesa), Italy (Varese), West Germany (1860 Munich), and England (West Ham United). Unfortunately, that would be the final year for the ISL due to a dispute with the USSFA. Once again, a U.S. soccer venture ends in court.

The American Challenge Cup, in which the previous year's winner returns to face the current year's winner, goes to Poland's Polonia Bytom, which has since fallen on hard times but, as of 2017, still has the trophy tucked away in a vault.[63]

1966–1967

With very little left of homegrown U.S. soccer aside from amateur and nominally (but not really) professional leagues, several groups take an interest in starting from scratch. Naturally, they can't get along.[64] Three proposed leagues are whittled down to two, with embittered ISL founder Bill Cox joining forces with would-be league founder Richard Millen to form the National Professional Soccer League (NPSL). The other organization leader is Jack Kent Cooke, owner of the NBA's Los Angeles Lakers and part owner (later sole owner) of the Washington NFL team.

Ironically, Cooke's league borrows Cox's idea of importing international teams, though they adopt U.S.-style nicknames. Stoke City becomes the Cleveland Stokers. Wolverhampton Wanderers become the Los Angeles Wolves. The league itself is called the United Soccer Association, or USA, a name that adds to the irony.

The USA opts to pay for USSFA (and, by extension, FIFA) sanctioning. The NPSL operates as an outlaw league, but lands a TV deal. But the squabbling ends after one year with a merger into one league—the soon-to-be-mighty North American Soccer League (NASL).

The ASL continues in obscurity, confined to its Baltimore-to-Boston crescent. The Ukrainian Nationals of Philadelphia win the Open Cup in 1966, the last ASL team to do so.

Broadcaster interest, though, is a big step forward. The 1966 World Cup final is broadcast on tape delay on NBC—something we would take for granted today, but the first seed in a barren landscape for the sport on American airwaves.

In the midst of all this hoopla, the USMNT doesn't play a single game, and the amateurs lose to Bermuda in Olympic qualifying.

Another youth organization forms. Soccer Association for Youth (SAY) sets up in Ohio in 1967 with 400 players. Like AYSO, the organization would eventually go national, and it would have company. Schisms in youth soccer—some philosophical, some cultural—were already common. A group of coaches (many Latino), disaffected with the AYSO's philosophy of sorting players into balanced teams, split from the AYSO to form the Golden State Soccer League.[65] Meanwhile . . .

. . . in the United States, the NFL and rival American Football League (AFL) play a game then called the AFL-NFL World Championship, but retroactively called Super Bowl I.

1968–1971

Having not played at all since World Cup qualifiers in 1965, the USMNT warms up for the next cycle with two games against Israel (one tie, one loss) and . . . they advance past the first round! The men open with a 4–2 loss to Canada but come back to beat their northern neighbors in Atlanta and take a pair of games from Bermuda. So with perennial qualifier Mexico automatically qualified as hosts and the first round of qualification behind them, the U.S. men have a golden opportunity to return to the World Cup. They face Haiti in a two-legged semifinal . . . and lose.

The NASL kicks off with 17 teams and no fans. It returns the next year with five teams and then survives 1970 with six teams—including Rochester and Washington, lured over from the ASL just as the older league was trying to expand geographically. In 1971, the ASL fields only one team from its traditional New York stomping grounds, with its other four teams in Boston, Philadelphia, Syracuse, and northern Virginia. But another team starts up in 1971 and joins the NASL—the New York Cosmos.

The Rochester Lancers win the NASL in 1970 and enter the 1971 CONCACAF Champions Cup, finishing fourth. But generally, the NASL ignores the CONCACAF tournament, just as it ignores the U.S. Open Cup. Meanwhile . . .

. . . in Mexico, the World Cup breaks its total attendance record, with 1,673,975 fans going to Mexican stadia. (The average of 52,312 tops all previous Cups except for Brazil in 1950.)[66]

. . . in the United States, your author is born.

1972–1974

Having not played at all since the World Cup qualifiers in 1969, the U.S. men are drawn into a first-round qualifying group with Mexico and Canada. One tie, three losses, no entry to the six-team CONCACAF final qualifying group. By 1973, the USMNT is 85th in the Elo ratings.

But U.S. Soccer finally starts to get serious. The Olympic team manages to qualify for the Munich Games. The USMNT cranks up with a full slate of games, winning three to break a losing streak dating back to 1968. In 1974, the federation changes its name to the U.S. Soccer Federation (USSF).

And the NASL creeps its way into the mainstream. The Philadelphia team averages more than 10,000 fans in 1973. Its players work their way into the USMNT. In 1974, the league debuts four teams on the West Coast—three of whom (San Jose Earthquakes, Seattle Sounders, Vancouver Whitecaps) are smashing successes.

The Open Cup, though, is virtually an all-amateur tournament. NASL teams don't enter, and the ASL has its own problems as it expands into the Midwest with little impact.

Youth soccer is getting bigger. The California-centric AYSO claims 40,000 members, while the Catholic Youth Conference of St. Louis boasts 100,000. A national body, U.S. Youth Soccer, forms in 1974.[67] Meanwhile . . .

. . . in the United States, Super Bowl ratings top 50 million for the first time.[68]

. . . in Costa Rica, Saprissa Stadium, the home of a powerful club of the same name, opens in San Jose. It eventually hosts musicians such as Andrea Bocelli (2005), Black-Eyed Peas (2006), Metallica (2010), Green Day (2010), Bon Jovi (2010), and Miley Cyrus (2011). It's also a place dreaded by every CONCACAF team, club or national.

. . . in Europe, Barcelona signs Dutch star Johan Cruyff from Ajax for a record transfer fee of £922,000, or more than $2.2 million in the exchange rate of the time and more than $12 million in 2018 money.

1975–1978

Pelé.

In later years, when Major League Soccer would sign a 30-something foreign star (from Lothar Matthäus to David Beckham), the league would be derided as a retirement league. Pelé had, in fact, retired before the New York Cosmos lured him back to play.

None of that mattered. He's Pelé. So when the New York Cosmos signed the Brazilian legend, it signaled an unprecedented ambition for the NASL—or at least the Cosmos and a few other teams that raced to sign their own foreign stars.

These stars weren't deterred by the NASL's decidedly nontraditional approach. While most of the world's leagues awarded two points (later three) for a win and one for a tie, the NASL gave six for a win. It eliminated ties in 1975, opting for a "shoot-out," in which attackers took the ball 35 yards from goal and went one-on-one with the goalkeeper. Teams also got a bonus point for each goal, up to three per game, so a team could claim as many as nine points in a given game. The league's teams also don't bother with the Open Cup, and many games take place on crude first-generation artificial turf.

The league boomed. Several teams averaged more than 20,000 fans per game, though the league as a whole never averaged more than 15,000.[69] Already up to 20 teams in 1975, the league expanded to 24 by 1978.

And yet the USMNT could make little progress. Having played many times since the last World Cup cycle, a nice change of pace, the U.S. men start qualification for the 1978 competition, once again in a first-round group with Mexico and Canada from which *two* teams would reach the CONCACAF final. They win once, lose once, and draw twice, setting up a tiebreaking match with Canada for a spot in the six-team final group. Canada wins 3–0.

In 1975, the USMNT's Elo rating hits rock-bottom—88th in the world.

The ASL, which might have been well advised to focus on being the best regional league it could be, instead reaches all the way across the continent. Four West Coast teams and Utah join in 1976. Teams shuffle about for another few years. Meanwhile . . .

. . . in the United States, the Public Broadcasting System (PBS) begins broadcasting the highlight show *Soccer Made in Germany*, bringing the Bundesliga to an American audience.

1979–1983

Soccer retreats inside.

Indoor soccer had been an occasional experiment over the years in the United States. Rules varied a bit, but indoor soccer eventually settled into a game conveniently set within a hockey rink's boards—obviously with turf instead of ice. Futsal, which takes place on a gym floor (or any available surface) without dasher boards, was growing in South America but was not yet firmly established as an international sport.

The Major Indoor Soccer League (MISL) finishes its first season in 1979, with the New York Arrows taking the title. It has all the things non-soccer fans claim they want in sports—high scoring, fast action, and the occasional fracas. It's not wildly popular in its first season, but five of the six teams return for the second year (a surprisingly high retention rate by U.S. standards), and the league expands to 10 teams. The St. Louis Steamers debut in that second year with average attendance exceeding 14,000. [70]

The NASL, which had played several indoor exhibitions over the years, doesn't cede any ground. Ten teams play an indoor 1979–1980 season, and most of the league returns the next year.

In 1980, all seems well in the outdoor NASL—24 teams, some averaging more than 20,000 per game and the Cosmos flying high with an average over 40,000, and lucrative games against foreign teams. But the departures start the next year. By 1982, the league is down to 14 teams.

The NASL's Jacksonville Tea Men flee for the ASL, which is well into a steep decline and a late-career identity crisis, no longer fielding a single team from its old Baltimore-to-Boston home grounds. Six teams—Jacksonville, Pennsylvania, Carolina, Dallas, Detroit, and Oklahoma

City—play in 1983 before the longest-standing non-local league in U.S. history says goodbye.

In 1980, the USMNT tries once again to reach the six-team CONCA-CAF final to qualify for the World Cup, again facing Mexico and Canada in the first round. They beat Mexico 2–1, but only after their mathematical elimination.

The federation makes a bold move, essentially entering the national team as its own entry in the NASL. The team, dubbed Team America, is unable to convince some of the top U.S. players to leave their current teams, and the experiment only lasts a year.

Opportunity knocks in 1982. Colombia bows out as host of the 1986 World Cup. The USA leaps at the chance to bid, as do Mexico and Canada. Longtime Cosmos fan and notorious foreign-policy man Henry Kissinger joins Pelé and Franz Beckenbauer in pressing the case, but FIFA chooses Mexico in a decision that *World Soccer* magazine would later describe as "skullduggery."[71]

The college game makes progress, with players taking unusual paths through campuses to the pro and international games. Ecuadorian immigrant Chico Borja plays and majors in architecture[72] at the New Jersey Institute of Technology, then joins the Cosmos and the national team. South African Roy Wegerle plays at the University of South Florida—and, quite importantly for his future happiness, citizenship, and national team decision, meets and marries an American woman—and goes on to the NASL, MISL, and then England, eventually getting U.S. citizenship and choosing to play for the USMNT over other options.[73] Meanwhile . . .

. . . in the United States, NBA TV deals inch past the $25 million/year mark, combining traditional broadcast networks with cable.[74]

1984

A classic good-news, bad-news year. Los Angeles hosts the Olympics and spreads its soccer tournament around the country to great success, capped by two crowds of more than 100,000 in the Rose Bowl. FIFA takes note when the United States bids a few years later to host the World Cup. And the mostly pro (the rules are complicated) U.S. team is competitive, beating Costa Rica 3–0, losing to Italy 0–1, and tying Egypt 1–1, barely missing out on the quarterfinals. The USMNT is making slow progress, finally climbing into the top 50 in the Elo ratings.

The bad news? The NASL is dying. The 1984 season proceeds with nine teams, none of them able to draw more than 15,000 fans per game. A couple of teams bolt for the MISL, and by early 1985 it's clear that's the only place to play. The leagues have been in a salary war—Chico Borja leaves the Cosmos before the team's demise, saying he would be paid twice as much to play for the MISL's Las Vegas Americans.[75]

A few ASL survivors and expansion teams form the United Soccer League (USL, no relation to the twenty-first-century USL), which plays with nine teams in 1984 and manages to lose seven of them after the season.

Amateur soccer still has some strong teams, most notably the New York Pancyprian Freedoms, who defeat Mexico's Puebla in CONCACAF Champions Cup play. Meanwhile . . .

. . . in Europe, Argentine playmaker Diego Maradona sets a new transfer-fee record, breaking the record set two years earlier by . . . Diego Maradona.

1985–1987

The nadir—for outdoor soccer, anyway.

The NASL is gone. The mighty Cosmos, fresh off withdrawing midway through the MISL season,[76] get partway through an exhibition schedule before dissolving with a whole lot of finger-pointing.[77] The USL, fielding only four teams for an abbreviated 1985 season, disappears as well. The only intercity league of note is the Western Soccer Alliance (WSA).

World Cup qualifying is revamped, and the USMNT finds itself just needing a draw at home against Costa Rica to reach the three-team final group. Players keep arriving through the campaign—defender Kevin Crow finishes up the MISL final series with the San Diego Sockers, then starts for the USMNT in the decisive game three days later. Costa Rica wins 1–0, a bitter blow to a reeling U.S. soccer community.[78]

The next year, former Buffalo Bills quarterback and future Republican vice presidential nominee Jack Kemp stands in opposition to a congressional resolution in favor of the United States' bid to host the World Cup, decrying soccer as a "European socialist [sport]" on the floor of the House of Representatives.[79]

At this point, the United States is an indoor soccer country. The MISL is chugging along with several teams averaging more than 10,000 fans per game. U.S. players might not be able to readjust to the longer runs, vast spaces, and limited substitutions of the outdoor game, but who cares?

The biggest competition for the MISL is another indoor soccer league. The American Indoor Soccer Association launches in the Midwest, including the Milwaukee Wave, a team that will stick around for a long time. A league with less ambition, the Southwest Indoor Soccer League (SISL), starts in Texas and Oklahoma. It would eventually morph into the USISL and later the USL, a dominant umbrella group for 100 or more pro and elite amateur teams.

The only saving grace is youth. U.S. Youth Soccer launched in 1974 with 100,000 players, but was well over 1 million by the mid-1980s on top of the numbers registered by the independent AYSO and SAY.[80] High school participation had grown from less than 50,000 boys (no girls) in 1969–1970 to nearly 200,000 boys and more than 85,000 girls in 1985–1986.[81] College soccer is slowly building for women. Title IX was passed in 1972, and slowly prodded colleges to add the sport for women through the 1980s before exploding to hundreds in the 1990s.

Men's college soccer has matured, with more than 180 schools sponsoring Division I teams. And the players are starting to have an impact, not just with the occasional import such as Wegerle or Borja. The old soccer hotbed of Kearny, New Jersey, sends three players to southern schools—Tab Ramos to North Carolina State, and John Harkes and Tony Meola to Virginia, where a young coach named Bruce Arena has shed his second gig coaching lacrosse to focus on building a soccer powerhouse. All three players would be a big part of the USMNT in the 1990s. Meanwhile . . .

. . . in England, full-fledged promotion and relegation between the semipro/amateur Football Conference and the sprawling Football League is introduced, replacing the old system of clubs running for election against the club at the bottom of the League ladder.

. . . in Mexico, the country hosts the World Cup for the second time.

1988–1989

Just when outdoor soccer was all but dead in the United States, the World Cup saves the day.

First—appropriately on Independence Day 1988—FIFA awards the 1994 World Cup hosting rights to the United States, barely beating a bid from Morocco that only had two of the 12 required world-class stadiums. [82]

And then, at last, the USMNT qualifies for a World Cup. Needing a win at Trinidad and Tobago, the U.S. men see a brilliant looping shot from Paul Caligiuri send the mullet-haired young men to the 1990 World Cup. After 40 years in the wilderness, the USA would play in the 1990 World Cup by qualification and the 1994 World Cup as hosts. (And the 1991 "1st FIFA World Championship for Women's Football for the M& M's Cup," which would retroactively be called the Women's World Cup.)

The players include the Kearny Three—Meola in goal, Harkes and Ramos in midfield. Meola is still at Virginia, being heckled by people like me at Duke. Others play in obscure outdoor leagues, a couple play indoors, and some are trying their luck in lesser-known European clubs. But with those outdoor leagues unable to pay serious salaries, many players are under contract with U.S. Soccer itself. One of those obscure outdoor leagues is yet another American Soccer League (ASL), which sets up shop on the East Coast.

The USA gets a surprising result at the youth level, where goalkeeper Kasey Keller helps the Under-20 team claim fourth place in the World Youth Championship. For the next 28 years, the USA would reach the quarterfinals of the biannual tournament several times, but never the semifinals.

1990

The inexperienced USMNT loses all three games at the World Cup. The best result is a 1–0 loss to host Italy. Still, it's better than not qualifying, and the experience would prove valuable.

The AISA, still challenging the MISL for indoor dominance, changes its name to the National Professional Soccer League (NPSL), not to be confused with the NPSL that fought the USA for outdoor supremacy in 1967 before merging into the NASL.

But the MISL still wields plenty of power, and it provides an important bloc of votes in the USSF presidential election. FIFA favorite Alan Rothenberg, a lawyer best known in soccer circles for organizing the successful 1984 Olympic tournament, unseats incumbent Werner Fricker.[83] Few in the sports world noticed the vote, but it would have a massive impact through the rest of the decade.

Outdoors, the ASL and WSA merge to form the American Professional Soccer League (APSL), which boasts 22 teams and some decent players—a couple of national teamers when available, a few NASL holdovers, and some good young talent. Meanwhile . . .

. . . in the United States, NBA TV rights (broadcast and cable combined) sail past the $200 million/year mark, an eightfold increase in eight years.[84]

1991

The U.S. wins the World Cup! U.S. Women, that is. With little professional play anywhere in the world, the Title IX-inspired U.S. college conferences are likely the best women's soccer leagues anywhere on the planet, and the U.S. women take their head start and run with it.

The men, led by colorful globe-trotting coach Bora Milutinovic, also win a nice trophy—the first CONCACAF Gold Cup. Playing at home in Pasadena and Los Angeles, the USMNT goes 3–0 in group play over Trinidad and Tobago (piling into taxis when their bus doesn't show),[85] Guatemala, and Costa Rica. Then the stunner—defender John Doyle and Peter Vermes score in a 2–0 semifinal win over Mexico. The defense and goalkeeper Tony Meola hold off Honduras in the final, and the USMNT takes the Cup.

The bad news: The APSL is already down to nine teams.

1992–1993

Now even the indoor leagues are failing. The MISL, which had briefly changed its name to MSL, collapses despite solid attendance—averaging more than 7,000 fans per game in six of seven cities.[86] The San Diego Sockers, an MISL powerhouse that actually launched outdoors in the NASL, moves with the long-standing Dallas Sidekicks to the new Continental Indoor Soccer League, an effort by NBA and NHL owners to fill arenas in the summers. It never really takes off, morphs into the Premier Soccer Alliance (PSA) in 1998 and World Indoor Soccer League (WISL) in 1999 before merging with the mostly stable NPSL in 2001.

But signs of life are appearing outdoors. The SISL transforms into the United States Interregional Soccer League (USISL) with a healthy coast-to-coast outdoor presence. The San Francisco Bay Blackhawks (APSL) and Dallas Rockets (USISL) make respectable runs in the 1992 CONCACAF Champions Cup.

And USSF must make good on its pledge to FIFA that in exchange for the World Cup, it would make sure the country had an honest-to-goodness professional league. It solicits bids and receives three. One is the APSL, whose case is damaged by having only seven teams, three claimed from the wreckage of Canada's defunct league.

The fun bidder is Jim Paglia's League One America. which is ahead of its time in terms of a single-entity structure (the league owns everything) and its desire to have soccer-specific stadiums. Less likely to catch on: Drastic rule changes that confined players to specific zones on the field (enforced by electronic monitors), and extra points for long-range shots or in a second set of goalposts outside the main goal.[87]

To no one's surprise, the winner is a plan drawn up by a team of Rothenberg appointees, including a lawyer in Rothenberg's firm (Mark Abbott) and an economist with a history of filling volunteer roles at many levels of soccer (Sunil Gulati). That league would be known as Major League Soccer (MLS). Meanwhile . . .

. . . in England, First Division clubs leave the Football League to form the Premier League. In some respects, it's business as usual, with promotion and relegation continuing between the tiers. But the Premier League has more freedom on the marketing and sponsorship front, and money begins to pour into the top of the English pyramid.

. . . in Europe, the European Cup morphs into the Champions League, adding a group stage and later allowing multiple entries from top countries.

1994

The World Cup comes to the United States and wins over many skeptics at home and abroad. Attendance is immense, averaging more than 68,000 per game.[88]

And the U.S. team isn't bad. Eric Wynalda scores in a 1–1 draw with Switzerland in the first World Cup match ever played inside, on temporary grass in the Pontiac Silverdome. Up against Colombia, the USMNT pressures the dark-horse tournament favorites into conceding an own goal (tragically, defender Andres Escobar was shot to death upon returning to Colombia). Then the team scores a signature goal worthy of any good national team, with a long buildup freeing Tab Ramos to send Earnie Stewart through on goal, 2–0 USA. The final would be 2–1.[89]

The USMNT's first World Cup win since 1950 would be its last for a while longer, though. A disappointing 1–0 loss to Romania caps the group stage, and the men miss a golden opportunity to advance past Brazil in the round of 16 on July 4 when the eventual tournament winners are reduced to 10 men for a brutal elbow that knocks Ramos out of the game. Though the USMNT gains the one-man advantage, losing Ramos unhinges the attack, and Brazil wins 1–0.

The Netherlands-born Stewart was one of the European Americans the federation had located, along with German American midfield general Thomas Dooley.

1995–1996

MLS kicks off. Eventually. The league delays its launch from 1995 to 1996, trading the opportunity to build off World Cup momentum for another year of lining up investors and infrastructure.

The delay gives many U.S. players a chance to capitalize on a surge in demand for their services, with many going to Europe or Mexico. Most would return to play in MLS in its debut season, but Stewart would remain in the Netherlands for many years, backup goalkeeper Juergen Sommer would stay in England for some time, and young midfielder Claudio Reyna would go on to be a standout in Germany, Scotland, and England.

The USMNT reconvenes as special guests in Copa America, South America's continental championship, and shocks everyone with a 3–0 win over Argentina after a brief labor stoppage. A penalty-kick win over fellow guest Mexico gets the team to the semifinals and a fourth-place finish, perhaps the most impressive result for the U.S. men in any tournament thus far.

In 1996, MLS blows its expectations out of the water. The Los Angeles Galaxy, with flashy Mexican goalkeeper Jorge Campos making frequent forays forward, can't handle the walkup crowd for its debut, eventually getting more than 69,000 fans through the turnstiles. The league averages more than 17,000 fans. That's impressive, but it sets unreasonable expectations moving forward.

And the U.S. Open Cup roars back from obscurity. Pro teams and USISL amateur teams enter in 1995, with the USISL's then amateur Richmond Kickers defeating the USISL Professional League's El Paso Patriots in the final. MLS teams enter right away in 1996, with D.C. United claiming the "double" of MLS and Open Cup trophies under the leadership of Bruce Arena, who has finally left the college juggernaut he built at Virginia. The USISL also launches the amateur W-League for women in 1995.

The United States hosts the Olympics again, but the men struggle in a tough group with Argentina and Portugal. The women, on the other hand, avenge their defeat in the 1995 World Cup to win the first Olympic women's tournament and continue to elevate Mia Hamm to celebrity status.

1997–1998

The USMNT qualifies for the World Cup with a bit less drama than in the past. But the Cup itself is a disaster, with three depressing losses amid infighting and tactical naivete.

MLS expands to 12 teams, and the new Chicago Fire team wins the championship in its first season. But attendance is dropping, and the league isn't showing much impact on the sports landscape.

The APSL, the one-time rival of MLS for Division 1 sanctioning, merges into the now-sprawling USISL, which has so many teams that it splits into three divisions, the top one now boasting the APSL's snazzy

"A-League" moniker. That league is now the official U.S. Division 2 league, while the USISL's second tier is Division 3 and the bottom tier is the amateur Premier Development Soccer League (PDSL). The USISL also still operates the W-League, though some teams split to form the Women's Premier Soccer League (WPSL, not to be confused with the Women's Professional Softball League, a name that goes into use in 1999).

CONCACAF decides to hold its Champions Cup in the United States, giving MLS teams a considerable advantage. In 1997, Los Angeles reaches the final and D.C. United reaches the semifinals. The next year, D.C. United becomes the first U.S. team to lift the trophy. It goes on to win the rarely contested Interamerican Cup, defeating Brazil's Vasco da Gama in a two-leg series held in the United States. Meanwhile . . .

. . . in the United States, NBA TV rights balloon past $600 million per year.[90]

1999–2000

Another World Cup in the United States—women's this time—and the U.S. team responds beautifully with a comeback past Germany in an epic quarterfinal and a win on penalty kicks in the final that puts Brandi Chastain on magazine covers all over your local newsstand. Average attendance surges from 4,315 in 1995 (host: Sweden) to 37,319, validating organizers' desire to put the games in large stadiums.[91]

MLS continues with unusual stability, neither moving nor folding a team in its first five years, a refreshing change from the revolving doors of the ASL and NASL. The Los Angeles Galaxy wins the CONCACAF Champions Cup, held entirely in Los Angeles. Lamar Hunt, who has been pushing pro soccer forward since the early NASL days, gets a soccer-specific stadium built in Columbus.

Promotion and relegation comes to a U.S. pro league for the first time—sort of. The USISL offers promotion between its divisions, but in reality, economic necessity trumps on-field performance, and clubs often opt to "self-relegate" to save money.[92] The USISL also continues its merry-go-round of brand names, switching to the United Soccer Leagues (USL).

The 1999 Open Cup goes to the underdog, as the well-supported Rochester Rhinos emerge from the A-League to upset several MLS teams and take the trophy.

U.S. youth teams take two fourth-place finishes. The 1999 Under-17s fall on penalty kicks in the semifinals, making enough of an impression for Landon Donovan to claim the Golden Ball (best player) and DaMarcus Beasley to take the Silver Ball. Donovan features again the next year in the Olympics, now featuring Under-23s plus three "overage" players per team, where Team USA beats Japan on penalties in the quarterfinals before bowing out to Spain.

Indoors, the Premier Soccer Alliance (PSA), a group of leftover teams from the CISL, changes its name to the World Indoor Soccer League (WISL). The "World" is intentional—the league plans to have a U.S. division and a European division, unhindered by the lack of any history (or perhaps any interest) in the turf-and-boards game in Europe.

2001

The idea that soccer is solely a women's sport in the United States is at its peak. The U.S. women are World Cup champions, plastered on every magazine cover and late-night talk show after their triumph. Their league, the WUSA, averages 8,103 fans in its first season, with two teams smashing the 10,000 mark.

MLS is on the brink of collapse. The USISL is seeing plenty of teams either folding or dropping down to its amateur PDL, which has dropped the obvious "S" from its name. The indoor game grasps for past glory. The NPSL reclaims the old MISL name and merges with the WISL (formerly CISL, briefly PSA). The San Diego Sockers and Dallas Sidekicks persist. Most of the teams have solid histories, but don't attract many fans.

Finally, the September 11 attacks shake the United States to its core. Soccer competitions are the least of anyone's concerns, but MLS manages to complete its season amid restricted air travel and a declining economy. Meanwhile . . .

. . . in Europe, Real Madrid pays $66 million ($93.7 million in 2018 money) for Zinedine Zidane, breaking the world record the club set the year before by spending $55 million ($80 million in 2018) for Luis Figo.

Big money is flowing into the top clubs in Europe through the Champions League and the domestic leagues.

. . . in Germany, the country responds to relatively disappointing performances in the 1998 World Cup and Euro 2000 with "Das Reboot," an ambitious program to overhaul youth development throughout the country, making sure no promising players are overlooked.

2002

Just when U.S. soccer needs it most, the stars align at the World Cup in South Korea and Japan. Claudio Reyna and John O'Brien are healthy. Tony Sanneh hits a career peak. (None of those three played in the Gold Cup in January, which the USA won for the first time since the inaugural event in 1991.) Landon Donovan and DaMarcus Beasley burst onto the World Cup scene a few years after lighting up the Under-17 World Championship. Portugal can't cope with the U.S. attack and then falls apart against South Korea, allowing the U.S. men to reach the round of 16 and outfox Mexico for a quarterfinal berth, where German goalkeeper Oliver Kahn has to be at his best to keep Bruce Arena's crew out of the semifinals.

At last, men's soccer has broken through. Fans pack bars in the middle of the night, stunning the handful of holdouts who thought the 1994 World Cup attendance numbers were a fluke. U.S. Soccer finances turn around.

MLS bounces back from the verge of extinction, in large part due to the formation of affiliate Soccer United Marketing, giving the league more pieces of the growing soccer pie. Two teams, Tampa Bay and Miami, are sacrificed. CONCACAF play becomes more difficult, with two-leg series replacing the single-site knockout tournaments and starting a long spell of futility in which Mexican and the occasional Costa Rican clubs knock out the MLS entries on a regular basis.

2003–2005

MLS takes a couple of cautious steps forward, adding a team in Salt Lake City and a second team in Los Angeles. The former takes root nicely. The latter, called Chivas USA as an outgrowth of the giant Mexican club, does not.

The USL's pro ranks are in free fall, with just 12 teams in the once-sprawling top division (now the less catchy "USL First Division" instead of the A-League) and nine in the USL Second Division.

The United States hosts another major tournament, taking over on short notice when the SARS (severe acute respiratory syndrome) epidemic hits China and the Women's World Cup returns to the United States in 2003. It comes too late to save the WUSA, which managed three seasons with the same eight teams but never managed to have enough impact to justify the giant piles of money shoveled into it in a fit of post-1999 optimism. And the U.S. women lose in the semifinals to a German team that has advanced past the athletic kick-and-rush style the American team employs—as it did in the early days of the men's national team. They rebound to win the 2004 Olympics in a last hurrah for many of the players who launched the program in the 1990s.

The NPSL name returns to the U.S. soccer landscape, though it's a rebranded amateur outdoor summer league (National Premier Soccer League) instead of the old indoor league.

2006–2009

Not a great World Cup for the U.S. men, though a battling 1–1 tie with a bruising Italy team is a highlight. But that tournament is sandwiched between two Gold Cup triumphs, the latter of which qualifies the team for the 2009 Confederations Cup.

And the USMNT is astounding in the Confederations Cup, ending Spain's 35-game unbeaten streak and taking a 2–0 lead in the final against Brazil before falling 3–2.

The U.S. women have one embarrassing tournament, a 4–0 semifinal loss to Brazil after the benching of controversial goalkeeper Hope Solo, and one brilliant showing, winning the Olympics for the third time.

In indoor soccer, the MISL drops to six teams, then expands to nine, then explodes in 2008. Four others form the Xtreme Soccer League (XSL), its name a nod to either a computer programming language, the X-Games, or the Poochie character on *The Simpsons*. Three form the nominally different National Indoor Soccer League (NISL). After one year, the XSL loses every team except Milwaukee, which returns to the NISL, which resurrects the MISL name. Again.

Another team joins the new pro division of the Premier Arena Soccer League (PASL), which is thinking globally. It's affiliated not with FIFA but with FIFRA—Federation International de Futbol Rapido, which plans its own international competitions.

MLS is moving ahead. For the first time, it signs a rights deal in which it collects a fee from the broadcaster, a change from the "hey, can we have some of the ad revenue?" deals of the past. The league moves across the northern border into Toronto, and grabs attention with substantial, lively crowds. It also drops the hammer on the San Jose Earthquakes, which were unable to find committed local ownership, and moves the team to Houston. New ownership immediately pops up to restart the Earthquakes, taking MLS to 14 teams. The biggest leap is a change in salary cap rules to allow people called "Designated Players" to sign for more money, which sounds boring but is made considerably more exciting when global megastar David Beckham signs with the Los Angeles Galaxy.

The USL has a few moments of glory, with a couple of teams reaching U.S. Open Cup semifinals, and turns into a breeding ground for MLS teams. The Seattle Sounders, a name that has been used in several leagues since the NASL days, move into MLS and immediately draw giant crowds to the stadium it shares with the NFL's Seattle Seahawks.

The league's teams continue to struggle in CONCACAF play, though the New England Revolution wins the 2008 edition of the gimmicky "SuperLiga" for MLS and Mexican sides.

After a five-year absence, women's professional soccer returns with a league called . . . Women's Professional Soccer (WPS). Expenses are scaled back from the lofty ambitions of the WUSA.

2010

England tries and fails to avenge the 1950 World Cup defeat, tying the U.S. men 1–1. Poor refereeing nearly keeps the USA out of the round of 16, but Landon Donovan scores at the death against Algeria to send them through, going viral in the process. Ghana then eliminates the USA for the second straight World Cup.

By this point, it's not unusual for a World Cup game to draw 10 million or more viewers on U.S. television, especially when Spanish-language broadcasts (often drawing more than the English broadcasts) are added. The dreary World Cup final between the Netherlands and Spain draws 24.7 million, a record that would stand until the *next* World Cup.[93]

MLS barely manages to avoid a labor stoppage, then plays a 16-team season with Philadelphia added to the mix.

The lower divisions have gone off the rails. For two years, a group of USL owners had sought a new direction for the top leagues. In late summer 2009, the organization is sold to something called NuRock Soccer Holdings instead of Jeff Cooper, a St. Louis attorney. Several teams announce plans to split from the USL. They decide to revive a name from the past—NASL.

But neither the NASL nor the remaining USL top-division teams have a critical mass of teams, so the USSF steps in to force 12 teams to play together as a second division for one year. Two of those clubs are already pledged to move into MLS in 2011 (technically somewhat different entities but carrying over some personnel, as the Seattle Sounders have already done).

The final irony for the year—a couple of months into the season, Jeff Cooper's St. Louis enterprise falls apart with the revelation that Cooper had called in funding from British investors who defaulted. The men's team continues playing, but the WPS team dissolves a few weeks into the season, scattering players like Hope Solo and Shannon Boxx elsewhere in the league.

Late in the year, in an effort to stabilize the lower divisions, U.S. Soccer updates its Professional League Standards. The Division 2 standards seem particularly difficult, including a principal owner worth at least $20 million.[94] The NASL teams embrace it and head off on their own. The USL retrenches as a Division 3 league, still also operating the W-League and the PDL.

Here's how the 2010 Division 2 teams disperse for 2011:

- MLS (2): Portland Timbers, Vancouver Whitecaps
- NASL (6): Carolina RailHawks, Puerto Rico Islanders, FC Tampa Bay (later to reclaim the name "Rowdies" from limbo), Fort Lauderdale Strikers (formerly Miami FC, not to be confused with the

club that would start a few years later), NSC Minnesota Stars, Montreal Impact
- USL (2): Rochester Rhinos, Austin Aztex (moved to Orlando)
- Oblivion (2): AC St. Louis, Crystal Palace Baltimore

2011–2013

MLS continues expansion, adding Montreal from the NASL in 2012.

Real Salt Lake comes close to ending the MLS drought in CONCACAF play, drawing 2–2 away to Monterrey in the first leg of the 2011 final but losing 1–0 at home.

The NASL takes the six holdovers from the Division 2 league and adds Edmonton and the Atlanta Silverbacks, which sat out the 2010 season, for 2011. It remains at eight teams in 2012 with the addition of the San Antonio Scorpions. But the NASL has a few problems, with much of it propped up by an organization called Traffic Sports. Reporting several years later by North Carolina journalist Neil Morris revealed that MLS was talking with the new league about an affiliation deal, but that NASL abruptly walked away in 2012. A couple of days later, the reborn New York Cosmos—reclaimed from intellectual-property hell and put back on the field as an exhibition team—announce plans to join the league in 2013.[95] The league plays a split season and earns a waiver from U.S. Soccer to play the first half of 2013 with only seven teams after Puerto Rico's departure.

The USL has a disastrous 2011 season, announcing an "international" division with three Puerto Rico clubs, an Antigua club, and the Los Angeles Blues. A few weeks into the season, the Puerto Rico experiment ends. But the league pounces when the NASL opts out of MLS affiliation, striking up a partnership between the two organizations that have occasionally feuded. In 2013, MLS clubs start loaning players to USL teams.

The indoor game also folds into the USL. After considering its own pro indoor league, going back to its SISL roots, and various indoor excursions over the years, the USL agrees to manage MISL 3.0, which has struggled to field more than five teams since the shakeup of 2008.

Women's soccer takes another big step forward and then a step off the cliff. The 2011 World Cup is filled with great moments, including an Abby Wambach goal deep into extra time's stoppage time in the quarterfinals versus Brazil, and a heartbreaking loss on penalties after a classic match with Japan in the final. WPS rides the momentum with great crowds after the Cup, then implodes.

The league's demise is sped along by the saga of the former Washington Freedom, which continued to play exhibitions and in the W-League between the WUSA and WPS. Freedom owners John and Maureen Hendricks, who were driving forces behind the WUSA, sell to South Florida entrepreneur Dan Borislow. See the legal chapter for that saga. The whole thing ends up in court, and the league folds after three seasons.

In 2012, a few clubs band together with some high-level WPSL teams to form the stopgap WPSL Elite League. The national team players are busy with the Olympics, in which they take another thrilling ride with an epic 4–3 win over Canada in the semifinals and revenge over Japan in the final. In 2013, the National Women's Soccer League (NWSL) launches, scaling back expenses from WPS, which had already scaled back expenses from the WUSA.

Scandal strikes CONCACAF, though some journalists would argue it was long overdue. Longtime president Jack Warner, also a FIFA vice president, resigns in the wake of a bribery scandal in June 2011.[96]

That was just the start. Chuck Blazer, a longtime U.S. soccer power broker and CONCACAF's general secretary from 1990 to 2011, had ruled the region with Warner for decades but is forced to order an investigation once the bribery evidence comes to light. A few months later, Blazer turns whistleblower. In a secret court session in 2013, Blazer confesses he and others in FIFA took bribes in exchange for their votes to give South Africa the 2010 World Cup hosting rights.[97] Meanwhile . . .

. . . in the United States, various contract renewals push domestic NFL broadcasting rights to a total around $7 billion starting in 2014.[98]

2014

Another round of 16 appearance for the U.S. men, who finally beat Ghana and have Portugal beaten before conceding a very late goal. Holding Germany to a single goal assures passage out of a "Group of Death," but the second-place finish consigns the USA to a date with an overwhelming Belgian team. Tim Howard's goalkeeping heroics get the game to extra time still scoreless, but Belgium wins 2–1.

MLS remains at 19 teams, and the lower divisions are relatively stable. The NASL raises a few points on a revised set of Pro League Standards, but works out the issues with the USSF.

Indoor soccer is more or less forgotten at this point, but the confused history takes one more strange turn. After three years under management of the USL, which started as the indoor SISL and continued to dabble in the indoor game, MISL teams decide they've had enough. They leave the USL and abandon the MISL once again, merging with the PASL's Pro Division (see 2006–2009 above) to form the Major Arena Soccer League (MASL). The league includes the Dallas Sidekicks and San Diego Sockers.

High school soccer is ubiquitous, with 432,000 boys and 375,000 girls[99]—numbers that are limited by available facilities more than interest, with big schools forced to cut a lot of prospective players who try out, even as club coaches try to keep their elite players out of scholastic soccer. Meanwhile . . .

. . . in the United States, Major League Baseball TV rights, split between Fox, ESPN, and Turner networks, go for roughly $1.5 billion per year.[100]

2015–2016

The Justice Department reaches across the Atlantic, working with Swiss authorities to raid FIFA offices on the eve of their 2015 general meeting. FIFA president Sepp Blatter is re-elected, but forced to resign.

And the scandal hits closer to home. CONCACAF president Jeffrey Webb is among those charged, ending up under house arrest at his home in the Atlanta suburbs. Also ensnared: Traffic Sports, the company that owns multiple NASL teams, and executive Aaron Davidson, the chairman of the NASL's Board of Governors.

The United States wins two World Cups. The first, a thrilling run by the U.S. women's team to reclaim the trophy it last won in 1999, draws considerable attention. The other, an indoor soccer World Cup held by the World Minifootball Federation, does not. That's the PASL's turf-and-boards soccer, not the wall-less game of futsal that has become the rage with youth coaches.

Orlando City is the latest to jump from the lower divisions to MLS. New York gets a second team, this one associated with Manchester City and the New York Yankees. The Chivas USA experiment ends. The NASL continues slow expansion, while the USL booms with the addition of many MLS reserve teams. The W-League, a sturdy second division and at times the de facto top division in U.S. women's soccer, folds after two decades.

In 2016, the United States hosts a special edition of the Copa America, usually the South American championship but expanded to include North America this year. The USMNT reaches the semifinals, and the tournament adds tons of money to the once-penniless but now powerful USSF.

2017

The debacle in Trinidad, ending the USMNT's streak of qualifying for the World Cup, caps a laborious campaign in which Jürgen Klinsmann was fired and Bruce Arena rehired. For the first time since 1986, the World Cup proceeds the next year without the United States. (The U.S. women have always made it, though one year wasn't easy.) Italy and the Netherlands also fail to make it.

MLS expands to Minnesota and Atlanta, the latter taking over attendance supremacy from the Seattle Sounders. The league's average attendance is now well over 20,000.

The big problem is the NASL. After putting on airs of challenging MLS head-to-head for a few years, the league drops from twelve to eight teams. Two teams join the USL, which is now bidding for Division 2 status alongside the NASL. The New York Cosmos are on the verge of selling to a buyer (later revealed to be Soccer United Marketing) that would close them down and keep the intellectual property until buyer Rocco Commisso emerges. San Francisco joins the league, wins the league, and folds. U.S. Soccer decides not to grant the NASL Division 2 status for 2018. Clubs leave, and all hell breaks loose in court.

PRESENT

Basically, the United States is finally pretty good at soccer. But the rest of the world is better.

We can look at the TV numbers. Major League Soccer is getting $90 million per year. That's $90 million more than it was getting 20 years ago, but it's nowhere near what other leagues generate.[101]

- "Big Five" European leagues generate nearly 17 billion euros (more than $19.5 billion) per year.
- NBC is paying $166 million per year ($1 billion over six years) just to broadcast the English Premier League in the United States.
- Champions League rights in the United States alone are worth $100 million a year ($65 million for English-language, $35 million for Spanish-language).
- Two networks pay $2.6 billion a year to broadcast the NBA.
- Individual college sports conferences command up to $300 million a year—each.[102]

We can look at attendance, which isn't that bad. MLS, propelled by giant crowds in Seattle and Atlanta, averaged more than 22,000 fans per game in 2017. (Naysayers often claim numbers are often inflated by counting "tickets distributed" rather than "tickets sold," and some people buy tickets but can't show up for the game, but other leagues' practices are generally similar.) Germany's Bundesliga is roughly twice that, England's Premier League isn't too far behind Germany, but Spain, Italy, and France aren't too far ahead of MLS.[103] Big-spending China and tradition-rich Mexico are also slightly ahead.[104]

We can look at statistical comparisons. FiveThirtyEight lists several MLS teams roughly equivalent to most second-tier European teams.[105] These metrics are all factors in the more general question: Where does the USMNT rank, and what are the chances it can win the World Cup?

The best—still flawed, but best—ratings in the world are the Elo ratings, using the same system that ranks chess players. The USMNT fell as low as 88th in 1975 and was out of the top 50 as recently as 1995. A good surge in early 1998, including a win over Brazil, got the team up to 22nd, though the World Cup later that year would drive it back down. A win over Germany in the 1999 Confederations Cup was good enough to take the 20th spot. In the 2000s, the team managed to spend a lot of time in the teens and even cracked the top 10 with the 2009 Confederations Cup win over Spain. But that was short-lived, and the team has been in the 20s or even lower through most of the 2010s.[106] The 2002 World Cup surely skewed some perceptions. But that team was the best the United States has sent to a men's World Cup, at least since 1930, and it still required a few breaks to make the quarterfinals.

Progress isn't linear. Nor are any of the factors supposedly benefiting the United States—a massive economy, a large population—necessarily an indicator of future success. Croatia, not China, made the World Cup final in 2018.

Want optimism? U.S. soccer has never gone completely underground. And now is a good time to be a fan. Or a lawyer.

7

WE'RE OBSESSED WITH THE QUICK FIX

To recap where we are so far: We've seen that the United States faces extraordinary difficulties in building a soccer power. We're a country full of stubborn individuals who either don't want to deal with soccer at all or want to do things their own way, which means we're as likely to end up shredding each other in court as we are to build anything that takes us closer to soccer greatness.

This bleak landscape hasn't stopped people from suggesting everything can be solved in an instant. If soccer in the United States was a show on the HGTV network, the crew would be impressed with some new kitchen fixtures but horrified by the cracks in the foundation. And yet so many people see a house that just needs an open floor plan to make it a $2 million dream home that puts the rest of the neighborhood to shame.

The most prominent solution is the third rail of U.S. soccer discussions. Previous chapters have alluded to how violent a discussion it can be, but now we need to get into it in detail to explain why it's not going to solve everything . . .

PROMOTION AND RELEGATION

Consider for a moment the oft-cited entrepreneurs of *South Park*—the Underpants Gnomes.

(Seriously—Google Scholar has more than 100 references to the Gnomes. Sometimes, the analogy is a stretch, though many of them are secondhand references to "Privacy and Antitrust: Underpants Gnomes, the First Amendment, and Subjectivity," which raises the Gnomes only to point out how they are *not* relevant. "The Relevance of Power in International Relations" also doesn't offer a sound reason for invoking the Gnomes. "The Balance Point: The Blacksmiths of the Digital Age or the Economics of Serials" is more intriguing. Outside Google Scholar, everyone from *Motley Fool* to Paul Krugman has invoked the Gnomes to point to holes in economic or political plans.)

The Gnomes are famous for their business plan:

Step 1: Collect underpants
Step 2: ?
Step 3: Profit

The analogue in the U.S. soccer world:

Step 1: Institute promotion and relegation
Step 2: ?
Step 3: Dominate world soccer

The United States is indeed unique (aside from Australia and some rather tiny countries) in having a league system that doesn't send the bottom teams down to a lower division and the top teams up the ladder or pyramid. Soccer isn't the only sport that uses this system around the world. Generally, if more than 20 teams are capable of playing at the same level, teams are promoted and relegated.

The folklore is wonderful. Supporters are thrilled when their clubs pull off an escape from relegation. Coventry City had an uncanny knack for getting the result they needed on the last day of the season. Jimmy Glass, an unheralded goalkeeper on an emergency loan to fill in Carlisle United's injury-riddled roster, turned into an English legend in 1999 when he raced forward into the opposing penalty area on a late corner kick and scored the goal that kept Carlisle in the fourth tier of English soccer in an era in which the fifth tier was virtual oblivion. Smaller towns like Barnsley and Blackpool revel in that one season in which they played in the Premier League and welcomed Manchester United, Arsenal, and all the other giants of England to their home grounds.

It's exciting. Before the days of the internet and TV networks beaming every bit of action into U.S. households, some of us wrestled with antennas on shortwave radios to hear the BBC crackling through the static to hear the last day of the season and track which clubs were moving up and down. And no one would dispute that pro/rel makes the lower divisions more interesting.

The big question is whether pro/rel is feasible in the United States. (If you answer "but it works everywhere else," I hope you've enjoyed this free sample, but you really should read the rest of this chapter and the rest of the book.)

But the argument pro/rel advocates make isn't just that it brings a romantic joy to the sport, and it's not just about feasibility. The argument is that if the United States and Australia went to a pro/rel system, their leagues would join the global soccer elite, and the men's national teams would follow. Right?

Here's where the Underpants Gnomes come in.

To be fair, some promotion and relegation advocates aren't quite as insistent in this argument. Some are just seeking opportunities for more communities across the United States to have a place in the pro game, thereby boosting the professional game's national footprint. They don't push the pro/rel panacea mantra. But we're talking about the national team in this book, and other prominent people do indeed claim pro/rel is the key to, or at least a necessary part of, changing the U.S. men's fortunes.

Consider Riccardo Silva, a sports media mogul who owns Miami FC, a team that started out in the North American Soccer League in 2016. His company, MP & Silva, made a grand statement in the summer of 2017, claiming to offer MLS $4 billion for 10 years of television rights on the condition that the league would institute pro/rel.

MLS said it wasn't interested, partially because its broadcast rights were already set through 2022, and the league really didn't want to look beyond that when Silva stepped into the office to chat. Critics may argue that the league's tangled relationship with its media arm, Soccer United Marketing, and the U.S. Soccer Federation played a role in that reticence to discuss anything else at this time. Or maybe they were skeptical of someone from the NASL, which had taken more and more of an adversarial stance toward MLS over the years, coming in with an offer. And, yes,

MLS hasn't been receptive to talk of pro/rel for reasons we'll get into below.

But the point became moot in 2018, when MP & Silva fell apart. Britain's High Court ordered the dissolution of the company's home office in London based on a petition from the French Tennis Federation, part of a long list of creditors. Italy's Serie A was initiating legal proceedings over unpaid rights fees. England's Premier League, Germany's Bundesliga, Formula 1, and the International Handball Federation also were among those whose deals collapsed into MP & Silva's black hole.[1]

Silva didn't make the offer to try to save the company, which still bore his name but had been majority-owned by Chinese investors since 2016. A vague pledge that MLS would consider handing over media rights to MP & Silva in 2022 would not have paid the bills in 2018.

Silva's true goal was obvious. It was public relations. Headlines around the world posited MLS as the league that turned down a massive increase in broadcast rights because it refused to institute promotion and relegation, and few of those news outlets followed up to point out the implausibility of that offer. But even if Silva's offer was what was called an "unvitation" on *Seinfeld*, never designed to be accepted, MLS was forced into being defensive. Score a PR point for Silva and the NASL, which had at least paid lip service to pro/rel without putting its money where its mouth was. (We'll get to that.)

A couple of journalists called the bluff:

> *Graham Parker:* "That assumes this is a good-faith offer in the first place. The timing, outlandish scale and key contingencies of the offer seem more a shot across the bow than genuine desire to work together."[2]

> *Michael Long:* "With the man himself refusing to comment on this week's reports, there is some talk that his outsized offer amounted to little more than grandstanding—a way to keep the topic of promotion/relegation in the public forum whilst rousing the interest of team owners throughout the North American soccer pyramid. After all, Silva must have known MLS couldn't possibly accept his proposal."[3]

The reason we're discussing Silva's offer here, though, is that he explicitly tied pro/rel to the fate of the men's national team, most forcefully in an October 2017 interview with ESPN's Gabriele Marcotti:[4]

Q: Back to promotion and relegation: Why do you think it's necessary for a deal this size?

A: We know how soccer works and we believe there would be more fan excitement and the quality would increase over time. There is no reason why the United States should not be among the top five or ten countries in the world and it's a pity to see them struggling against Costa Rica and Honduras when they have all they need to be at the top level, competing with the likes of Germany, France or Spain.

Q: And you need promotion/relegation to do that?

A: We believe one of the reasons is the lack of an open system. The U.S. will only be able to compete when the third division in the U.S. is able to compete with the third division in Germany, France, or Spain and the second division can do the same with the second division in those countries and the first and so on. The natural consequence will then be that the national side will be at a comparable level to their national teams.

Here's another voice—Chris Hummer, founder of *SoccerWire* (for which I've written), writing the day after the USA's ill-fated World Cup qualification campaign came to an end with a loss in Trinidad:

> Without promotion and relegation in our domestic league, players on teams not in the playoff hunt have no reason to compete beyond simply earning a paycheck or their next contract offer. . . . Which means we lose to teams like we did last night in the most important game we've played in over 30 years—against a "B" team with nothing to play for (other than becoming legends like they just did).[5]

Hummer goes on to put it in bluntest terms: "Without promotion and relegation in our domestic league, we will never win a World Cup."[6] But why?

Silva's argument is "natural consequence," which again calls to mind the Underpants Gnomes. Others are more detailed.

Pressure Makes Diamonds

Eric Wynalda—Hall of Fame player, longtime TV pundit, and 2018 U.S. Soccer presidential candidate—is fond of telling a story about his time playing in Germany. After a loss, he decided to joke around a bit to lighten the mood in the locker room. A teammate flung a boot at him.

The moral of the story is supposed to be about the threat of relegation forcing players to treat their jobs with the utmost gravity. We have no way of knowing, though, whether the shoe-flinging is a result of relegation pressure or German soccer culture. If you follow Ian Plenderleith's lively *Referee Tales* blog, about his experiences reffing games in the lower reaches of German amateur soccer, you'll probably conclude it's the latter.

Hummer's argument is also along these lines. Without relegation, Hummer argues, MLS teams don't have much to play for down the stretch.

The first problem with such arguments is that MLS teams are rarely out of playoff contention. Perhaps that's a bug, not a feature, of the MLS system of taking far too many teams in the playoffs, but MLS generally has as many teams playing relatively meaningless games down the stretch as European leagues do. In European leagues, those teams are in the middle of the table—too far down to reach the promotion spots or the qualification berths for the Champions League or Europa League, too far up to worry about relegation. In MLS, the only teams with nothing at stake are those that can't reach the playoff spots, and most teams aren't out of the running until late in the season.

The second problem with the argument is that players are always playing for their jobs. Always. And coaches are always coaching for *their* jobs.

The third problem is that players from other countries don't seem to have a problem excelling with *their* national teams after playing in MLS. As MLS has expanded, the league's clubs have signed more players from other countries, including regional rivals in North America and the Caribbean. The 2018 World Cup proceeded without the United States but with 18 players from MLS, including 14 with teams that advanced ahead of the United States in CONCACAF qualifying. (The totals were 19 and 15 until Costa Rica's Ronald Matarrita was ruled out due to injury.)

Meanwhile, most U.S. national team players have spent at least part of their careers in Europe or Mexico. The vast majority of the starting lineup on that fateful 2017 night in Trinidad that sealed the USA's elimination in World Cup qualifying had played outside MLS, many of them with clubs in the midst of relegation battles.

So the idea that the USA faltered in World Cup qualifying because other teams' players are more accustomed to the pressure of relegation battles simply doesn't hold up. The U.S. players who failed had lived through relegation drama. The players that beat the USA had lived through MLS playoff battles.

MLS: Money Left Sidelined?

The idea here is that Major League Soccer is leaving a lot of money on the table. If the league opened up to pro/rel, more investors would step forward, and that money would trickle down to the youth level because clubs would rev up their academies.

One piece of evidence: Many American moguls have bought clubs overseas. The Glazer family, which owns the Tampa Bay Buccaneers but declined to bail out original MLS team Tampa Bay Mutiny, owns Manchester United. Fenway Sports Group, the ownership group of the Boston Red Sox, owns Liverpool. Stan Kroenke owns a majority share of Arsenal in addition to the MLS Colorado Rapids, the Los Angeles Rams, the Denver Nuggets, and a whole lot more. The guy even owns a team in the Overwatch League. (Ask your kids. Or your brother who spends all day on the computer.)

A few U.S. owners have bought clubs that aren't quite as big. The results were financial quagmires:

- Ellis Short had a nine-year run with Sunderland, plowing tons of money into the club to see it engineer a few escapes from Premier League relegation before plummeting to the third tier of English soccer. An economist called his tenure "a bit of a car crash," but he took steps to wipe out debts before selling, a gesture that surely enhanced his legacy in the northeastern city.[7]
- A group appropriately known as American Partners owned Derby County for a few years before selling to Mel Morris, who made a fortune on the mobile game Candy Crush Saga. The U.S. group

bought the club just before it dropped from the Premier League, then handed over tens of millions of dollars to try to boost the club back up the ladder. [8]

- Shahid Khan, who may one day own an American football team in London if the persistent rumors of the Jacksonville Jaguars moving come to fruition, has been more persistent. He bought Fulham, where American players Brian McBride and Clint Dempsey were standouts and fan favorites, and saw it relegated despite firing a couple of managers. Khan stuck with the club through a few years in the second-tier Championship and saw it promoted in 2018. A few months later, the club fired another manager.

A few U.S. moneybags own some clubs scattered around the world, including semipro English side Alfreton Town. [9] But they don't seem to be under the illusion that their clubs will rocket up to global prominence.

The most unsettling cautionary tale of an American owner overseas is the saga of Randy Lerner with Aston Villa. Lerner inherited two prominent positions upon the death of his father, Al Lerner, in 2002. He became the chairman of credit-card monolith MBNA, which was later subsumed into the complex mergers and acquisitions of the high-powered financial world. He also inherited the NFL's Cleveland Browns.

The latter was the result of a quirk of American sports. The once-mighty Browns declined after their 1950s heyday, and in 1995 owner Art Modell moved the team to Baltimore—with minority owner Al Lerner playing a role in making the deal. The Baltimore team, filling a void left when the Maryland city lost the Colts to Indianapolis, would technically be an expansion franchise and took on the name Ravens.

The Browns' intellectual property was kept in reserve in case someone stepped forward to restart the team. Al Lerner stepped forward, and the Browns returned to the field in 1999 after a three-year absence.

Randy Lerner certainly had big shoes to fill in the financial world and in Cleveland. But he also wanted to go a bit farther. Having acquired a taste for soccer while studying at Cambridge, he eagerly jumped at the chance to own a Premier League team, buying Aston Villa in 2006 for $118 million.

For a few years, Lerner's investment looked great. The team played well. The American owner invested in everything from the club's training facilities to a pub next to Villa Park. Writer and Villa supporter Simon

Inglis gushed about Lerner to the *Guardian* in 2008: "With his tastes and philanthropy, Randy Lerner has qualities sadly rare in football club chairmen. Lerner seems to have appreciated that heritage is not a luxury but an intrinsic part of football clubs. In fact, after so many years of disappointment, he seems almost too good to be true."[10]

The honeymoon continued into 2010, with the *Telegraph*'s Sandy Macaskill contrasting Lerner with other American owners who were reviled:

> The banners at Old Trafford and Anfield recently sum up the state of mind of supporters under the Glazer regime at United and Tom Hicks and George Gillett administration at Liverpool: "Thanks, but no Yanks." The antithesis of their kind is just down the M6. Randy Lerner, the philanthropist who contributes to the National Portrait Gallery, the quiet American who bought Aston Villa for £63.6 million in 2006, has transformed his club in 3½ years to the point that they are on the cusp of a trip to Wembley for their first major final in a decade.[11]

Lerner's commitment to Aston Villa played well in England, but it was a source of resentment in Cleveland, where he was seen as an unenthusiastic absentee owner. In 2012, he sold the Browns for roughly $1 billion to Jimmy Haslam. (The Browns and Haslam would figure into a couple of ironic twists in Major League Soccer. When Columbus Crew owner Anthony Precourt seemed set to move the Crew to Austin, Texas, local officials sued under a law limiting the power of an owner to make such a move if that owner's facility or club received any governmental benefits. That law is called the "Art Modell Law" and was passed in the wake of Modell's move to Baltimore. Under severe pressure from lawyers and fans, not just in Columbus but nationally, the Crew managed to find a new ownership group—including Jimmy Haslam. Small world.)

But the good times were already ending in England. After finishing sixth for three straight seasons and ninth after that, a great run for a club that isn't quite one of the giants, Villa had to fight to stave off relegation in the 2011–2012 season and didn't fare much better the next season. In 2014, Lerner said he was putting the club up for sale, only to find buyers weren't lining up as they would for an NFL franchise.

"Don't forget, you're looking at £200m, plus in my opinion £100m for players to save Villa from their annual flirtation against relegation and one of these days they will drop off the edge unless this is sorted out," said BBC reporter Pat Murphy. "And where are the multi-billionaires around who would go for what is now, a middle-ranking club in the Premier League?"[12]

The sale, though, would take two years. In his last season, 2015–2016, the team had clearly given up the ghost by the midway point and fell out of the Premier League with a thud, garnering only three wins and 17 points, half of the next-lowest team's total. All the while, fans chanted and waved "LERNER OUT" signs.

But Lerner wasn't entirely despised. A retrospective in the British paper *Metro* credited Lerner with his facility upgrades and his decision to hand over the prime advertising space on the club's jerseys to a children's hospice.[13] A *Birmingham Mail* column recognized that Lerner was sincere in his efforts to sell the club to a good steward for its future, with the sub-headline "Those who think Lerner didn't care about the claret and blues need to think again."[14]

Villa fans complained that Lerner didn't spend enough on the club. And yet he plowed tons of money into the club with little return. Writing at *Forbes*, Mike Ozanian pegged Lerner's losses at $400 million.[15] Different accounts disagreed on the exact numbers, but agreed that he sold Aston Villa for less than he paid for it, at least after adjusting for inflation, even after pumping hundreds of millions of dollars into the club.

"The total of Villa's annual operating losses over the 10 years of Lerner ownership came to more than $260 million," the *Wall Street Journal* reported. The same story painted a dreary portrait of English football in the 2010s: "Team owners are so spooked by the prospect of the drop—and the financial sinkhole that comes with it—that some say in private that they have knowingly made short-term decisions, from gambling on aging or unreliable players to suddenly firing the manager, just to appease their fans."[16]

It's safe to say Lerner didn't buy Aston Villa with the intent of relishing the fray of a relegation battle. And it's difficult to conclude that pro/rel had a direct or indirect effect on the decisions to invest in all these clubs, big or small. The big ones—Manchester United, Liverpool, and Arsenal—aren't at all likely to fall into the second-tier English Championship. Generations ago, when the clubs were all competing for a pool of mostly English players, relegation among this group was rare but plausible. In the last 20 years, with the Premier League's big-money era firmly established, those three teams haven't finished outside the top eight.

More likely than relegation is a relegation-free European Super League. German newspaper *Der Spiegel* found documents suggesting several European powerhouses were indeed discussing such a league in 2018.[17] Jonathan Clegg and Joshua Robinson added a few more details in their 2018 book, *The Club: How the English Premier League Became the Wildest, Richest, Most Disruptive Force in Sports*, starting with a meeting in, naturally, a New York restaurant. At the table were the American owners of Manchester United and Liverpool, along with Arsenal executive Ivan Gazidis (a former MLS executive). Stan Kroenke, the American sports-team collector who spent part of 2018 raising his majority stake in Arsenal to a full ownership, had "summoned Gazidis across the pond," Clegg and Robinson said.[18]

"It was now clear that the most serious existential threat to the Premier League, itself formed by a breakaway in 1992, was, improbably, another breakaway," Clegg and Robinson wrote in a *Guardian* piece with an excerpt from the book and a bit of bonus material such as this dire conclusion.[19]

A few other big European clubs have U.S. investors. Frank McCourt bought Olympique Marseille in 2016 with the goal of getting back to European prominence, which the well-established club managed quickly. In 2018, an American business group bought FC Girondins de Bordeaux, another club that tends to look up toward European continental competitions rather than looking down at the drop to Ligue 2. Italian club Roma is in the same situation.

That's a limited sample size, but it's certainly not enough to prove a thirst for getting involved in relegation battles. The biggest exception is Vincent Volpe, who spent much of his business career in Europe and is now determined to get Le Havre promoted to the top tier in France.

So, once again, we have to ask whether European clubs are attractive investments because of the soccer culture or because promotion/relegation makes things exciting. For many U.S. owners in Europe, the lure is the Champions League, the competition for top teams from each European league that offers bountiful fame and fortune. Others, like Lerner, show how much money can be flushed into a soccer club with little to show for it but a bunch of angry supporters.

Meanwhile, MLS isn't exactly hurting for investment from the United States and elsewhere. Expansion owners pay $150 million to join the league, a cost that has many fans crying foul (or "Ponzi scheme") but effectively keeps new owners from taking a free ride on the investments that the league's previous owners have made. As of 2018, both New York teams were owned by global groups—Red Bull also owns clubs in Germany, Austria, and elsewhere, while NYCFC's City Football Group is an Abu Dhabi organization that built Manchester City into an English power and now has a global empire on which the sun never sets.

Even without promotion and relegation, the lower divisions are seeing investment, though some of it is driven by the prospect of MLS expansion. Longtime Chelsea star Didier Drogba moved to North America to play for the Montreal Impact in MLS, then finished his playing career with the USL's Phoenix Rising, of which he also had an ownership stake. Cincinnati, Sacramento, and North Carolina's Triangle region also have seen investment driven in part by a desire to enter the MLS sweepstakes, with Cincinnati getting its ticket for the 2019 season.

Some other investments, particularly Spanish club Rayo Vallecano's efforts to run an NASL team in Oklahoma, have been unproductive attempts at brand-building. Other investments are driven simply by a desire to have a community club. "We want people to come and enjoy *futbol*, but moreover as a club and as a business we want to give back to the community of Memphis in any way we can," said Memphis 901 FC advisor Tim Howard, known to most of the world as the longtime goalkeeper for Everton and the U.S. national team.[20]

The second-tier United Soccer League also has seen its expansion fees and expenditures increase exponentially through the 2010s. *SocTakes'* Nipun Chopra pegged the franchise fee at a 47-fold increase in nine years (up to $7 million in 2018) and the expenditures for a first-year team climbing 10-fold up to more than $10 million, though he cautioned that this spending could just be another cycle in the USL's decades of boom and bust.[21]

Meanwhile, the idea that investors are waiting to jump into U.S. pro soccer if pro/rel takes hold doesn't have a lot of empirical proof. We have vague suggestions that broadcasters will suddenly jump into the game if pro/rel were involved, though none of those broadcasters has said anything to that effect or tried to help the NASL and other pro/rel-minded leagues build up into something substantial. The notion of all this money just waiting to be poured into U.S. soccer is, like so many political claims, unfalsifiable.

Silva wasn't the only NASL owner to issue an "unvitation" contingent on pro/rel. Rocco Commisso, the combative media mogul (see chapter 5 on lawsuits) who rescued the New York Cosmos from oblivion in 2017, told U.S. Soccer in 2018 he was willing to spend up to $500 million over 10 years to build an alternative to MLS.

But Commisso's offer had more strings attached than all the guitars in the arsenal of Cheap Trick's Rick Nielsen. Exemption from the Pro League Standards. Deadlines. Changes to the relationship between MLS, Soccer United Marketing, and U.S. Soccer.

Conversely, we have no reporting to suggest adidas demanded such things before the company invested $700 million in MLS. Or that the clubs spending a combined couple hundred million on training facilities demanded such things.

Low-Risk Investments and Youth Academies

A country as vast as the United States would surely benefit from having scores of professional clubs with affiliated youth academies scattered throughout the country. More kids could be seen by talent scouts. More kids could get access to well-trained coaches. More kids would play low-cost or free youth soccer. The assumption, though, is that clubs will automatically pop up with youth academies if the clubs have a chance of climbing the ladder. And the evidence for that assumption is shaky.

Across the Atlantic, academies are not the sure bets you'd expect if you listen to pro/rel advocates. In England, Huddersfield Town and Brentford ditched most or all of their academies, figuring they can just get the leftovers from larger clubs. Other English clubs have closed the bulk of their academy programs, at least temporarily—Dagenham and Redbridge, Torquay, Wycombe, Crawley, and Yeovil. When a club is relegated, the academy is threatened.[22]

In Germany, pro/rel didn't make clubs in the top two tiers form academies. The federation did, as part of the much-lauded "Das Reboot" of the early twenty-first century. The federation also set up hundreds of regional training centers to find and develop players who weren't in those academies.[23]

Surely somewhere in Europe, clubs are investing in their academies to try to climb the ladder by developing players and then either putting them in the first team or selling them for a nice profit. Promotion, then, might provide an incentive. But relegation can provide a reason to pull the plug.

Meanwhile, in the United States, we're starting to see MLS clubs making big investments in youth soccer *because* they know those investments are safe. Atlanta United opened a training facility that cost $60 million, and it's safe to say that facility isn't just for the first team. Many MLS clubs have free academies.

MLS has also teamed up with the USL to make a solid development pathway. MLS reserve teams play in the USL, just as reserve teams play in lower divisions elsewhere in the world, and players gain valuable experience before moving up to the MLS club. Tyler Adams and Aaron Long have progressed from New York Red Bulls II to the national team. Chris Durkin, who played in the 2017 Under-17 World Cup, spent much of that year with the Richmond Kickers. Alex Bono, Danilo Acosta, Cristian Roldan, and Justen Glad also have moved through USL to MLS to national team consideration.

The USL-MLS pathway is also developing players for other countries. The most notable is Canadian Alphonso Davies, who moved through the Vancouver system and debuted for the national team at age 16. He has since transferred to Bayern Munich. (Noteworthy: Vancouver will earn solidarity payments. The rules against such payments are set by the United States, not MLS—a clear demonstration that pro/rel is not a condition for participating in the worldwide player market.) Nouhou Tolo developed with Seattle Sounders 2, and quickly moved into Cameroon's national team.[24]

No MLS team is making money on its reserve team or USL partner. They're not box-office smashes. That relationship exists just to develop players.

The next question: Does a pro/rel league offer incentive for teams to *play* younger players in important games? With all the complaints about MLS leaving its teens and 20-year-olds on the bench, would those players get more opportunities if teams were faced with relegation?

Comprehensive evidence is tough to find. You'd have to compute the mean and median ages, not just of each team's rosters, but of their lineups. Maybe someone at FiveThirtyEight could scrape all the data of minutes-played-per-year-being-alive and analyze it.

We'll need to look to knowledgeable people to weigh in. Here's Hugo Perez, possibly the best player on the U.S. national team in the 1980s and then a youth national team assistant coach, who frets about young players getting little time in MLS but sees a systemic issue elsewhere: "In a lot of the countries, including Mexico, it's difficult because they're fighting for promotion and relegation," Perez said while participating in a Front Row Soccer panel. "So, a lot of the teams don't play a lot of young players because they are under pressure not to go down."[25] More Perez from the same story:

> Promotion and relegation has to do more with how important games are to clubs. But it doesn't have to do with developing players. Promotion and relegation, when you hear those words, it just puts more pressure on the coaches that they say, "If I have a 30-year-old that is more experienced, it's going to help me win to stay in the first division than to play a 16-, 17-year-old who is coming up." He's probably going to pick the 30-year-old.[26]

That's one person. But it's also common sense. Relegation battles tend to feature gritty games in which experience counts. In MLS, on the other hand, a team that's playing out the string of a lost season can throw its kids on the field and build for next year.

Risk and Feasibility

A year prior to his bold media-rights offer, Silva had commissioned a report by consulting firm Deloitte, which duly confirmed the notion that pro/rel would be a boon for U.S. leagues. But Silva and his backers didn't do much to heed the report's warnings. The Deloitte report says quite clearly that any transition would need to be carefully managed: Mitigate risks. Impose cost-control measures. Implement "new equity structures and revenue distribution models."[27]

And perhaps U.S. Soccer, to the chagrin of those who say otherwise, cannot impose such a system from the top down. Deloitte cites the importance of "the continued development and stability of a second tier competition to develop clubs capable in management and football terms of joining the first tier" as a preliminary step. In other words, the way to create promotion/relegation is to create enough clubs to have promotion/

relegation. The final word: "US club soccer is not immediately ready for promotion and relegation."[28]

Repeat . . . the United States is not ready, according to a report that speaks of the concept in glowing terms.

Plenty of MLS critics have similar cautions. Andrew Zimbalist was an expert witness against the league when its players sued in an effort to break up the "single-entity" structure, offering the astonishing testimony that players' salaries would be huge if only U.S. Soccer had allowed two Division 1 leagues to compete. *Soccer America* columnist Paul Gardner, himself no MLS apologist, referred to Zimbalist's testimony as "Alice in Wonderland" and a "totally fictitious exercise" based on "a whole series of improbable conditions" that never existed.[29] In 2015, Stefan Szymanski said that Major League Soccer would collapse sooner rather than later.[30] In 2017, he wrote an expert declaration on behalf of the NASL in the lawsuit discussed in chapter 5.

The two economists joined forces in 2005 to write the book *National Pastime*, cited several times in this book, showing why the United States diverged from the world's sports in favor of soccer. Naturally, that includes a discussion of "open leagues," or those with promotion and relegation. And they said this: "Open leagues thus generate a number of desirable characteristics from the standpoint of the fans, but as we shall see, the operation of the promotion/relegation system in Europe has created significant incentive and financial problems."[31]

The problem is financial insecurity. In the United States, this discussion is often painted as unwarranted concern over the wealth of the oligarchs who own the league and its clubs. But Szymanski and Zimbalist see a greater danger arising from instability, connecting it to horrific incidents such as widespread hooliganism and the 1985 fire in Bradford City's unsafe wooden stand that killed 56 fans. English clubs that didn't have guaranteed revenues didn't invest in basic safety measures.

> As recently as 1990, most stadiums in England had been little altered since their construction in the first two decades of the twentieth century. Most clubs lacked the resources to invest in upgrading facilities, and municipal government was usually not allowed to support such investments. The gradual decay of stadiums in England was not just a safety hazard; it also discouraged supporters, and between 1950 and 1985 total attendance fell by more than half (from 41 million per season to 18 million). The audience for soccer became concentrated

among young men on low incomes who were increasingly involved in violent confrontations with the fans of rival teams. By the mid-1980s, with most teams close to bankruptcy, the hooligan problem was so pressing that Margaret Thatcher's government contemplated closing down professional soccer altogether.[32]

Today, those clubs are investing, but that's a function of the growth of the game. The difference between England 1984 and England 2019 is not promotion and relegation, which has existed nearly as long as the professional game in England.

So we're talking about risky business here. With their league status uncertain, football clubs might not make the necessary investments in facilities and youth programs. MLS have been making those investments throughout the 2010s.

Does Pro/Rel Make Other Countries Great?

A few conversations from over the years:

First: "Japan showed you could add pro/rel to your league system and do OK."

The J-League is indeed OK. FiveThirtyEight's global club ranking has its clubs pretty much on par with MLS clubs, as of December 2018. Attendance tracks a little less than MLS, but not too far. Revenue between the two leagues is close. And the Japanese national team's performance this century is roughly comparable to the USA's. A couple of rough World Cups, and a couple of appearances in the round of 16.

Japan, though, isn't fully open for top to bottom. "Open" is really a spectrum, anyway. Many countries have a barrier between "pro" and "amateur" that isn't fully permeable. For generations, England had a divide between "League" (the top four tiers, fully professional) and "Non-League" (anything below that). England still has criteria, some merely to provide proper lighting and some designed to avoid tragedies such as the Bradford fire, that each club must meet to move up. While those criteria aren't much of a barrier in England, Japanese clubs aren't always able to meet the requirements.[33]

The Japanese system could provide a model for moving forward gradually and conservatively. The strict criteria control the flow of clubs upward, and the third tier is expanding to become a network of regional leagues from which it will be difficult to be relegated for the foreseeable future. So Japan might provide the "how" for pro/rel. It doesn't really provide the "why."

Second: "China proved you could do it with a big land mass."

China has a population of more than 1.3 billion people, and has never won a game in the men's World Cup.

Third: "Russia also proved you could do it with a big land mass."

Russia, like China, is a state built on central planning that can make things happen without too much concern over the consequences. Its national team also isn't particularly successful, a run to the quarterfinals at home in 2018 notwithstanding.

Could the USA Even Make It Happen?

For all the issues they have with Major League Soccer and its closed, single-entity system, Szymanski and Zimbalist write this: "The lesson we draw from these baseball and soccer examples is that an unrestrained monopoly will inevitably lead to the exploitation of fans and taxpayers, while a system of unrestrained competition will, as we will explain, lead to financial pressures that may threaten the health of the league."[34]

That's a good moderate approach, suggesting an "open" system might work if we keep it well-regulated like Japan has done. The problem is that Americans generally don't do moderation. Furthermore, we can't seem to get anywhere without casting people and entities as heroes or villains. The NASL, especially when Commisso and Silva started leading the charge, was seen as heroic. And yet the USL, which many in the pro/rel movement consider Major League Soccer's puppet, is closer to pro/rel reality. League president Jake Edwards has long taken a coy attitude in answering questions about the potential of promotion and relegation. For the 2019 season, the league rebranded so that its three divisions are called the Championship, League One, and League Two, mimicking the English nomenclature, and the league hasn't exactly slammed the door on the idea: "With League One about to enter its first season, implementation of competitive movement between the two leagues is certainly quite a few years away as the new division establishes itself as a strong competitive level on the North American landscape."[35]

Why hasn't anyone else put something together? See chapter 4. We can't agree on things even when we're supposedly aligned ideologically.

In the late 2010s, several leagues—NASL, NISA, NPSL, and UPSL—claimed to be pushing promotion and relegation forward. Nothing was stopping them from getting together and creating a pyramid with a well-funded league at the top. If they joined forces, surely they could make pro/rel a reality and force MLS to compete, adapt, or join in.

They would not, could not join forces.

Pro/Rel: The Final Word

The truth is that promotion and relegation isn't the *cause* of a thriving soccer culture. It's a *symptom*.

Promotion and relegation will happen in the United States if the country has a critical mass of professional clubs and if the people pushing for it could get on the same page. They would need to discuss ways to account for everything that's unique about the United States, from its giant land mass to the paucity of existing infrastructure. All parties would need to agree on a structure that won't make owners and municipalities wary of investment in stadiums, training facilities, and youth development.

They would need to account for the billions of dollars MLS owners have poured into the league, including stadiums and other facilities as well as an increasing and improving talent pool. Even the Deloitte report, hailed by pro/rel advocates as proof that the system would be a boon in the United States, stresses the need to protect or compensate for the investments that have already been made in the pro game. The report reminds us to be patient. Once again, directly from the report: "US club soccer is not immediately ready for promotion and relegation."[36]

Do all of these things, preferably without getting too many lawyers involved, and the United States might be able to come up with a promotion and relegation system that gives everyone an opportunity to move up.

It *won't* happen as long as so many people in the soccer community are at each other's throats and can't even hold a rational discussion of all the issues. Here, we have conspiracy theories in which some document is unearthed (the so-called Fricker Plan, whose importance to U.S. pro soccer history was adequately debunked by historian Steve Holroyd[37]) and people think the powers that be are against pro/rel for the sake of being against it, or that they're holding back soccer's growth because they want the NFL to remain supreme. Here, we have zealots who have an all-or-nothing approach. They insist that U.S. Soccer must force pro/rel into existence up and down the pyramid, even though some countries (Japan, the Netherlands) have been hesitant to open the amateur-to-pro gateway and England needed nearly a century to open it. If the United States follows the English model, the system will be fully opened in 2095.

And it won't make the national team great. The differences between the United States and the traditional soccer powers go far beyond the pro league system. See chapter 1. Chapter 2. Chapter 3. Chapter 4. Chapter 5 . . .

END PAY TO PLAY

This idea is a little less controversial. Who could possibly object to reducing costs for soccer families? Better yet, let's eliminate them all together! No more "pay to play."

That won't take much money, right? Well, let's run some numbers . . .

U.S. Youth Soccer counts more than 3 million players registered. AYSO counts 400,000. Maybe another 500,000 for U.S. Club Soccer. Another 100,000-plus for SAY Soccer, then a few more for the U.S. Specialty Sports Association. Some of these registrations overlap, so we'll say it's a total of 4 million.

Of those, we'll say 3 million are recreational players. Rec soccer costs somewhere between $100 and $200 per season, so we'll split the difference and say $150 per season. Most programs have two seasons in a year, so that's $300. Multiply 3 million by $300, and we're looking at a tidy $900 million.

We'll say another 800,000 play mid-level travel. Some programs keep costs down around $1,500, while others are closer to $3,000. We'll be generous and say $2,000 per player. Multiply 800,000 by $2,000, and it's $1.6 billion.

The other 200,000 play high-level travel, which might be $3,000 per year but is often northward of $5,000. We'll say $5,000. Multiply 200,000 by $5,000 to get another billion.

Add up all three tiers, and that's maybe $3.5 billion. *Per year*.

Suddenly that much-ballyhooed $150 million surplus that U.S. Soccer accumulated, maybe two-thirds of it over a long period of growth and one-third of it off the Copa America Centenario in 2016, doesn't look like the answer to our prayers, does it?

Suddenly the notion that community clubs will raise those billions through transfer fees and solidarity payments, even as English clubs trim their academies, seems a bit more far-fetched. Clubs don't really climb to the top through youth academies, anyway. They just get enough money to keep going, and maybe solidify long enough to move up from the fourth tier to the third. The biggest story of an amateur club racing up the ladder to the big time is German club Hoffenheim, which shot through the lower divisions when software mogul Dietmar Hopp decided it would be fun to spend the money it would take to get his childhood club into the Bundesliga.

Bill Gates has a net worth of maybe $95 billion, so he could float the bill for about 20 years. Alas, the Microsoft mogul seems intent on spending that money on things like "education" and "wiping out malaria."

How do other countries go without "pay to play"? In many cases, they don't. Recreational soccer still costs a bit of money to defray some fixed costs such as facilities and referees. In France, that might be $150 to $200.[38] Clubs may also do some creative fund-raising, including one English club that has worked a deal akin to Amazon Smile—a small percentage of your purchase goes to a charity of your choice—but with condom- and sex toy-maker Durex.[39]

What American soccer has that other countries often don't is that middle level of "travel" that isn't recreational but isn't a pro club's academy. England has a few private programs if parents insist on being separated from their money to chase pro dreams—or U.S. college scholarships—and some smaller youth clubs may have professional coaches and higher fees, but the U.S. standard $2,000-a-year travel program is far from the norm.

At the higher levels, there are professional clubs that run academies that develop future players for the club or who can be signed to a pro contract and then sold elsewhere. See the pro/rel discussion above to see how the United States is making progress but won't immediately have 100 or so club academies as they have in the United Kingdom.

Where a federation *can* step in with its financial war chest is in trying to get professional coaches out to as many players as possible. Germany has put training centers all over the country, giving recreational players opportunities to be identified and developed.

If the soccer community is looking for massive subsidies, the tough sell in the United States will be why soccer gets such support while other activities do not. Sunil Gulati, longtime U.S. Soccer Federation president and longtime U.S. soccer scapegoat, was widely ridiculed for mentioning that U.S. parents pay a lot for piano lessons. It's not really clear why he brought it up, but it's also not really clear why Gulati's critics were howling at the comparison. The most prevalent argument was that the comparison was elitist—soccer is supposed to be for people from all walks of life, while piano is for . . . only the upper classes? Wait a minute. Who's being elitist here—the people making the comparisons to piano lessons, or the people implying that the rabble should play soccer, not piano?

And for the record, if you take weekly piano lessons for $50 each (a bargain), 50 weeks a year, that's $2,500. Other programs in the arts can easily run $5,000. So can hockey.

All of which raises the question—if parents are willing to spend $2,000 a year, should we really turn away that money? In many cases, that money subsidizes financial aid that allows more kids to play.

At the top level, the goal is to have 100 or more free academies in the United States. Perhaps that will come about through professional clubs that generate the revenue to do it themselves. Perhaps it will come about through youth clubs that harness the spending power of their parents who pay at the lower levels. Or, perhaps, some combination of the two.

Reducing costs for those who need it is certainly a worthwhile goal, and expanding the available talent pool is certainly a good thing. Finding the right path to get there isn't so simple, and the money needed to pull it off won't materialize out of thin air.

OTHER QUICK FIXES

How about a new national team coach? Maybe Jürgen Klinsmann can come in and fix everything from the national team down to the grassroots. That didn't work. Nor should it. At best, a national team coach can help an underdog team overachieve, and no one person can overhaul a country's entire soccer culture.

No one U.S. Soccer president can make such a change, either. Large organizations have checks and balances for a reason, which means a president can only do so much to change the organization's governance and policies.

Better coaching education will help. Seeing the benefits will require patience, and we'll all have to agree on the definition. Again, we don't do "agree" well.

Any substantive change is going to take a while. And there's no road map for changing the soccer fortunes of a large country with the history and unique circumstances of the United States.

But we're fertile ground for hucksters selling everything from ideology to phony medicine. Why should soccer be any different?

8

WE'RE TOO SERIOUS TO SUCCEED AT A SPORT BUILT ON JOY

"Some people believe football is a matter of life and death. I am very disappointed with that attitude. I can assure you it is much, much more important than that."

Those words, or some variants thereof (those were the days before everything was recorded and uploaded to the internet, allowing a precise transcription), are attributed to one Bill Shankly, the manager who led Liverpool out of its late 1950s doldrums and won three English top-flight championships along with a couple of FA Cups and a UEFA Cup. He and assistant Bob Paisley, who took over upon his retirement, laid the ground-work for a European juggernaut.

Like the Bible, this quote can be taken at face value or interpreted in context, and which one you choose says a lot about how you approach soccer. (Or, if you're like many Americans who don't realize people in different countries use words differently, you might think he's talking about American football.)

The evidence suggests Shankly was just being witty. The Scottish people, including Shankly, are known for dry wit. "Like many of his witticisms, the quote lost its context over the years," argues Neil Humphreys in FourFourTwo.[1]

Daryl Grove, an Englishman who lives in Virginia and cohosts the rollicking *Total Soccer Show* podcast, put Shankly's quote alongside 29 other memorable quotes, many of them similarly witty. (My personal favorite: "Tommy Smith wasn't born, he was quarried.") Grove puts the "life and death" quote in the context of "the fraternal love and rivalry" between crosstown rivals Liverpool and Everton and gives a longer account of Shankly's quote: "I am not saying they love each other. Oh, no. Football is not a matter of life and death . . . it's much more important than that. And it's more important to them than that. But I've never seen a fight at a derby game. Shouting and bawling . . . yes. But they don't fight each other. And that says a lot for them."[2]

Shankly himself put his famous quote in a more somber context: "Asked if he regretted that absence he said: 'I regret it very much. Somebody said: "Football's a matter of life and death to you." I said, "Listen it's more important than that." And my family's suffered. They've been neglected.'"[3]

All compelling evidence. But that's not enough to keep some Americans from treating soccer as a Very Important Thing, whether Shankly meant the "life or death" bit or not. We have a spectrum anchored by two poles:

1. Soccer is a wonderful activity for youngsters, instilling good habits of teamwork and exercise. It encourages players to have both the discipline to learn skills and the ability to be creative—as former U.S. men's coach Bruce Arena once said of accomplished U.S. player Clint Dempsey, to "try shit." Perhaps it's no surprise that Hall of Famer Alexi Lalas is also a musician, putting the hard work and creativity he honed on the soccer field to good use in a recording studio.

2. Soccer is an endeavor in which "a portion of people's very identity and self-esteem is hinged on their clubs and national teams" and "clubs and national teams across the world represent people at a social, political, economic, and cultural level. It is their flag." The phrase "it's just a game," in this school of thought, isn't just a reminder to people to have some perspective and avoid serious conflict with opponents and officials. It's the foundation of American mediocrity.

The latter of those poles includes several direct quotes[4] from Gary Kleiban, a flame-throwing critic of all things U.S. soccer, whom you may remember from chapter 3, in which he accused those who "fight against pro/rel" as defenders of "white culture." He and his brother, Brian, are highly regarded coaching gurus, and Brian has pragmatically put aside his brother's anti-establishment rants to be employed with a couple of MLS clubs' Development Academy programs.

Kleiban also finds fault with the media (including me):

> Incumbent American soccer media has been practically curated by the establishment. An establishment that naturally doesn't want to be critically examined, particularly not at the foundational level. Hence, it neuters its media. How does it accomplish this? Well, it holds a monopoly over the ecosystem. Anyone who doesn't align with its foundational narrative, its founding culture, is in danger of losing access.[5]

"Access journalism" criticism is common these days, sometimes directed at the White House press corps, rather implausibly. It's also a common complaint in sports journalism, fanned by sports site Deadspin and its "Sports News without Access, Favor, or Discretion" tagline. It's always a false dichotomy. The only answer to the question of whether we need credentialed journalists or non-credentialed journalists is "yes." The journalists who watch from afar bring valuable perspective; the journalists who talk with sweaty players after a game humanize athletes so we're not just looking at them as pieces of meat or video-game avatars.

And "access journalism" critiques are often easily refuted. Lalas, now a Fox Sports commentator, wasn't kicked out of press areas when he called U.S. men "soft, underperforming, tattooed millionaires."[6] (We'll get back to that. The derivation of the term: Lalas is a bit of a heavy metal fan, and *Tattooed Millionaire* is a solo album by Bruce Dickinson—not the fictional character Christopher Walken played in the legendary *Saturday Night Live* "More Cowbell" sketch, but the longtime lead singer of Iron Maiden.)

Kleiban conveniently says such critiques are "fake." So the soccer media can't win. Anything positive or neutral we say demonstrates that we're mere lapdogs. Anything else is "fake."[7]

Whatever your thoughts on the soccer media, which do seem to have some attention-deficit disorder at times, this is not the happy soccer experience your local club offered you when your kid turned five.

And yet, the Kleiban brothers are anything but anti-fun. Video of Brian's youth teams and their mesmerizing possession skills is popular on YouTube. They certainly seem to be having fun. Brian's thoughts on younger age groups are certainly not as dour as Gary's blog posts and Twitter arguments would suggest. "The kids need to have fun within the sessions and the game," Brian Kleiban told *Soccer America*'s Mike Woitalla. "As coaches, we need to inspire them to want to be different than the rest. Have passion for the game!"[8]

Kids today can see that passion—on the internet, where "freestyle" artists do tricks with soccer balls and the highlights of the latest sublime Messi move are readily available. If the United States wants to have more players in those videos that kids emulate in South America and Africa as well as New York and Los Angeles, they'll have to have a mix of the discipline to play in a team and the freedom of expression to "try shit."

CUTTING PASSION AT THE EARLY AGES

"I have, behind my back, the most coveted toy in the world," I told a group of youngsters gathered for their first soccer practice of the season. They were intrigued. What could it be?

I swung my arm back to the front for the big reveal. I was holding a soccer ball. They were less intrigued. (I never said my coaching tactics worked.)

Kids in the USA have a lot of distractions. Video games. YouTube. Homework. If only U.S. kids had no computers. Or school.

Video games, oddly enough, have helped build the U.S. soccer community. Well, *one* video game. For the younger generation, "FIFA" isn't just the organization that governs soccer around the world. It's a coveted video game. And thanks to license agreements, the EA Sports video game—updated each year to become FIFA 15, FIFA 16, FIFA 17, and so on—is also an interactive database of soccer clubs and players. Kids with a gaming console can take charge of Barcelona or Liverpool (or the Los Angeles Galaxy), change the formation and personnel, and pass and shoot with real names attached.

Even Andrei Markovits, the scholar who attributed the U.S. soccer community's difficulties to American exceptionalism, sees FIFA (the game) bringing soccer further into the mainstream, as he explains with coauthor Adam Green in an abstract to a 2016 academic paper:

Our study analyzes how a particular venue—EA Sports' FIFA video game series—has contributed to this fascinating ongoing development (of soccer popularity's growth in the USA). While at this temporal stage, soccer's popularity in following (in notable contrast to playing) continues to lag behind that of America's "Big Four" of football, baseball, hockey and basketball, recent events, aided by the burgeoning proliferation of FIFA the video game, may catapult soccer's cultural presence into the Big Four's in coming years.[9]

So a kid encounters soccer through FIFA and decides to try it out. Mom and Dad take him out to the local club for a couple of years of recreational soccer. And then the club cuts the player from the travel team. Sorry, kid. You don't get the nice warmup jacket. You don't get the fun trip to the hotel with the swimming pool. (That was the highlight of the one annual overnight stay on one of my son's teams.)

Cutting players from the team is part of the professional experience. College teams don't just let everyone walk on to the team, and some high school teams are difficult to make. The most elite youth teams at the older age groups also don't have room for everyone. But U.S. clubs are cutting kids at age ten. Age nine. Age eight. They can still play in the recreational program, of course, but access to coaches who can help them develop is curtailed.

Traditionally, European clubs also have tryouts at early ages. Not always. "We believe it is not good for a nine-year-old to play [regularly] for a professional football club because it changes the reasons why he plays football," Freiburg administrator Sebastian Neuf said in one of many pieces extolling the virtues of Germany's youth football overhaul.[10]

Overachieving Iceland also keeps players in the game. "Clubs have an open-door policy with regards to participation and training, as any individual up to 18-years-old, regardless of his or her footballing level, can train with any club in Iceland," reports Tryggvi Kristjánsson in *These Football Times.*[11]

Early-year cuts are also biased toward kids whose bodies have matured quickly, including those who are old for the age group. By the time players are 16 years old, a 10-month difference in age might not make a difference. But a kid who's 8 years and 11 months old has a significant advantage over one who's 8 years and 1 month old. It's called relative age effect, a popular topic of discussion among everyone from youth coaches to data scientists publishing papers in medical journals.

U.S. Soccer, at least, is aware of the issue. The Development Academy put together a set of "bio-banding" games, following a trend seen overseas, in which players are grouped by "biological maturity" rather than age.

But that doesn't help the eight-year-old who's cast out because an older, bigger eight-year-old was too much of an obstacle to show off the skills and passion that might prove useful down the road. Youth clubs will often pick the star athletes instead of the kids who truly love the game.

In Brazil, maybe that player hits the streets and beaches with renewed determination to get into that academy. In the United States, that player takes up lacrosse, music, Overwatch, or something else while maybe—maybe—continuing to play rec soccer.

POVERTY AND PLAYING "SOFT"

Let's get back to the Lalas "tattooed millionaires" rant, delivered on a Fox Sports MLS broadcast on September 10, 2017, when the U.S. men's World Cup qualifying campaign was teetering after an embarrassing home loss to Costa Rica and slightly better draw in Honduras. Here's what he said about the team as a whole:

> What are you guys gonna do? Are you going to continue to be a bunch of soft, underperforming, tattooed millionaires? You are a soccer generation that has been given everything. You are a soccer generation who's on the verge of squandering everything. So, now it's time to pay it back. Make us believe again. You don't owe it to yourselves, you owe it to us. [12]

The key here is this: "You are a soccer generation that has been given everything."

These are players who grew up long after youth soccer went mainstream. They had the opportunity to turn professional as teenagers and earn a decent living—in many cases, far more money than players of Lalas's generation could have imagined. Players before that generation were lucky if they could make a bit of money playing indoors.

Did desperation make players better? Maybe. Jon Townsend, writing in *These Football Times*, looked back on older generations and found they worked harder because opportunities in the sport were so scarce:

> The national team players from decades past knew struggle, ate failure on a daily basis, and showed back up at the buffet line of adversity for second helpings. When it came to competing with better footballing nations, those generations of players may have lacked the skill, tactical nous and overall ability to play teams off the park, but they weren't outworked or outfought. [13]

But then the U.S. player can't win. If the infrastructure isn't there, we can't develop the skills we need to compete, but if the infrastructure *is* there, we won't develop the grit? More generally—if players have everything they need, do they actually lose what they need most of all: the competitive drive to practice hard and play harder?

Inevitably, this argument veers into the socioeconomic realm, where we find English football writers figuring out why Brazil has the impudence to keep doing better than England in the game England invented.

"Rocky Road to Brazil: Poverty—The Creator of Superstars," read the headline in the *Independent*,[14] which rounded up the usual stories of heartbreaking desperation—along with one kid who sold his video-game console to finance a trip to try out for a professional club, which doesn't quite have the same ring to it as the typical old-school Olympics story of an eastern European walking uphill in the snow to practice figure skating.

It's not just England. The piece on Brazilian poverty and success starts with a quote from French legend Thierry Henry, who spent the end of his playing career in the United States: "When I was a kid I wanted to play football all day, but my dad told me I had to study first," Henry said. "In Brazil they play football from eight in the morning to six o'clock at night."

The response from the *Independent*'s James Young: Henry offended Brazilians. And yet ("unwittingly," in Young's words), he was right. By the end of his piece, Young concludes that the gradual improvement of Brazil's economy may indeed hurt that country's soccer culture. One aspect is land use—as neighborhoods are redeveloped, the space for kicking soccer balls everywhere shrinks. But he sees the potential for Brazilian kids to be a bit more like their counterparts farther north because "poorer Brazilians have greater access to higher education than ever before, and the internet and video games compete with football for the leisure time of Brazilian youth."

So maybe if the U.S. economy crashed at a massive scale—call it the Even Greater Depression—we'd be better at soccer. Right?

You probably won't find anyone arguing in favor of tanking the economy just to win a few soccer games. In any case, the relationship between poverty and soccer is complicated. Part of the sport's global appeal is that it can be played without much equipment. All you really need is something round that can be kicked. Kids can play in the street using walls as goals. They can play on patches of dirt using anything—shirts, piles of rocks, whatever is at hand—as goal markers. Ice hockey requires ice and skates, American football and rugby require a bit of open space, and cricket requires that space to be flat. Even basketball, perhaps the most accessible sport after soccer, requires a hoop firmly anchored to a pole, an overhead support, or a garage.

But Simon Kuper and Stefan Szymanski cast cold water on the notion that poorer nations have an advantage: "The best bets for the future are probably Japan, the US, or China: the three largest economies on earth. . . . In the new world, distance no longer separates a country from the best soccer. Only poverty does."[15]

The other poverty-related argument is that young players will be drawn to sports that pay well, just as Brazilians see soccer as a lifeline out of wretched neighborhoods. The professional pot of gold, the argument goes, is an incentive to get players to dedicate their lives to the sport at an early age, and when soccer pays as much as baseball or basketball, more athletes will choose soccer.

The idea that the United States would dominate in soccer if better athletes flocked to the sport is more than a little shaky. The towering height of a pro basketball player or the girth of an NFL linebacker would not be an asset in soccer, where sky-scraping players are rare and bulky players are nonexistent. And Kuper and Szymanski, once again, have a counterargument:

> The game has thrived as a pastime for upscale families in part precise-ly *because* there is no big soccer in the US. Many soccer moms are glad soccer is not a big professional sport like basketball or football. Like a lot of other Americans, they are wary of big-time American sports, whose stars do lousy and unethical things like shooting their limousine drivers.[16]

SOCCER IN SCHOOLS

Scholastic sports are, with all due respect to the Oxford-Cambridge Boat Race, a uniquely American phenomenon. England has "schoolboy" soccer, and a handful of half-decent professionals have played it, but the U.S. norm of going through high school and college sports to reach the professional ranks is rare elsewhere in the world.

This pathway relates to poverty and economics because it, unlike traditional pro academies, gives athletes a Plan B. While NCAA football (the American kind) is often seen as mere practice for the NFL, it's also a chance for many athletes to obtain a college degree—in many cases becoming the first person in their families to do so.

That's not the English way. When former NASL commissioner and Welsh football player Phil Woosnam passed away, many obituaries took note of the fact that he, unlike the overwhelming majority of players in England's top flight, had a university degree. And according to Robin Dutt, then of Germany's football federation, representatives from English club Aston Villa were dumbfounded to find that teen prospects in Germany spent 34 hours a week in school. The Villa representatives, in Dutt's account, said their kids only spent nine hours a week in school because they had to decide whether to be professionals or not.[17]

The notion of getting soccer prodigies in school has at last worked its way across Europe. A 2012 study of pro clubs' academies found three-quarters of them were affiliated with a school, and half of them were affiliated with a university.[18] But the notion of simultaneously prepping for the white-collar workforce and professional soccer is still a mostly American thing. And it's under attack.

College soccer certainly has its flaws. The season is crammed into a couple of months in the fall, leaving little recovery time. Substitutions are nearly unlimited, which is good for keeping everyone happy with playing time, but not great for preparing players for the rigors of 90-minute games. Teams also may veer toward the "physical" side of the game, trotting out players to run for 15-minute bursts and maybe whack the other team's star player before returning safely to the bench. And if you have kids applying to college, you may well ask why non-athletes have to post astronomical grades and test scores to get in while a future bench-warmer on a soccer team (let alone the fourth-string tight end on the football team) who may or may not take school seriously waltzes through the admissions process.

Sports have taken over Title IX, a 1972 law intended to stop gender discrimination in U.S. schools. While it has indeed offered protection against discrimination and sexual harassment, it's known mostly as a springboard for the powerful U.S. women's teams in soccer and basketball. The law pushes universities to demonstrate a commitment to women's athletics, often based on how many women attend the university—paradoxically, the quota will be lower at a mostly male engineering school like Georgia Tech, which therefore doesn't need to offer as many teams for women, while a school like North Carolina, a dominant power in women's soccer and very strong in other women's sports, scrambles to comply because its student body is nearly 60 percent female. In practice, Title IX might not get women into engineering. But it does get women into sports. No one would argue against the benefits of having female role models on ESPN or the cover of *Sports Illustrated*, but shouldn't it also produce the next generation of masterminds such as the NASA mathematicians celebrated in the film *Hidden Figures*?

Some college coaches are pushing to reform the game. But its importance in the soccer landscape is waning as pro clubs sign more teenagers each year. To those in the Development Academy, a college career has become a consolation prize rather than the goal.

The Development Academy impact also is putting pressure on the next level of scholastic soccer—the high school game. Academy kids aren't supposed to play for their school teams. The same criticisms apply to high school soccer and college soccer alike—short season, physical play—but that's a loss on several fronts.

First, high school soccer extends the sport's talent pool. If a major problem with club soccer is that many families are priced out of such an expensive and time-consuming endeavor, then why wouldn't we take advantage of a low-cost (often free) pathway in which kids simply remain at school rather than being ferried to a club practice elsewhere? And are college coaches missing talented players by attending club showcases almost exclusively, rather than looking for kids who lack the time or money for club soccer? Scouting high schools shouldn't be *that* hard. If American football coaches can find the best players in the country at small schools—Herschel Walker, one of the best college players ever, attended a tiny high school in rural Georgia and was highly recruited a couple of decades before the internet could spread the word about such players—can't soccer scouts find a few players there as well?

Second, we're losing a social outlet. Essayist Andrew Guest sees what we could lose: "School soccer can serve an important mediating function: immigrant children can play a game they know and love from their birthplace, while also engaging in the distinctly American ritual of school sports."[19] Guest sees the Development Academy in a more sinister light:

> The explanation [for skipping high school soccer] highlights how U.S. Soccer sees youth development as a matter of "competing in a global marketplace." In this framing youth players are not people learning a game; they are commodities being prepared for competitive exchange—which is particularly significant when elite soccer clubs in the United States have long been an expensive endeavor funded by participation fees. . . . Is youth development about maximizing specialized talents, or is it about gathering experiences that serve both educational and social functions?[20]

In other words, school soccer offers many benefits. One of them: It's *fun*. The Development Academy might not be as fun. And as it gets more serious, the players might not be getting any better.

Steve Gans ran for U.S. Soccer president with Development Academy concerns among his many tenets. His own son dropped out of the DA after several years because he was losing his passion for the game, and Gans saw others in the same boat. The players who stayed, in Gans's view, often lost a bit of what made them great in the first place.

"We are indeed producing more technically sound players, but at a great cost," Gans told *Soccer America*'s Mike Woitalla. "So we are producing more technically sound players, but many of those players come out of the DA robotic in playing style and/or having lost the passion and joy for the game."[21]

We overcoach players. All the time. Coaching education teaches us to avoid "joystick coaching" so we can let players make their own decisions and solve their own problems, but we just can't help ourselves. The old saying "The game is the best teacher" is too often ignored.

Here's another coaching guru, Todd Beane, who is related by marriage to Dutch legend Johan Cruyff and has worked with him to spread Cruyff's coaching philosophy:

At times, our children are over-drilled. Drilled to boredom and drilled in a way that fails to honor the innate desire of children to learn through play.

Some of the greatest players to have ever played the game learned the game on the streets—the humble streets of cities worldwide. Streets void of whistles and coaching tips.

As Johan Cruyff said: "I trained about 3–4 hours a week at Ajax when I was little. But I played 3–4 hours every day on the street. So where do you think I learned to play football?"[22]

Let's go back to the beginning of this chapter. We shouldn't think of soccer as "just a game," we're told. It's how we prove ourselves to the rest of the world. That point may come as news to the kids who play soccer in the streets *because it's fun*.

THE REST OF THE WORLD

That point may also come as a surprise to the grownups who play on Brazilian beaches *because it's fun*. Or the people in *Pelada*, the wonderful film in which Gwendolyn Oxenham and Luke Boughen travel the world finding people of all walks of life playing pickup games *because it's fun*.

Go back to the World War I example. British and German troops on Christmas Day didn't hop out of the trenches to play a game of soccer because of their national identities. National identity was why they spent the other 364 days of the year lobbing shells at each other. They were playing *because it's fun*.

Granted, a teammate in Germany threw a shoe at Eric Wynalda. But Germany has actually gotten better internationally *since* then, and they've done so while making sure their kids go to school and don't get too serious too soon. Besides, the official Bundesliga YouTube channel regularly features blooper reels, so *someone* in Germany has a sense of humor.

In Brazil, soccer is simply a way of life. Style matters almost as much as winning.

England had a reputation for overzealous fans called "hooligans" who took advantage of soccer passions to set up massive fights. You may have noticed that English professional soccer has become a global colossus since the hooligans were quieted. Violence in the stands was largely replaced by supporters getting through losses by singing Monty Python's "Always Look on the Bright Side of Life."

One factor in England's growth is similar to what's building up sports in the United States. On this side of the Atlantic, it's fantasy sports. A few decades ago, that meant a bunch of friends getting together for a "rotisserie" draft, mostly in baseball but spreading to football and basketball. In 2017, the Fantasy Sports Trade Association claimed $7 billion in revenue, with a spike in the 2010s as "daily" fantasy games came in and straddled the line between traditional fantasy sports and outright gambling. In England, where gambling laws are less restrictive, online betting sites offer all sorts of odds that can change during a game, and updated odds may scroll on advertising boards along the side of a field while the game is in progress. The UK Gambling Commission reported more than £1 billion ($1.27 billion) in remote football betting alone in a 12-month span ending March 2018,[23] a sizable part of an industry that claims nearly half of the country gambled in a four-week span in 2016.[24]

So if you want to build a soccer culture that equals that of Brazil, England, Germany, or any other soccer power, you'd better make damn sure the game is fun. Otherwise, kids are going to stick with their video games. Or skateboarding. Or math.

Besides, math is a better way out of poverty in the first place. Only the best of the best can be professional soccer players, and only 23 players can make a World Cup roster. This country needs more than 23 people who can understand calculus.

Also, we're even worse at math these days than we are in soccer. At the end of 2015, the U.S. men's Elo rating (a comprehensive analysis of results based on . . . math) was 30th out of 238 countries. That's not great. In a 2015 global assessment of math skills, the United States ranked 38th out of 71 countries.[25] That's a whole lot worse. And that should embarrass us a lot more than conceding a bad goal in Trinidad.

We could make soccer a national priority from the top down. We could have congressional inquests every time the U.S. men flop in the World Cup or Gold Cup. We could sell inner-city kids on the idea that soccer is their way out.

We already start culling the herd at age eight. We specialize far too soon, risking burnout and overuse injuries. While previous generations of men and women, the latter including World Cup and Olympic champions, played high school and college soccer, we shove kids into academies. We get hyper-serious top-down mandates from U.S. Soccer. We pay tons of money for coaches from overseas to come in and coach our kids.

And we're not better. We *still* won't win the World Cup. We might even take a few steps further back.

9

BUT WILL THE WOMEN KEEP WINNING?

You've read earlier about soccer being "crowded out" of the U.S. sports landscape. In the women's team sports landscape, soccer broke out before it could be crowded out.

The story in women's sports is different. At the Olympics, women's basketball and the restored sport of women's softball join women's soccer on the stage. But no single-sport women's event compares to soccer's World Cup. The U.S. women's basketball team won its 10th World Cup in 2018, a competition in which it has finished no worse than third since 1975, and hardly anyone noticed. Women's softball draws little attention outside the Olympics, and it suffered from being omitted at the 2012 and 2016 Games.

No other U.S. women's team sport has created as many mainstream highlights as women's soccer: Brandi Chastain converting the final penalty kick and tossing off her jersey in the 1999 final. The "Mia vs. Michael" Gatorade ads, in which Mia Hamm squared off in several sports against her fellow North Carolina alumnus Michael Jordan, one of the most recognizable athletes of the twentieth century. The golden generation of Hamm, Joy Fawcett, and Julie Foudy bowing out with gold in 2004. Carli Lloyd clinching the 2008 gold with a squeaker and scoring a stunner from midfield in 2015, capping a four-goal outburst, three from Lloyd alone, in the first 16 minutes of the final. Megan Rapinoe placing a 45-yard cross on the head of the most dangerous aerial player in the game, Abby Wambach, in the final minute of extra time against Brazil in 2011.

The controversies have also hit the mainstream. Talk shows have debated the latest Hope Solo escapade or Rapinoe's decision to follow Colin Kaepernick's lead in kneeling for the national anthem. (Rapinoe ruffled a few feathers in U.S. Soccer and the pro league, the National Women's Soccer League, but unlike Kaepernick, she's still employed.)

In men's soccer, the best run for any national team belongs to Brazil from 1958 to 1970, when the team won three of the four World Cups on offer. Brazil also had another nice run from 1994 to 2002, winning two World Cups and finishing second in the other while winning two Copa America championships.

In women's soccer, dating back to the first World Cup in 1991, the best run is just as obvious. It's the United States. Of the first four international championships available (first three World Cups, first Olympics), the USA won three, matching Brazil's 1958–1970 run. And like Brazil, the USA has had other great runs as well. Unlike Brazil, the U.S. women have never really had a down period.

Women's soccer joined the Olympic program in 1996, and unlike the men's game, it features full-fledged national teams. Since then, women's soccer has settled into a series of two-year clusters with a World Cup followed by the Olympics—1995/1996, 1999/2000, 2003/2004, and so on. In each of those clusters, the USA has won one major tournament—1996 Olympics, 1999 World Cup, 2004 Olympics, 2008 Olympics, 2012 Olympics, 2015 World Cup. And throughout women's soccer history, dating back to the 1991 World Cup, the USA had never finished lower than third.

Until 2016. Let's take a closer look at what happened in the Olympic quarterfinal in Brasília.

You may consider the USA's loss to Sweden, led by former U.S. coach Pia Sundhage, a fluke. The U.S. Soccer website ran the game report under the headline "Dominant USA Falls to Sweden 4–3 in Penalty Shootout After 1–1 Draw in 2016 Olympic Quarterfinals," emphasizing the shot count—27 for the USA, six for Sweden. The USA put six of those shots on goal to two for Sweden.[1]

But that was Sweden's plan. Sundhage is a clever coach, having found a way to push the USA to 2008 Olympic gold despite a calamitous World Cup the year before and an injury to Wambach just before the Games. She had her Swedish team sit back and dare the USA to beat it. When the

USA committed too many players forward, Sweden was deadly on the counterattack.

The game went to extra time, in which each team had a goal controversially ruled offside. Then it went to penalty kicks, the tiebreaker in which the USA faltered badly after the sensational 2011 World Cup final against Japan. (The team did beat Brazil on penalties in that year's quarterfinals after Wambach's last-minute equalizer.) Goalkeeper Hope Solo used a bit of gamesmanship, changing her gloves to make Lisa Dahlkvist wait to take the decisive kick, but the unfazed Dahlkvist calmly made the shot.

So the USA never even made it to Rio, having played its group-stage games in Belo Horizonte and Manaus. A few issues popped up in those games as well. The USA wasn't seriously threatened by scrappy underdog New Zealand but only converted two of twelve shots. (If any stay-at-home defender, even the great Becky Sauerbrunn, is named Woman of the Match,[2] you can't claim to have a scintillating attack.) France, one of the world's top teams, outshot the USA 14–7 but fell to a goal by clutch scorer Carli Lloyd. Then unheralded Colombia scored first and last in a 2–2 draw, admittedly against a U.S. team that only needed a draw to win the group and was resting several starters.

Solo provided a convenient distraction from the Olympic postmortem. The ever-controversial goalkeeper called the Swedes "cowards" for sitting back in a defensive posture instead of sending forth waves of attackers. U.S. Soccer used that bit of petulance as the pretext for the unusual step of both suspending her (six months) and terminating her contract (indefinitely).

The reality is that U.S. Soccer put up with Solo's shenanigans as long as she was the near-unanimous pick as the world's best goalkeeper. She was benched in the 2007 World Cup for murky reasons, though it's safe to say no one buys the argument that the team preferred rusty 1999 World Cup keeper Briana Scurry for their comparative on-field form, then threw Scurry under the bus with the infamous "I would have made those saves" postgame interview. But Solo was back—and played brilliantly—in the 2008 Olympics, the 2011 World Cup, and the 2012 Olympics. A few more incidents played out over the years—everything from rash accusations against other people to run-ins with the police—and she was never severely punished. With Solo aging and perhaps slipping a bit in form, she didn't seem likely to be the goalkeeper in the 2019/2020 cycle, so the federation had little incentive to give her another second chance, even if the final offense was the weakest of the bunch.

Moving on from a veteran is not something the women's team does well. Thanks to a mix of convoluted contracts and a few marketing concerns, the roster is often calcified, with little space left open for newcomers. In the 2015 World Cup, Wambach had already departed from club soccer and eventually filled a substitute's role. Coach Jill Ellis may have been too sentimental in keeping Rapinoe on the 2016 Olympic roster despite months of inactivity after a knee injury, and Ellis had to take the unusual step of substituting for a substitute in the fateful game against Sweden when Rapinoe wasn't fit enough to last through extra time. (That said, once Rapinoe was fully recovered, she started playing some of the best soccer of her career.)

THE WORLD CATCHES UP

Judging a team, let alone an entire program, by a bounce of a ball here and there is never completely fair. The U.S. women have rarely pulverized the world's top teams, even when few countries took women's soccer seriously. The Scandinavian countries gave the American team fits in early competitions, with Norway taking the 1995 World Cup title and Sweden and Denmark often posing problems. China was also a formidable rival in the 1990s, falling by a thin margin in the 1996 and 1999 finals. Had the USA not rallied from a 2–1 deficit against Germany in a fantastic quarterfinal that those of us in attendance will never forget, the wave of publicity that made household names of Hamm and Chastain never would have happened. And had the referee not been lenient with Scurry stepping off her line on her penalty-kick save against China, the USA might not have won the 1999 final.

The streak of semifinal appearances in every major championship was threatened again in 2011 until Rapinoe's majestic cross to Wambach and a clinical set of penalty kicks advanced the USA past Brazil. In 2012, the USA's semifinal win over Canada was tinged with controversy, as the U.S. women rallied with the help of a surprising call against Canadian goalkeeper Erin McLeod for holding the ball more than six seconds—a rule that is enforced about as often as cars are pulled over for driving 56 miles per hour in a 55-mph zone.

The USA could have lost any of those games. And it could have won the game against Sweden. We can't draw too many conclusions from any single result.

What we can say, though, is that many more countries are taking women's soccer seriously. Heading into the 2019 World Cup, only four countries had won either the World Cup or Olympic gold—the USA, Germany, Japan, and Norway. Not many other countries had reached the final—just Sweden, Brazil, and China. Those countries are no longer a sure bet to qualify for the big tournaments, much less win them.

Consider the competition to make the small 2012 Olympics field. In Europe, the competition is so fierce that perennial power Germany failed to qualify. In Asia, China failed to advance despite hosting the final round, and a strong Australian team also missed out. The competition went down to the wire in South America, with Colombia edging past Chile and Argentina.

And if the World Cup field was as small as the Olympics field, the USA would have missed the 2011 tournament. Mexico upset the USA in CONCACAF qualifying for that World Cup, forcing the eventual finalists to beat Costa Rica and then edge Italy in a home-and-away series.

With the World Cup now expanded to 24 teams, the major powers shouldn't worry too much about qualifying. But we have more major powers now than we used to. Germany, Norway, and Sweden all failed to make the 2017 European Championship semifinals, in which the Netherlands beat Denmark in the final and England and Austria reached the last four.

"It used to be parity in the top five—or top three, *then* top five," said longtime U.S. women's team defender Kate Markgraf on ESPN's online soccer show, *ESPN FC*, in 2018. "The level of depth and quality is now top 10. . . . It's not a huge drop between the No. 1 and the No. 10 team compared to how it used to be."[3]

One factor: Europe has surpassed the United States in professional women's soccer. In 2001, the Women's United Soccer Association launched to great fanfare in the United States, even figuring into the action of the film *Bend It Like Beckham*, and attracted most of the world's top players because few other countries offered professional play. As recently as 2011, Germany's Frauen-Bundesliga was semiprofessional.[4] England also was semipro and didn't go fully professional until 2018, when the Football Association imposed strict licensing criteria on its top division.

The WUSA collapsed after three years, leaving the European leagues to steadily build up around their best players. The United States launched another pro league (Women's Professional Soccer) in 2009, but it also lasted just three years. The National Women's Soccer League launched in 2013 and has remained stable, though it has done so by tightening the wallet.

In 2017, the NWSL lagged behind three European soccer leagues (plus the WNBA, Denmark's handball league, and the peculiar Australian sport of netball) in a global Sporting Intelligence survey of sports salaries.[5] The average salary in the NWSL was $27,054, which trailed France ($49,782), Germany ($43,730), and England ($35,355), the last of which was rapidly scaling up its efforts.

Those averages are slightly skewed because they cover the whole league. An outlier like French power Lyon can average close to $200,000 per player, and rival Paris Saint-Germain isn't too far behind. The rest of the league ranges from barely professional to not professional. Germany is more egalitarian, but still has some big-money clubs in Wolfsburg, Bayern Munich, Frankfurt, and Turbine Potsdam. Sweden has a mix of paid and unpaid players in its top division.

Mexico is also trying to ramp up the professional game. Liga MX Femenil launched at the end of 2016, and while it naturally ranked lower than the European giants in the Sporting Intelligence survey a few months later, solid attendance may push wages higher. The league averaged 2,743 fans in its first season,[6] and a staggering 51,211 attended the 2018 Clausura final.

Rewind less than two decades. Of the 11 All-Stars in the 2003 World Cup, only German goalkeeper Silke Rottenberg, Swedish midfielder Malin Moström, and Swedish forward Victoria Svensson had not played in the WUSA. The WUSA even drew players from then powerful China— 2003 All-Star Wang Lipeng and co-Player of the Century Sun Wen among them. In the 2011 World Cup, the FIFA Technical Study Group picked a set of the 23 best players.[7] Five were from the U.S. team and had all played in the NWSL. Only two others had played in the NWSL, though three more joined later. Three more played in WPS, but not the NWSL. One more, oddly enough, had played in the W-League (the lower-tier U.S. league, not the Australian league), but in no fully professional

U.S. league. Seven more had never played in the United States. The most curious resumes belonged to Lucy Bronze and Kadeisha Buchanan, who played college soccer in the United States but went to Europe to play professionally. The top U.S. pro league is no longer guaranteed its pick of top collegiate talent. Many NWSL draft picks never play in the league or play only briefly—some because they don't make the small rosters of each team, some because the options are simply better in Europe.

It's not that the United States has completely stopped developing and attracting more than its share of talented players. In 2018, the *Guardian* teamed up with *The Offside Rule* podcast to rank the top 100 women's footballers in the world.[8] The newspaper assembled a panel of judges from 30 countries, many of whom had experience coaching or playing on multiple continents. The United States accounted for 16 of those players. England and Germany had 11 each, followed by France with 9. The NWSL had 30 of the players, followed by France's top league with 21 (the overwhelming majority of those at Lyon) and Germany's Frauen-Bundesliga with 18.

But Europe also has its top teams in the Champions League, which includes more than half of the players on the list. Barring changes in the winter transfer window, the March 2019 quarterfinal series between Lyon and Wolfsburg would include 24 of the top 100. Each of those teams has a roster full of international players, thanks to the free movement around the European Union. (England might not have that free movement in the future, depending on how Brexit pans out down the road.)

Suddenly the United States doesn't seem quite as intimidating. And its competition is no longer just Scandinavia, France, Canada, Brazil, and whichever country is the best in Asia at the moment. It's England. Australia. The Netherlands. France, which has a couple of semifinal appearances in major tournaments. North Korea, if it can ever translate its youth success to the senior level.[9] And Spain, which is also building up its women's league.

No one who has ever played for the U.S. national team is going to begrudge the rest of the world for taking women's soccer more seriously. Some U.S. players have played overseas, or pushed to close the gender gap in the pro game around the world. But with the competition getting better, the United States needs to get better, too. And that might not be happening.

THE KIDS ARE NOT ALRIGHT

November 21, 2018. The U.S. women are eliminated from the Under-17 World Cup.

The 4–0 loss to Germany is a little deceiving. The USA had more shots—25 to Germany's 13. But only eight of those shots were on target, and none got past Germany goalkeeper Wiebke Willebrandt. And no matter how well things go in midfield, the object of the game is to put the ball over a line, under a crossbar, and between two posts.

More concerning: This isn't the first game in this tournament in which the USA was shut out. North Korea simply tore the Americans apart. Twenty-two shots on goal to the USA's five. Shots on goal: 9–2. Goals: 3–0.

Even more concerning: This is the fifth straight time the Under-17s have failed to advance to the World Cup quarterfinals. The USA didn't even qualify for the 2014 tournament, losing to Mexico in the CONCA-CAF semifinals, or the 2010 tournament, losing to Canada at the same stage.

The Under-20s have done slightly better, but the trend is also pointing downward. Since winning the Cup for the third time in six tries in 2012, the USA has had one early exit, one run that stopped in the quarterfinals, and one fourth-place finish. No medals.

Don't panic just yet. The United States is still producing excellent women's soccer players. The 2016 Under-20 team that lost to Japan and North Korea included Mallory Pugh, who quickly became a key attacker on the senior national team. Teammate Emily Fox also made her USA debut before finishing college.

We also might not have much of a correlation between youth national team success and full national team success. A FiveThirtyEight analysis showed "about three-quarters of the variation between countries in World Cup success is explained by something other than youth-level results in the years beforehand,"[10] but the sample size was small. Another mitigating factor to add: A country that figures prominently in that sample is North Korea, which has a sort of *Logan's Run* thing going on, rarely fielding players older than 25.

Yet another mitigating factor: U.S. youth teams are cobbled together from a diverse array of clubs and schools, and they don't have a lot of time to mesh as a team. Other countries' soccer landscapes aren't as spread out, geographically and figuratively. We can't be too surprised when North Korea, which for all we know has its Under-17s in a camp all year, or a pro academy-driven country like France or Germany beats a U.S. All-Star team. "(U.S.) players play at different club teams, so bringing them together and asking them to play a certain way when they're not used to it makes it very challenging," former U.S. Under-17 coach Albertin Montoya told *Soccer America*'s Mike Woitalla. "Other countries have a fairly set way of playing." [11]

The bottom line: We don't know how bad the U.S. youth teams' struggles really are. We just know they're not good.

So what in the name of Mia Hamm is going on here?

NOT THE EQUALITY YOUTH SOCCER WANTED— PROBLEMS FOR BOYS *AND* GIRLS

Start with the Great American Turf War of the 2010s: the Elite Clubs National League (ECNL) versus the Development Academy.

The Development Academy will always have the fundamental advantage of being directly associated with U.S. Soccer, giving its players plenty of opportunities to be seen by national team staffs. In boys' soccer, add in the decade-long head start the DA had over the ECNL, and the latter has little chance of competing head to head.

In girls' soccer, the ECNL is the one with the head start. It launched in 2009; the DA left the starting gate in 2017. And clubs liked the ECNL— so much so that some clubs returned to it after only one season in the DA.

"USSF declined to start the GDA 10 years ago," tweeted Anthony DiCicco, son of former national team coach Tony DiCicco and a soccer educator in his own right. "The ECNL stepped in. Built something great. Instead of investing in the ECNL, they wanted control over the pathway & decided to compete with it. But they haven't built a better mousetrap, just one with more restrictions & constraints." [12]

The biggest of those restrictions is on high school soccer. With a few exceptions for players who have scholarships or preferential admission (called "consideration" in the 2018–2019 Development Academy Rules and Regulations) at private schools, DA players are not allowed to play for their high school teams.

The high school ban has proven to be a tough sell for young players. DA coach and World Cup veteran Brandi Chastain sees why some players would opt out of high school play—the team might not be worth-.while, or the fields may be substandard—but she has reservations about an outright ban:

> I hope they look at it again and provide some flexibility. Maybe the rule is too stringent. I coach high school boys' varsity soccer and I see it is a different environment. Some of the players may not be the leaders on their club team, but they are in high school. They have to take on new roles. They get to listen to a new voice. It is a valuable experience. There are lots of young memories. To be amongst your peers and wear the school letter has a wonderful social element as well. Some people say the level of soccer is not good enough, but there are a lot of positives. How do you go from being a role player to THE player in high school? That's an important experience. [13]

The overriding message is one of choice. The Development Academy isn't about choice. From the high school restrictions to coaching methodology to playing in outside competitions, the ECNL is the one offering greater freedom. The DA can and will argue that its regulations are necessary to mimic the professional environments seen elsewhere in the world.

Clubs are left with a dilemma. Do they go against U.S. Soccer and opt for the ECNL? Or do they go against the wishes of many of their players and parents who want to play high school soccer and a few traditional tournaments?

Perhaps the DA/ECNL split is simply healthy competition. And perhaps U.S. Soccer really is keeping tabs on every competition—DA, ECNL, traditional U.S. Youth Soccer championships, the Olympic Development Program, and more—to make sure no players are overlooked in their scouting. The federation also has a roving Training Center program, since renamed Youth National Team Identification Centers, that tries to extend the U.S. Soccer scouting department's reach.

But duplicating efforts between the DA, ECNL, and the clubs that have remained in traditional leagues is surely a sinkhole of time, effort, and money. Check the websites for each organization for a small taste of wasted energy—each organization devotes plenty of space toward spin-heavy press releases, as if they're still trying to convince clubs and families to go in one direction or the other.

And as we've seen on the boys' side, the travel requirements are absurd. In the 2018–2019 season, Minnesota had two clubs playing at the DA/ECNL level in girls' soccer—Minnesota Thunder (ECNL) and Shattuck-St. Mary's (DA). They don't play each other or the other Minnesota teams that Youth Soccer Rankings lists ahead of several Thunder and Shattuck teams. Same thing in Oklahoma, which has one club in the DA and two in ECNL. And Kansas. And Nebraska. And so on.

Below the national level, the turf wars are playing out on smaller scales. The typical region has a traditional U.S. Youth Soccer league versus an upstart U.S. Club Soccer league. A league that uses club-to-club scheduling (all of one club's A, B, or C teams play another club's A, B, or C teams), versus a league that uses promotion and relegation for parity. To be fair, these divisions aren't totally driven by ego. Maybe only 50 percent. Maybe 80 percent. But not totally.

The DA's mantra of professional environments isn't just marketing hype. Above the U-14 level, teams must train four days a week, and they play no more than one game per day. (The "one game per day" rule was not followed in the 2018 Dallas Cup, one of those rare events in which DA teams are allowed to mingle with ECNL teams and others.) Players are technically allowed to play other sports, but only if they do not conflict whatsoever with those four practices per week 10 months a year and the travel. Teams are generally allowed to make seven substitutions per game, but players can't re-enter the game once they're out, a policy that DA officials say prepares players to make decisions on their own and push through an entire game without coaching interference or a rest. Games at the pro or international level also have no re-entry, so the DA games prepare players for those games as well.

The ECNL allows re-entry for substitutions, which gives coaches a chance to emphasize a particular point. ECNL clubs have more flexibility to move players to B teams if they're not going to get playing time in a particular game or weekend, a stark contrast with the DA practice of simply leaving kids at home with no opportunity to play at all. (The DA does have rules forcing teams to make sure each player gets a set percentage of playing time over the course of a season, but with substitutions limited to five per game at the oldest age group, it's still entirely possible to make a long road trip and not play a single minute.) ECNL players can play high school sports, including soccer, though their teams' winter schedules might make it difficult to sign up for the basketball team.

Meanwhile, U.S. Youth Soccer leagues offer their own national league and cup, all driven by how well a team does rather than a selection of club names. And the teams have nobody telling them how often to practice in the winter or what high school sports the players can and can't do. The only question is how they can attract the attention of college scouts.

Muddled competitions. Confused parents. And players who decide to bag it all and play lacrosse instead.

To be fair to all the parties involved, though, the United States needs to do *something* to keep up. The European clubs are signing players to pro contracts in their teens. They're playing games that are a little more sophisticated than the high school and college games that prepped previous generations of U.S. players.

The U.S. college game is unfairly derided at times, but we have legitimate questions about how well it prepares players for the pro and international game. Frequent substitutions are good for keeping players and parents happy, but they interrupt the flow of a game and encourage teams to rely on short bursts of running rather than possessing the ball. Some college teams have developed a reputation for skillful play—Akron's men in the Caleb Porter days, Virginia's women under Steve Swanson—but the stereotypes of putting too much emphasis on "physical play" (a euphemism for fouls or plays that *should* be fouls) exist for a reason.

The good news is that the NCAA is finally loosening the reins a bit. College teams are experimenting with a short spring season in addition to the traditional fall season, and they've played some of those games under FIFA substitution rules. A mix of rules between fall and spring may seem confusing, but it lets college coaches juggle the twin goals of playing everyone on the roster and acclimating players to the 90-minute game without hockey-style line changes.

But the old ways of doing things are fading, whether soccer leagues legislate that change or not. Though the ECNL tries to leave the door open, the old American ethos of playing three high school sports each year is dying. Some athletes are still able to manage the football/baseball double in high school and even college, but many athletes are simply specializing if they see a future in one particular sport. Several organizations are trying to hold back the tide by stopping specialization *before* high school, but they're not likely to be successful.

Blowing everything up and starting fresh isn't a viable option. Besides, if college soccer were completely useless, we wouldn't see so many people coming over from other countries and playing. Florida State's 2018 NCAA championship team included players from Ireland (a player who also played the arcane sport of Gaelic football), England (a former Arsenal Ladies player), Venezuela (Dayna Castellanos, who made the *Guardian*'s top 100 list), Costa Rica, Finland, Canada, and China.

In women's soccer, even more so than in men's soccer, college is going to be the apogee of most players' careers. Men's soccer players and parents have started to buy into the notion of signing contracts in their teen years, usually for decent money. In women's soccer, signing early is going to be a tougher sell, especially when the only players making six-figure salaries are on the national team or in France. We can't expect many U.S. women to buy into the European club academy model. A couple of players have bypassed college—Lindsey Horan gave up a chance to play at North Carolina to go pro at Paris Saint-Germain, and Mallory Pugh left UCLA without playing a game—but that's likely to be the exception rather than the rule for years to come.

The difference between women and men when it comes to going pro early: In men's soccer, a prospect who isn't on the national team radar will go pro, while in women's soccer, the teen professionals are either being groomed for the national team (Horan) or already established on it (Pugh). The NCAA's insistence that a player who took a risk on professional soccer can't turn around and play college soccer doesn't help. Women usually aren't willing to risk a college scholarship for a chance at playing professionally at an earlier age. You could say that's because the money is lower in women's soccer, or you could say it's because women are smarter than men. Maybe both.

THE CHECKLIST

So let's review. Take the other chapters in this book, each one naming a reason while the U.S. men won't win the Cup. How many of them apply to women?

We play too many other sports. Not as much of an impact, but don't be surprised if lacrosse starts to siphon off some of the girls who had been playing soccer.

We watch too many other soccer leagues to focus on our own. Not really a factor. The men's soccer league gets more attention than the women's soccer league in every country, and the bigger question is how well they coexist. In the United States, they coexist pretty well. You'd also be hard-pressed to find someone who watches European or Australian women's soccer in the winter who doesn't turn around and watch the NWSL in the summer.

We're insecure about our identities. Not an issue at all. Women's soccer fans were never in it for indie cred.

We can't agree on anything. A problem. Youth soccer is chaotic and divided. Adult amateur soccer is chaotic and divided. Pro soccer has issues as well.

We can't stop suing each other. Women's soccer was pretty prominent in that chapter, wasn't it? Labor disputes aren't any less likely in the future than they have been in the past. The NWSL is proceeding peacefully for now, but that could always change.

We fell behind by 100 years. Not true in women's soccer, where the United States benefited immensely from being ahead of the curve.

We're obsessed with the quick fix. We'll see what happens when something really needs fixing at the top level.

We're too serious to succeed at a sport built on joy. A slight issue. Most of the coaches who want to turn youth soccer into a glum, Darwinian exercise have focused on boys' soccer. But young girls can be cut out of the game at early ages as well, and the "club versus school" debate is raging in the DA-ECNL split.

The trick is going to be for the various forces in U.S. soccer to get together and figure out a consistent but flexible set of pathways that give opportunities to as many people as possible, striking a balance between soccer as a scholastic activity and a professional pursuit, all while minimizing travel costs and making the sport's expenditures of money and time feasible for all.

If we could do all that in this country, this book wouldn't exist.

CONCLUSION

Keep Trying!

Here's the good news: We're not that bad.

We're getting better. Mostly.

We have a women's soccer team that has won several World Cups and Olympic gold medals.

We have a men's professional league signing some of the top players in the Americas and the occasional star from Europe, not necessarily when they're far past their peak.

We have a women's professional league signing some of the top players in the world (many of whom are actually from here).

Being a soccer *fan* in the United States is no longer a lonely existence fed by the occasional tidbit of news or delayed video of a sole European game.

And we've pretty well wiped out the cavemen of prior generations, particularly in the media, who couldn't stand the sport. The typical general-sports talk show actually addresses soccer from time to time. And not just to bash it. Consider one soccer Luddite—provocative Boston media personality Gerry Callahan. Here's his writing in 1992:

> Soccer is a terrific game for 8-year-old girls who need something to do when Brownie season is over and high school boys who are too skinny to play football. It is a nice, cheap, easy-to-understand way for parents to enjoy their child's athletic experience. That doesn't mean that American sports fans are waiting eagerly to be converted. [1]

It gets worse. From the same column: "There is still the theory that the World Cup is a big sting operation by the Department of Immigration, which will toss a net over each stadium on game day and demand to see green cards."

By 2014, Callahan was at least admitting that he watched the Cup:

> I will watch today, and if the U.S. pulls off the upset, I'll watch again on Saturday. And I'll admit: Something is happening here, and it's not just an over-the-top ESPN production. I'll concede that soccer is making great strides in this country and we are gaining on the rest of the world, and in the United States, the next World Cup will be bigger than this one.[2]

He may still gripe on his radio show that an Egyptian soccer star (Mo Salah) was on the cover of *Sports Illustrated*.[3] But by now, Callahan might as well be waving a white flag.

Even the anti-immigrant brigade isn't resistant to soccer. Among the recent players for D.C. United's academy program is one Barron Trump, son of a president who shut down the government because he wanted to build a wall along the border with Mexico.

The biggest enemy to soccer's progress in the United States is no longer the soccer basher. It's no longer cultural antipathy. The enemy is *us*. The U.S. soccer community.

We've let our civil disagreements spin into endless ego battles and lawsuits. We turned reasonable reflection over the 2018 World Cup qualifying failure into a web of conspiracy theories and a reform movement that all but disappeared when it didn't get what it wanted right away. (The 2018 U.S. Soccer presidential election had eight candidates, plus one or two more who didn't get the necessary nomination letters. The 2019 vice presidential election had one candidate, plus one who didn't get the nomination letters.)

We tear each other down, trying to win internal battles on Twitter rather than finding common ground and common cause.

In short, soccer politics has become U.S. politics. That's not a good thing. But it doesn't have to define us.

We've built a soccer culture. It doesn't have the history that soccer in other countries has. It's not as dominant or prevalent as we see in other countries, and it's a little more chaotic and fractious than most. But it's ours.

And the men's national team's progress? Consider this: Simon Kuper was present for a USA-Romania friendly in Santa Barbara, California, in 1993. After the game, Kuper recounts, a local journalist asked Romanian coach Cornel Dinu for his impressions of the Americans. Dinu's response: "They're very nicely dressed. They'll need a hundred years to play soccer. The Americans only scare us if they bring aircraft carriers."[4]

Actually, the U.S. record against Romania was already pretty good, though Romania took its revenge the next year with a win en route to the 1994 World Cup quarterfinals. Romania reached the round of 16 the next time around in 1998, but hasn't qualified for the tournament since then. USA's World Cup record is considerably better, and no coach has resorted to aircraft carriers.

The U.S. men beat World Cup dark-horse pick Colombia in 1994. They beat Argentina and reached the Copa America semifinals in 1995. They beat World Cup dark-horse pick Portugal and reached the World Cup quarterfinals in 2002. They beat Spain, then on a 35-game unbeaten streak, to reach the Confederations Cup final in 2009.

Whatever happens down the road, we'll always have Pasadena. And Paysandú. And Suwon. And Bloemfontein. And if you want to go back to 1950 and the win over England, Belo Horizonte.

Winning the World Cup requires much more than that. The team would need to string together three or four of those in a row. Think of it as the Premier League. Burnley, Southampton, Watford, Wolverhampton Wanderers, and Bournemouth have the same chance of winning the league as the U.S. men have of winning the World Cup. Supporters turn up anyway.

That's literally a foreign concept to fans of American sports. Our leagues are built on parity. Over a 20-year span in the MLB, the NFL, or the NHL, fans can expect at least 10 different teams to win. (The NBA, in which one or two star players can transform a team in an instant, has more teams that win multiple championships in a short span, but will also see teams veer wildly from top to bottom. See any team pre– and post–LeBron James.)

The World Cup qualification now draws more than 200 national teams. As of my 50th birthday, only six teams have won the Cup in my lifetime. England, birthplace of the game and host of a global superpower of a professional league, is not one of them. The best players of the twenty-first century, Argentina's Lionel Messi and Portugal's Cristiano Ronaldo, haven't won it.

To match the shared wealth of the American Big Four pro leagues, with more than half of the existing teams claiming a trophy at some point in league history, the World Cup would have to exist for at least 400 more years. We'll surely have messed up civilization and regressed to the Dark Ages by then.

But if soccer fandom were limited to those who were successful, it wouldn't be the global sport. It wouldn't be played on dusty African streets. It wouldn't inflame passions in Central America and the Middle East. We wouldn't see English supporters hopping on the train on a Saturday to travel 100 miles to see their third-tier club play a dreary game against another third-tier club.

At times, you may think the game hates you. That's no reason to hate it right back. You can find joy from every pickup game to every unexpected success.

And if the circumstances align, and the United States produces more Christian Pulisics and Tim Howards, and if an opposing goalkeeper has a lapse of concentration, then maybe . . .

If soccer can break through the pack of sports in the United States to be at least the third or even second most popular sport, and if MLS can establish itself on at least the next tier down from the Premier League, making us less secure about where we stand in the soccer world . . .

If we can at least agree on a framework that makes sense for everyone moving forward, from the youth level to the pros, and if we can at least agree to stop dragging each other to court when we don't get our way . . .

If we can quit looking for a quick fix to make up for a soccer history that is nowhere near the histories of the game's elite countries. And if we can lighten up a bit and avoid turning youth soccer into a horrible experience that drives young players to lacrosse, basketball, or Fortnite . . .

If we can do all of those things, the U.S. men might be consistently in the top 10. Maybe even the top five. And the U.S. women will stay there.

Make it into the top five, and the U.S. men's chances of winning any given World Cup will still be less than 20 percent. But at that point, perhaps we won't say "never."

Maybe we can finally say "maybe."

NOTES

INTRODUCTION

1. David Wangerin, *Soccer in a Football World* (London: When Saturday Comes Books, 2006), 209.

1. WE PLAY TOO MANY OTHER SPORTS

1. "Most Popular Sports," accessed October 29, 2018, http://mostpopular sports.net/.

2. Steven Kutz, "NFL Took in $13 Billion in Revenue Last Season—See How It Stacks Up against Other Pro Sports Leagues," *MarketWatch*, July 1, 2016, https://www.marketwatch.com/story/the-nfl-made-13-billion-last-season-see-how-it-stacks-up-against-other-leagues-2016-07-01.

3. "2018 MLB Attendance & Team Age," Baseball Reference, accessed February 18, 2019, https://www.baseball-reference.com/leagues/MLB/2018-misc.shtml.

4. "Statistical Data" (translated into English), Nippon Professional Baseball, accessed February 18, 2019, http://npb.jp/statistics/2018/attendance.html.

5. "NHL Attendance (1975–76 through 2017–18)," NHL.com, accessed February 18, 2019, https://records.nhl.com/history/attendance.

6. "NBA Breaks All-Time Attendance Record for Fourth Straight Year," NBA.com, April 12, 2018, http://www.nba.com/article/2018/04/12/nba-breaks-attendance-record-fourth-straight-year.

7. Brandon McClung, "NFL Attendance Lowest Since '10 Despite Chargers Rebound," *SportsBusiness Daily*, January 2, 2019, https://www.sportsbusiness

daily.com/Daily/Issues/2019/01/02/Leagues-and-Governing-Bodies/NFL-attendance.aspx.

8. "Premier League 2017/2018 >> Attendance >> Home Matches," world-football.net, accessed February 18, 2019, https://www.worldfootball.net/attendance/eng-premier-league-2017-2018/1/.

9. "2018 MLS Attendance," *Soccer Stadium Digest*, accessed February 18, 2019, https://soccerstadiumdigest.com/2018-mls-attendance/.

10. McClung, "NFL Attendance Lowest Since '10 Despite Chargers Rebound."

11. Elena Holmes, "Bundesliga Remains Most Watched Soccer League in the World," *Sports Pro Media*, June 25, 2018, http://www.sportspromedia.com/news/bundesliga-most-watched-soccer-league-world.

12. "Premier League 2017/2018 >> Attendance >> Home Matches."

13. John Stensholt, "Record Crowds Fuel AFL Clubs," *Australian*, August 28, 2018, https://www.theaustralian.com.au/sport/afl/record-crowds-fuel-afl-clubs/news-story/311e0190fa065a7dbc55c27c78003bcf.

14. "Statistical Data" (translated into English), Nippon Professional Baseball, calculation of total (25,550,719) divided by number of games (858).

15. "2018 MLB Attendance & Team Age."

16. "Average per Game Attendance of the Biggest European Soccer Leagues from 1996/97 to 2017/18 (in 1,000s)," Statista, accessed February 18, 2019, https://www.statista.com/statistics/261213/european-soccer-leagues-average-attendance/.

17. "2018 MLS Attendance & Team Age."

18. "Almost 75m Tickets Sold for UK Sports Events in 2017," Deloitte, December 15, 2017, https://www2.deloitte.com/uk/en/pages/press-releases/articles/almost-75m-tickets-sold-for-uk-sports-events-in-2017.html.

19. Jim Norman, "Football Still Americans' Favorite Sport to Watch," Gallup, January 4, 2018, https://news.gallup.com/poll/224864/football-americans-favorite-sport-watch.aspx.

20. "Q: What Is Your Favorite Sport to Watch?" *Washington Post*, October 20, 2017, https://www.washingtonpost.com/politics/polling/basketball-football-baseball-soccer/2017/10/20/b6643ab4-930b-11e7-8482-8dc9a7af29f9_page.html.

21. Mitch Metcalf, "Skedball: Weekend Sports TV Ratings 10.28.18," ShowBuzzDaily, October 30, 2018, http://www.showbuzzdaily.com/articles/skedball-weekend-sports-tv-ratings-10-28-2018.html.

22. Collin Werner, "Most-Watched Soccer Games on U.S. TV for October 22–28, 2018," World Soccer Talk, November 2, 2018, http://worldsoccertalk.com/2018/11/02/watched-soccer-games-us-tv-october-22-28-2018/.

23. More listings from the *Miami Herald* can be seen at https://www. miamiherald.com/sports/sports-on-the-air/article220690555.html; more listings from the *Washington Post* are available at https://www.washingtonpost.com/ sports/tv-and-radio-listings-october-27/2018/10/27/2c000366-d99c-11e8-a10f-b51546b10756_story.html.

24. Christopher Harris, "Barcelona-Real Madrid Clásico TV Rating Down 35% on beIN SPORTS," World Soccer Talk, November 5, 2018, http:// worldsoccertalk.com/2018/11/05/barcelona-real-madrid-clasico-tv-ratings-down-35-percent-on-bein-sports/.

25. More listings from the *Miami Herald* can be seen at https://www. miamiherald.com/sports/sports-on-the-air/article220732040.html; additional ratings are available from Mitch Metcalf, "UPDATES: SHOWBUZZDAILY's Top 150 Sunday Cable Originals & Network Finals: 10.28.2018," ShowBuzzDaily, October 30, 2018, http://www.showbuzzdaily.com/articles/showbuzzdailys-top-150-sunday-cable-originals-network-finals-10-28-2018.html.

26. Mitch Metcalf, "Skedball: Weekend Sports TV Ratings 7.22-23.2017," ShowBuzzDaily, July 25, 2018, http://www.showbuzzdaily.com/articles/ skedball-weekend-sports-tv-ratings-7-22-23-2017.html; Collin Werner, "Most-Watched Soccer Games on US TV for July 18–23, 2017," World Soccer Talk, July 27, 2017, http://worldsoccertalk.com/2017/07/27/watched-soccer-games-us-tv-july-18-23-2017/.

27. Darren Rovell, "NFL Television Ratings Down 9.7 Percent During 2017 Regular Season," ESPN, January 4, 2018, http://www.espn.com/nfl/story/_/id/ 21960086/nfl-television-ratings-97-percent-2017-regular-season.

28. "NASCAR 2018 TV Ratings," ESPN, November 28, 2018, http://www. espn.com/jayski/pages/story/_/id/22408275/nascar-2018-tv-ratings.

29. Paulsen, "Ratings, MLB Season Wrap, Thursday CFB, NBA," Sports Media Watch, October 6, 2018, https://www.sportsmediawatch.com/2018/10/ fox-mlb-ratings-college-football-nba/.

30. Daniel Holloway, "NBA Regular-Season Ratings Hit 4-Year High," *Variety*, April 13, 2018, https://variety.com/2018/tv/news/nba-ratings -1202752848/.

31. Paulsen, "Ratings, MLB Season Wrap."

32. "Record 39.3 Million Americans Tuned into NBC Sports' Coverage Of 2017–18 Premier League Season on the Networks of NBCUniversal," NBC Sports Group (press release), May 17, 2018, http://nbcsportsgrouppressbox.com/ 2018/05/17/record-39-3-million-americans-tuned-into-nbc-sports-coverage-of-2017-18-premier-league-season-on-the-networks-of-nbcuniversal/.

33. Paulsen, "NHL Regular Season Up on NBC, Down Overall," Sports Media Watch, April 12, 2018, http://www.sportsmediawatch.com/2018/04/nhl-viewership-nbc-nbcsn-regular-season/.

34. Paulsen, "Ratings, MLB Season Wrap."

35. Ibid.

36. "The MLS 2018 TV Thread," last edited November 1, 2018, BigSoccer, http://www.bigsoccer.com/threads/the-2018-mls-tv-thread.2080174/page-37.

37. "The Top Tens of 2017," Broadcasters' Audience Research Board, accessed November 21, 2018, https://www.barb.co.uk/download/?file=/wp-content/uploads/2018/04/Barb-Viewing-Report-2018_pullout_spreads_FINAL_LR.pdf.

38. This statement is based on an analysis, too complicated to reproduce here, of Broadcasters' Audience Research Board data, available at https://www.barb.co.uk/viewing-data/four-screen-dashboard/.

39. Joe Anderton, "Match of the Day Will Remain on BBC One for Another Three Years," Digital Spy, January 30, 2018, http://www.digitalspy.com/tv/news/a848770/match-of-the-day-remain-bbc-one-another-three-years/.

40. Nicholas Earl, "Premier League Broadcasting: What Is the Future of the 3pm Kick-Off and the TV Blackout?" City AM, September 13, 2018, http://www.cityam.com/262876/premier-league-broadcasting-future-3pm-kick-off-and-tv.

41. "Premier League: Third of Fans Say They Watch Illegal Streams of Matches-Survey," BBC, July 4, 2017, https://www.bbc.com/sport/football/40483486.

42. Gary Levin, "2018 in Review: The Year's Most Popular TV Shows According to Nielsen," USA TODAY, December 17, 2018, https://www.usatoday.com/story/life/tv/2018/12/17/2018-review-nielsen-ranks-years-most-popular-tv-shows/2339279002/.

43. R. Thomas Umstead, "Fox Sports Finishes World Cup Coverage on High Note," Multichannel News, July 17, 2018, https://www.multichannel.com/blog/fox-sports-finishes-world-cup-coverage-on-high-note.

44. "World Football Report," Nielsen, November 6, 2018, https://www.nielsen.com/uk/en/insights/reports/2018/world-football-report.html.

45. "Dent McSkimming—1951 Inductee," National Soccer Hall of Fame, accessed November 2, 2018, https://www.nationalsoccerhof.com/builders/dent-mcskimming.html.

46. Franklin Foer, How Soccer Explains the World (New York: HarperCollins, 2004), 245.

47. Ian Tyrrell, "What, Exactly, Is 'American Exceptionalism'?" The Week, Oct. 21, 2016, https://theweek.com/articles/654508/what-exactly-american-exceptionalism.

48. Stefan Szymanski and Andrew Zimbalist, National Pastime: How Americans Play Baseball and the Rest of the World Plays Soccer (Washington, DC: Brookings Institution, 2005), Kindle edition, chapter 3.

49. Simon Kuper, *Soccer against the Enemy* (New York: Nation Books, 1994), 191.

50. Steven Apostolov, "Everywhere and Nowhere: The Forgotten Past and Clouded Future of American Professional Soccer from the Perspective of Massachusetts," *Soccer & Society* 13, no. 4 (2012): 510–35, https://www.academia.edu/892364/Everywhere_and_nowhere_the_forgotten_past_and_clouded_future_of_American_professional_soccer_from_the_perspective_of_Massachusetts.

51. "Boston Bruins Yearly Attendance," HockeyDB.com, accessed Nov. 22, 2018, http://www.hockeydb.com/nhl-attendance/att_graph.php?tmi=4919.

52. Szymanski and Zimbalist, *National Pastime*, chapter 2.

53. Tim Arango, "Myth of Baseball's Creation Endures, with a Prominent Fan," *New York Times*, November 12, 2010, https://www.nytimes.com/2010/11/13/sports/baseball/13doubleday.html.

54. Szymanski and Zimbalist, *National Pastime*, chapter 3.

2. WE WATCH TOO MANY OTHER SOCCER LEAGUES TO FOCUS ON OUR OWN

1. Stefan Szymanski, "MLS TV Ratings a Concern Given They Account for Just 6% of Soccer TV Viewings," World Soccer Talk, April 19, 2018, http://worldsoccertalk.com/2018/04/19/mls-tv-ratings-concern-given-account-just-6-soccer-tv-viewing/.

2. Mike Koeshartanto, "Soccer on U.S. Television in 2017—Year in Review," Gilt Edge Soccer, January 24, 2018, http://www.giltedgesoccer.com/soccer-on-u-s-television-in-2017-year-in-review/.

3. Jonathan Tannenwald, "A Historical Look at MLS Salary Data," *Philadelphia Inquirer,* October 1, 2015, http://www2.philly.com/philly/blogs/thegoalkeeper/A-different-way-of-looking-at-MLS-salary-data.html.

4. "Salary Guide," MLS Players Association, updated September 15, 2018, accessed January 17, 2019, http://mlsplayers.org/resources/salary-guide. Previous years are archived, so the 2018 figures should remain available from that page.

5. Boys Development Academy, FC Dallas, accessed January 17, 2019, https://www.fcdallas.com/youth/academy.

6. Paul Kennedy, "Americans Comprised Less Than One-Third of Starting Field Players in MLS's Week 8," *Soccer America*, April 24, 2018, https://www.socceramerica.com/publications/article/77650/americans-comprised-less-than-one-third-of-startin.html.

7. Yes, a reporter asked Schweinsteiger if his arrival would help Chicago win the World Cup. See the video "Bastian Schweinsteiger Left Confused after Being Asked if Chicago Fire Can Win the World Cup—Video," *Guardian* (citing MLS), March 29, 2017, https://www.theguardian.com/football/video/2017/mar/30/confusion-reigns-as-bastian-schweinsteiger-asked-if-chicago-fire-can-win-world-cup-video.

8. Steven Kutz, "NFL Took in $13 Billion in Revenue Last Season—See How It Stacks Up against Other Pro Sports Leagues," *MarketWatch*, July 1, 2016, https://www.marketwatch.com/story/the-nfl-made-13-billion-last-season-see-how-it-stacks-up-against-other-leagues-2016-07-01.

9. I downloaded the CSV file available at "Global Club Soccer Rankings," FiveThirtyEight, accessed November 27, 2018, https://projects.fivethirtyeight.com/global-club-soccer-rankings/.

10. Gregor Aisch, Kevin Quealy, and Rory Smith, "Where Athletes in the Premier League, the N.B.A. and Other Sports Leagues Come From, in 15 Charts," *New York Times,* December 29, 2017, https://www.nytimes.com/interactive/2017/12/29/upshot/internationalization-of-pro-sports-leagues-premier-league.html.

11. Another study showed that foreign players account for 61.2 percent of playing time in the Premier League. See PA Sport, "Premier League Third-Most Reliant on Foreign Players in All of Europe—Study," ESPN, October 9, 2017, http://www.espn.com/soccer/english-premier-league/story/3224746/premier-league-third-most-reliant-on-foreign-players-in-europe-study.

12. Peter Welpton, "The Business of FC Dallas Takes Losses Off the Field," *Dallas Morning News*, August 30, 2016, https://sportsday.dallasnews.com/soccer/soccer/2016/08/30/business-fc-dallas-takes-couple-losses-field.

13. J. R. Eskilson, "Pro Prospects: Eight-Year-Old Heads Abroad," Top Drawer Soccer, December 19, 2012, https://www.topdrawersoccer.com/club-soccer-articles/pro-prospects:-eight-year-old-heads-abroad_aid28264.

14. Feel free to Google the Bosman case or read a lengthy legal analysis: Christina Lembo, "FIFA Transfer Regulations and UEFA Player Eligibility Rules: Major Changes in European Football and the Negative Effect on Minors," *Emory International Law Review* 25, no. 1 (2011), http://law.emory.edu/eilr/content/volume-25/issue-1/comments/fifa-transfer-regulations-uefa-eligibility-rules-european-football-minors.html.

15. "The Squads in Stats," FIFA, June 5, 2018, https://www.fifa.com/worldcup/news/the-squads-in-stats.

16. "The Economic Impact of the Premier League," Ernst and Young, accessed November 28, 2018, https://www.ey.com/Publication/vwLUAssets/EY_-_The_economic_impact_of_the_Premier_League/%24FILE/EY-The-economic-impact-of-the-Premier-League.pdf.

17. "How Clubs' 2018/19 UEFA Champions League Revenue Will Be Shared," UEFA, June 5, 2018, https://www.uefa.com/uefachampionsleague/news/newsid=2562033.html.

18. Beau Dure, "Messi, Lahm and . . . Sidwell? How Much Would Pelé's New York Cosmos Cost Today?" *Guardian*, November 28, 2016, https://www.theguardian.com/football/2016/nov/28/pele-new-york-cosmos-1970s-equivalent.

3. WE'RE TOO INSECURE
IN OUR IDENTITIES

1. Ted Berg, "U.S. Soccer Player Rogers Retires, Comes Out in Blog Post," *USA TODAY*, February 15, 2013, https://www.usatoday.com/story/gameon/2013/02/15/robbie-rogers-retires-comes-out/1923165/.

2. John Branch, "Note the Moment, Note the Man," *New York Times*, May 27, 2013, https://www.nytimes.com/2013/05/28/sports/after-robbie-rogerss-debut-whats-next.html; see also a video of Rogers's Galaxy debut at https://www.youtube.com/watch?v=Jau29R53hig.

3. Gary Kleiban, Twitter post, November 21, 2014, 10:13 a.m. ET, https://twitter.com/3four3/status/535813197253455873.

4. David Rudin, "Why the #ProRelForUSA Movement is So Utterly Ineffective," *Paste*, March 16, 2017, https://www.pastemagazine.com/articles/2017/03/why-the-prorelforusa-movement-is-so-utterly-ineffe.html.

5. Alan Siegel, "'Open Wide for Some Soccer!': The Simpsons' Brilliant Parody of the Beautiful Game," *Slate*, June 2, 2014, https://slate.com/culture/2014/06/simpsons-soccer-parody-the-episode-the-cartridge-family-is-historys-best-soccer-satire.html.

6. Benjamin James Dettmar, "'Fast-Kicking, Low-Scoring and Ties': How Popular Culture Can Help the Global Game Become America's Game," in *Soccer Culture in America: Essays on the World's Sport in Red, White and Blue*, edited by Yuya Kiuchi (Jefferson, NC: McFarland, 2014), 96.

7. Drew Magary, "Who Are the Bitchiest, Most Defensive Fans in America?" *Deadspin,* March 19, 2014, https://deadspin.com/who-are-the-bitchiest-most-defensive-fans-in-america-1542968511.

8. Ibid.

9. Franklin Foer, *How Soccer Explains the World* (New York: HarperCollins, 2004), 239.

10. Ibid., 243.

11. Alexi Lalas, personal email to author, November 30, 2017.

12. David Keyes, "Making the Mainstream: The Domestication of American Soccer," in *Soccer Culture in America: Essays on the World's Sport in Red, White and Blue*, ed. Yuya Kiuchi (Jefferson, NC: McFarland, 2014), 21.

13. Foer, *How Soccer Explains the World*, 237.

14. Mike Woitalla, "Earnie Stewart to Supervise U.S. Soccer's Style of Play Vision," *Soccer America*, June 6, 2018, https://www.socceramerica.com/publications/article/78239/earnie-stewart-to-supervise-us-soccers-style-of.html.

15. Mike Woitalla, "Tony Meola on the USA Style of Play Quest, Youth National Team Success, and Young Americans Going Abroad," *Soccer America*, October 3, 2018, https://www.socceramerica.com/publications/article/79828/tony-meola-on-the-usa-style-of-play-quest-youth-n.html.

16. Beau Dure, "For U.S. Soccer, It's a Matter of Style," ESPN, January 27, 2011, http://www.espn.com/sports/soccer/news/_/id/6061681/us-soccer-matter-style.

17. Jonathan Clegg, "The Problem with American Soccer Fans," *Wall Street Journal*, June 6, 2014, https://www.wsj.com/articles/why-i-hate-american-soccer-fans-1402012291.

4. WE CAN'T AGREE ON ANYTHING

1. Sam Roberts, "Listening to (and Saving) the World's Languages," *New York Times*, April 29, 2010, https://www.nytimes.com/2010/04/29/nyregion/29lost.html.

2. Parker Cleveland, "Pundits Should Stop Trying to Blame 'Diversity' for USMNT Failures," SB Nation, November 20, 2017, https://www.starsandstripesfc.com/2017/11/20/16660526/pundits-stop-blaming-diversity-usmnt-failures.

3. Les Carpenter, "Common Goal: How Soccer Helped Heal the Area at the Centre of the LA Riots," *Guardian*, June 6, 2018, https://www.theguardian.com/cities/2018/jun/06/common-goal-how-soccer-healed-a-gang-and-riot-hit-la-community.

4. Andrew Keh, "Jesse Marsch's Study Abroad Program," *New York Times*, January 18, 2019, https://www.nytimes.com/2019/01/18/sports/jesse-marsch-rb-leipzig.html.

5. Stefan Szymanski and Andrew Zimbalist, *National Pastime: How Americans Play Baseball and the Rest of the World Plays Soccer* (Washington, DC: Brookings Institution, 2005), Kindle edition, chapter 2.

6. Andrew Crossley, *Fun while It Lasted* (blog), accessed January 19, 2019, http://funwhileitlasted.net.

7. Steve Holroyd, "Pro/Rel and the 'Fricker Plan': Killed or Never Was?" *Philly Soccer Page*, September 10, 2015, http://www.phillysoccerpage.net/2015/09/10/prorel-and-the-fricker-plan-killed-or-never-was/.

8. Raphael Honigstein, "How German Football Rose from the Ashes of 1998 to Become the Best in the World," *Guardian,* September 5, 2015, https://www.theguardian.com/football/2015/sep/05/germany-football-team-youth-development-to-world-cup-win-2014.

9. A century of professional soccer (1909–2010) has been compiled by David Litterer, American Soccer History Archives, accessed January 18, 2019, http://homepages.sover.net/~spectrum/.

10. The early history is covered by Mike Woitalla, "U.S. Club Soccer Has Changed Radically in 10 Years," *Soccer America*, May 12, 2011, https://www.socceramerica.com/publications/article/42202/us-club-soccer-has-changed-radically-in-10-years.html.

11. "History | US Youth Soccer National Championships," U.S. Youth Soccer, accessed January 18, 2019, http://championships.usyouthsoccer.org/nationals/History/.

12. "League History," Virginia Premier League, accessed January 18, 2019, https://www.vapremierleague.com/page/show/2802833-league-history.

5. WE CAN'T STOP SUING EACH OTHER

1. Teri Thompson, Mary Papenfuss, Christian Red, and Nathaniel Vinton, "Soccer Rat! The Inside Story of How Chuck Blazer, Ex-U.S. Soccer Executive and FIFA Bigwig, Became a Confidential Informant for the FBI," *Daily News* (New York), November 1, 2014, https://www.nydailynews.com/sports/soccer/soccer-rat-ex-u-s-soccer-exec-chuck-blazer-fbi-informant-article-1.1995761.

2. Matt Apuzzo, Stephanie Clifford, and William K. Rashbaum, "FIFA Officials Arrested on Corruption Charges; Blatter Isn't Among Them," *New York Times,* May 26, 2015, https://www.nytimes.com/2015/05/27/sports/soccer/fifa-officials-face-corruption-charges-in-us.html?smid=tw-nytimes.

3. "FIFA Frantically Announces 2015 Summer World Cup in United States," *Onion*, May 27, 2015, https://sports.theonion.com/fifa-frantically-announces-2015-summer-world-cup-in-uni-1819577826.

4. "Webb Parties as Watson Starts 7-Year Stretch," Cayman News Service, February 8, 2016, https://caymannewsservice.com/2016/02/webb-parties-as-watson-starts-7-year-stretch/.

5. Loretta Lynch, interview by Stephen Colbert, *The Late Show with Stephen Colbert*, CBS, March 10, 2016, https://www.youtube.com/watch?v=tOr5TqTSc6A.

6. The facts of the Radovich case, as explained in recent accounts, reveal a few logical flaws. The complaint alleges that "This black-listing effectively prevented his employment in organized professional football in the United States" (as stated in 1957 Supreme Court decision posted by Cornell University's Legal Information Institute at https://www.law.cornell.edu/supremecourt/text/352/445), and Radovich's obituary in the *Los Angeles Times* (Sam Farmer, "Bill Radovich, 87; NFL Star Blacklisted after Court Case," March 12, 2002, http://articles.latimes.com/2002/mar/12/local/me-radovich12) claims that Radovich tried to join the Clippers after the AAFC folded. This is incorrect. The AAFC continued to play through the 1949 season. It seems that the court did not consider the possibility that Radovich simply could have continued his playing career in the AAFC. MLS might consider itself lucky that the court *did* consider such a thing in *Fraser v. Major League Soccer*, though given MLS's arguments, the court really didn't have a choice.

7. Ted Philipakos, *On Level Terms: 10 Legal Battles That Tested and Shaped Soccer in the Modern Era* (Chicago: American Bar Association, 2015), 31.

8. Glenn M. Wong, *Essentials of Sports Law*, 4th ed. (Santa Barbara, CA: Praeger: Imprint of ABC-CLIO, 2010), 515.

9. Wong, *Essentials of Sports Law*, 522.

10. Beau Dure, *Long-Range Goals: The Success Story of Major League Soccer* (Washington, DC: Potomac Books, 2010), 92,

11. *Fraser v. Major League Soccer, LLC*, No. 97-10342-GAO (Massachusetts District Court, 2000), summary judgment issued April 19, 2000.

12. Ridge Mahoney, "MLS Goes to Federal Court," *Soccer America*, November 14, 2000, https://www.socceramerica.com/publications/article/13425/mls-goes-to-federal-court.html. This page doesn't credit Mahoney, but the article was also published at the now-defunct CNNSI under Mahoney's byline.

13. Paul Gardner, "Enough Already with the Court Cases," *Soccer America*, December 25, 2000, https://digital.la84.org/digital/collection/p17103coll2/id/18411/rec/1.

14. *Fraser v. Major League Soccer*, LLC, No. 01-1296 (1st Cir. 2002), accessed January 19, 2019, athttps://caselaw.findlaw.com/us-1st-circuit/1441684.html.

15. Liviu Bird, "U.S. Soccer Presents Youth Clubs with Vital Document; More Meeting Details," *Sports Illustrated*, October 19, 2015, https://www.si.com/planet-futbol/2015/10/19/us-soccer-ussf-youth-clubs-solidarity-compensation-fifa-transfers.

16. Christian Hambleton (a former high school soccer coach) and Michael K. Wheeler, "Guest Post: Are U.S. Youth Clubs Leaving Money on the Table?"

JETLaw, June 20, 2014, http://www.jetlaw.org/2014/06/20/guest-post-are-u-s-youth-clubs-leaving-money-on-the-table/.

17. Miki Turner, "What Exactly Is Preventing US Soccer and MLS from Participating in the FIFA Solidarity/Training Compensation System?" SocceRESQ, July 7, 2018, https://socceresq.com/2018/07/07/what-exactly-is-preventing-us-soccer-and-mls-from-participating-in-the-fifa-solidarity-training-compensation-system/.

18. Terence D. Brennan, "Would Enforcing Training Compensation and Solidarity Really Violate US Law?" *Medium*, February 3, 2018, https://medium.com/@terryblaw/would-enforcing-training-compensation-and-solidarity-really-violate-us-law-2d9c37a48533.

19. Kevin Draper, "Moving from Buyer to Seller, Major League Soccer Tests a New Revenue Stream," *New York Times*, August 1, 2018, https://www.nytimes.com/2018/08/01/sports/soccer/major-league-soccer-alphonso-davies.html.

20. Liviu Bird, "U.S. Soccer Answers to Senate over Youth Club Compensation Dispute," *Sports Illustrated*, September 10, 2015, https://www.si.com/planet-futbol/2015/09/10/us-soccer-senate-youth-club-compensation-solidarity. A full transcript of U.S. Soccer's answers was posted at https://cdn-s3.si.com/s3fs-public/download/cantwell-us-soccer.pdf.

21. Jeff Carlisle, "Tottenham Pushing Back on Solidarity Payment Claim for DeAndre Yedlin," ESPN, December 9, 2018, http://www.espn.com/soccer/tottenham-hotspur/story/3723535/tottenham-pushing-back-on-solidarity-payment-claim-for-deandre-yedlin.

22. Jorge Arangure Jr., "U.S. Youth Club Petitions FIFA for Right to Collect Fees on DeAndre Yedlin," *Vice*, June 29, 2015, https://sports.vice.com/en_us/article/qkqyym/us-youth-club-petitions-fifa-for-right-to-collect-fees-on-deandre-yedlin.

23. Mike Woitalla, "MLS Players and Youth Clubs in War of Words over Lawsuit," *Soccer America*, July 1, 2016, https://www.socceramerica.com/publications/article/69425/mls-players-and-youth-clubs-in-war-of-words-over-l.html.

24. See https://twitter.com/AlexiLalas/status/1081184624477380611; also confirmed through the author's personal communication with Foose.

25. Stefan Szymanski, "The Economic Arguments Supporting a Competition Law Challenge to the Transfer System," FIFPro, July 2015, https://fifpro.org/attachments/article/6242/Embargoed%20Stefan%20Szymanski%20Transfer%20System%20Analysis.pdf. For a concurrent summary of the report, see "New Study: Abusive Transfer System Is Failing," FIFPro, October 15, 2015, https://fifpro.org/news/szymanski-report-available-now/en/.

26. *United States Soccer Fed'n Inc. v. United States Nat'l Soccer Ass'n*, No. 15-3402 (US Court of Appeals for the Seventh Circuit, 2016), https://law.justia.com/cases/federal/appellate-courts/ca7/15-3402/15-3402-2016-09-22.html.

27. "About the USNSTPA," U.S. National Soccer Team Players Association, accessed January 19, 2019, https://ussoccerplayers.com/about-the-usnstpa.

28. *United States Soccer Federation, Inc. v. United States Women's National Soccer Team Players Association*, No. 1:16-cv-01923 (Northern District of Illinois, Eastern Division, 2016).

29. Julie Foudy, "Why Isn't the USWNT Using Its Fair-Pay Clause?" ESPNW, April 4, 2016, http://www.espn.com/espnw/voices/article/15131346/why-uswnt-using-fair-pay-clause.

30. Cindy Boren, "Spanking, Dehydration among Allegations against Former MLS Coach," *Washington Post*, January 7, 2016, https://www.washingtonpost.com/news/early-lead/wp/2016/01/07/spanking-dehydration-among-allegations-against-former-mls-coach/?utm_term=.7d21cfa7c627.

31. Wong, *Essentials of Sports Law*, 475.

32. "NASL v. NFL case brief," Law School Case Briefs, November 2013, http://www.lawschoolcasebriefs.net/2013/11/nasl-v-nfl-case-brief.html.

33. Philipakos, *On Level Terms*, 60.

34. Many of the court filings in this case are available at https://www.scribd.com/lists/3364972/Borislow-WPS-legal-exhibits.

35. Beau Dure, "Remembering Dan Borislow," SportsMyriad, July 22, 2014, archived athttps://duresport.com/2014/07/22/remembering-dan-borislow/.

36. FIFA Statutes 2018, accessed January 19, 2019, at https://resources.fifa.com/image/upload/the-fifa-statutes-2018.pdf?cloudid=whhncbdzio03cuhmwfxa.

37. "FIFA to Tackle Areas of Concern," FIFA, March 12, 2008, https://www.fifa.com/womensyoutholympic/news/y=2008/m=3/news=fifa-tackle-areas-concern-709098.html.

38. Terence D. Brennan, "Does U.S. Soccer's League Set-up Violate FIFA Rules?" *Medium*, February 9, 2017, https://medium.com/@terryblaw/does-u-s-soccers-league-set-up-violate-fifa-rules-ceec15f54244.

39. Steven A. Bank, "Will U.S. Soccer Be Forced to Adopt Promotion and Relegation?" *Journal of Legal Aspects of Sport* 28 (2018): 3–18, https://doi.org/10.18060/22316.

40. Ed Farnsworth, "That USL/TOA/NASL Thing, Part II," *Philly Soccer Page*, December 17, 2009, http://phillysoccerpage.net/2009/12/17/that-usltoanasl-thing-part-ii/.

41. Neil Morris, "NASL League and Club Officials, Including Aaron Davidson, Shed Revealing Light on D1 Aspirations," WRALSportsFan, September 16, 2015, https://www.wralsportsfan.com/nasl-league-and-club-officials-including-aaron-davidson-shed-revealing-light-on-d1-aspirations/14903504/.

42. Paul Crowder and John Dower (directors), *Once in a Lifetime: The Extraordinary Story of the New York Cosmos* (Miramax Films, 2006).

43. *North American Soccer League v. United States Soccer Federation, Inc.*, No. 1:17-cv-05495 (Eastern District of New York, 2017). The NASL complaint is posted at https://www.scribd.com/document/359361983/Anti-Trust; my summary of various documents, along with news reports and USSF minutes, is posted at https://rantingsoccerdad.com/2017/10/24/timeline-how-did-nasl-dispute-come-to-this/.

44. Dick Shippy, "Marinaro Pleads His Case with Vengeance," *Akron Beacon-Journal*, November 10, 1990.

45. *Rough Riders Soccer LLC v. USISL, Inc.*, No. 2:07-cv-00915, 449, PACER (Eastern District of New York, 2007).

46. Phil Ball, "Dimitri Sparring," *When Saturday Comes*, May 2003, https://www.wsc.co.uk/the-archive/923-Europe/2511-dimitri-sparring.

47. *Piterman v. USISL, Inc.*, No. 8:12-cv-00208, PACER (Middle District of Florida, 2012).

48. Philipakos, *On Level Terms*, 77.

49. *Der Spiegel* staff, "Documents Show Secret Plans for Elite League of Top Clubs," *Der Spiegel*, November 2, 2018, http://www.spiegel.de/international/world/football-documents-show-secret-plans-for-elite-league-of-top-clubs-a-1236447.html. Stillitano also discussed the potential for the Super League a few months earlier on the World Soccer Talk podcast available at https://www.youtube.com/watch?v=cVph6gSXO84.

50. Paul Kennedy, "U.S. Soccer Sued by U.S. Soccer Foundation Regarding 'Hijack' Threat Over Trademarks," *Soccer America*, December 6, 2018, https://www.socceramerica.com/publications/article/80620/us-soccer-sued-by-us-soccer-foundation-regardi.html.

51. Les Carpenter, "Common Goal: How Soccer Helped Heal the Area at the Centre of the LA Riots," *Guardian*, June 6, 2018, https://www.theguardian.com/cities/2018/jun/06/common-goal-how-soccer-healed-a-gang-and-riot-hit-la-community. Disclaimer: I worked with U.S. Soccer Foundation president/CEO Ed Foster-Simeon at *USA TODAY*.

52. *United States Soccer Federation Foundation, Inc. v. United States Soccer Federation, Inc.*, No. 1:18-cv-02856 (D.C. District Court, 2018).

6. WE FELL BEHIND BY 100 YEARS

1. Terry Gilliam and Terry Jones (directors), *Monty Python and the Holy Grail* (EMI Films, 1975).

2. David Wangerin, *Soccer in a Football World* (London: When Saturday Comes Books, 2006), 31.

3. Clemente A. Lisi, *A History of the World Cup: 1930–2014* (Lanham, MD: Rowman & Littlefield, 2015), 17.

4. Roger Allaway, "Were the Oneidas Playing Soccer or Not?" American Soccer History Archives, updated February 14, 2001, http://homepages.sover. net/~spectrum/oneidas.html.

5. David A. Litterer, "The History of Professional Soccer in New England," American Soccer History Archives, updated April 26, 2010, http://homepages. sover.net/~spectrum/NewEngland.html.

6. "The History of the FA," the Football Association, accessed January 19, 2019, http://www.thefa.com/about-football-association/what-we-do/history.

7. Julian Humphrys, "5 Facts about the History of Football," History Extra, July 14, 2018, https://www.historyextra.com/period/victorian/facts-birth-football-history-first-international-match/.

8. "About the Borough of East Newark," Borough of East Newark, accessed January 19, 2019, http://www.boroughofeastnewark.com/History.html.

9. "Canadians the Victors," *New York Times*, November 29, 1885, https:// timesmachine.nytimes.com/timesmachine/1885/11/29/103642445.pdf.

10. "Other Football Games," *New York Times*, November 28, 1886, https:// timesmachine.nytimes.com/timesmachine/1886/11/28/106305049.pdf.

11. "League Players Barred," *New York Times*, September 18, 1894, https:// timesmachine.nytimes.com/timesmachine/1894/09/18/106916004.pdf.

12. Steve Holroyd, "The First Professional Soccer League in the United States: The American League of Professional Football (1894)," American Soccer History Archives, updated September 4, 2000, http://homepages.sover.net/ ~spectrum/alpf.html.

13. Ed Farnsworth, "Philadelphia and the Other First Professional Soccer League in the U.S.," *Philly Soccer Page*, October 23, 2015, http://www. phillysoccerpage.net/2015/10/23/philadelphia-and-the-other-first-professional-soccer-league-in-the-u-s/.

14. "Association Football League," *New York Times*, December 15, 1894, https://timesmachine.nytimes.com/timesmachine/1894/12/15/106917548.pdf.

15. "To Play Association Football," *New York Times*, December 14, 1894, https://timesmachine.nytimes.com/timesmachine/1894/12/14/106917385.pdf.

16. David Litterer, "History of Soccer in Greater Los Angeles," American Soccer History Archives, updated August 12, 2011, http://homepages.sover.net/ ~spectrum/losangeles.html.

17. David Litterer, "History of Soccer in the San Francisco Bay Region," American Soccer History Archives, updated June 9, 2010, http://homepages. sover.net/~spectrum/sanfrancisco.html.

18. "From 1863 to the Present Day," FIFA, accessed January 19, 2019, https://www.fifa.com/about-fifa/who-we-are/the-laws/index.html.

19. David Litterer, "The Year in American Soccer—1909," American Soccer History Archives, updated June 19, 2010, http://homepages.sover.net/~spectrum/year/1909.html. One error on the 1909 page says the second Pilgrims loss was against Haverford, but a newspaper account clearly states a Hibernian win: "Hibernians Stop Winning Streak of the Pilgrims," *Philadelphia Inquirer*, November 5, 1909, accessed at https://www.newspapers.com/image/169039178/?terms=pilgrims.

20. "Corinthians—Taking the Beautiful Game Across the Globe," Corinthian-Casuals Football Club, accessed January 19, 2019, http://www.corinthian-casuals.com/corinthian-tours.html.

21. Katie Zezima, "How Teddy Roosevelt Helped Save Football," *Washington Post*, May 29, 2014, https://www.washingtonpost.com/news/the-fix/wp/2014/05/29/teddy-roosevelt-helped-save-football-with-a-white-house-meeting-in-1905/?utm_term=.d566b1b58c01.

22. "Governing Soccer Body Admits America," *San Francisco Call*, August 16, 1913, https://www.newspapers.com/clip/21608338/usfa_joins_fifa.

23. "History of FIFA—FIFA Takes Shape," FIFA, accessed January 19, 2019, https://www.fifa.com/about-fifa/who-we-are/history/fifa-takes-shape.html.

24. "Soccer Body and Amateur Union Are Now Affiliated," *Pittsburgh Press*, December 1, 1913, accessed at https://www.newspapers.com/clip/21607607/usfa_and_aau_align/.

25. "Greatest Football Crowd Ever, Sees Big Match," *Day* (New London, Connecticut), November 21, 1914, accessed athttps://news.google.com/newspapers?id=SfogAAAAIBAJ&sjid=bXUFAAAAIBAJ&pg=6342%2C2362626.

26. "90-Year Anniversary Articles: Soccer Wire Decades (1920–1929)," U.S. Soccer Federation, February 3, 2003, https://www.ussoccer.com/stories/2014/03/17/11/30/90-year-anniversary-articles-soccer-wire-decades-1920-1929.

27. "Bethlehem Steel F.C. Scandinavian Tour," BethlehemSteelSoccer.org, accessed January 19, 2019, http://bethlehemsteelsoccer.org/scandinavia.html.

28. Anna Doble, "The Secret History of Women's Football," BBC, June 9, 2015, http://www.bbc.co.uk/newsbeat/article/33064421/the-secret-history-of-womens-football.

29. David Ornstein, "Billie's Brethren Bring Back Memories of the White Horse Final," *Guardian*, May 18, 2007, https://www.theguardian.com/football/2007/may/19/newsstory.sport6.

30. "History: 1921–1930," NFL, accessed January 19, 2019, http://www.nfl.com/history/chronology/1921-1930.

31. "46,000 See Hakoah Lose at Soccer, 3–0," *New York Times*, May 2, 1926, https://timesmachine.nytimes.com/timesmachine/1926/05/02/100072960.pdf; Steve Holroyd and David Litterer, "The Year in American Soccer—1926," American Soccer History Archives, updated May 19, 2010, http://homepages. sover.net/~spectrum/year/1926.html.

32. Roger Allaway, "What Was the Soccer War?" Society for American Soccer History, May 11, 2015, http://www.ussoccerhistory.org/what-was-the-soccer-war/.

33. Jonathan Wilson, "The Forgotten Story of . . . Spain 4–3 England," *Guardian,* May 14, 2009, https://www.theguardian.com/sport/blog/2009/may/14/england-first-defeat-continental-spain.

34. "World Football Elo Ratings: Year 1929," EloRatings.net, accessed January 19, 2019, https://www.eloratings.net/1929.

35. "History of FIFA—The First FIFA World Cup™," FIFA, accessed January 19, 2019, https://www.fifa.com/about-fifa/who-we-are/history/first-fifa-world-cup.html.

36. David Litterer, "American Soccer League I (1921–1933)," American Soccer History Archives, updated June 1, 2011, http://homepages.sover.net/~spectrum/asl.html.

37. Wangerin, *Soccer in a Football World*, 51.

38. Neil Morrison, "British 'FA XI' Tours," Rec.Sport.Soccer Statistics Foundation, updated January 4, 2018, http://www.rsssf.com/tablesb/britishfatours.html#1935SCO.

39. "World Football Elo Ratings: United States," EloRatings.net, accessed January 19, 2019, https://www.eloratings.net/United_States.

40. "Archive," Scottish FA, accessed January 19, 2019, https://www.scottishfa.co.uk/scotland/archive/.

41. David Litterer, "National Junior Cups," American Soccer History Archives, updated August 14, 2011, http://homepages.sover.net/~spectrum/juniorcups.html.

42. "90-Year Anniversary Articles: Soccer Wire Decades (1930–1939)," U.S. Soccer Federation, March 5, 2003, https://www.ussoccer.com/stories/2014/03/17/11/18/90-year-anniversary-articles-soccer-wire-decades-1930-39.

43. Paul Brown, "Scotland 3 England 1," *Blizzard*, June 1, 2015, https://www.theblizzard.co.uk/article/scotland-3-england-1.

44. Héctor Villa Martínez and Macario Reyes Padilla, "Mexico—List of Champions," Rec.Sport.Soccer Statistics Foundation, updated January 10, 2019, http://www.rsssf.com/tablesm/mexchamp.html.

45. "IRELAND BEAT U.S.A.: Creditable Display by the Visiting Team," *Belfast News-Letter*, August 12, 1948, accessed at the British Newspaper Archive, https://www.britishnewspaperarchive.co.uk.

46. David Litterer, "The Year in American Soccer—1948," American Soccer History Archives, updated May 30, 2008, http://homepages.sover.net/~spectrum/year/1948.html.

47. James Montague, "Stars of David," *Blizzard*, June 1, 2011, https://www.theblizzard.co.uk/article/stars-david.

48. Steve Holroyd and David Litterer, "The Year in American Soccer—1949," American Soccer History Archives, updated December 3, 2017, http://homepages.sover.net/~spectrum/year/1949.html.

49. Michael Strauss, "English: Irked Over Day's Delay, Down U. S. Soccer All-Stars, 6–3," *New York Times*, June 9, 1953, https://timesmachine.nytimes.com/timesmachine/1953/06/09/93605069.pdf.

50. "History: 1941–1950," NFL, accessed January 19, 2019, http://www.nfl.com/history/chronology/1941-1950.

51. Mike Janela, "World Cup Rewind: Largest Attendance at a Match in the 1950 Brazil Final," Guinness World Records, June 12, 2018, http://www.guinnessworldrecords.com/news/2018/6/world-cup-rewind-world-cup-rewind-largest-attendance-at-a-match-in-the-1950-brazil-final.

52. "History of FIFA—More Associations Follow," FIFA, accessed January 19, 2019, https://www.fifa.com/about-fifa/who-we-are/history/more-associations-follow.html.

53. Jon Carter, "How It Began in Africa," ESPN, January 19, 2012, http://www.espn.com/soccer/columns/story/_/id/1007858/rewind-to-1957:-how-it-began-in-africa.

54. Beau Dure, "The Trailblazing Trophy That Started a Soccer Trend in the U.S.," FourFourTwo, July 19, 2017, https://www.fourfourtwo.com/us/features/american-challenge-cup-soccer-william-cox-poland-trophy-history.

55. Emmet Malone, "Euro Moments: General Franco pulls Spain from 1960 Tournament," *Irish Times*, April 21, 2016, https://www.irishtimes.com/sport/soccer/international/euro-moments-general-franco-pulls-spain-from-1960-tournament-1.2614698.

56. Karel Stokkermans, "Copa Libertadores de América," Rec.Sport.Soccer Statistics Foundation, updated December 13, 2018, http://www.rsssf.com/sacups/copalib.html.

57. Wes Gaffer, "Britons Boot to 10–0 Win," *Daily News* (New York), May 28, 1964, accessed at https://www.newspapers.com/clip/21850496/daily_news/. (No, England is not "Britons," given the existence of separate national teams for Scotland, Wales, and Northern Ireland.)

58. Steve Holroyd and David Litterer, "The Year in American Soccer—1962," American Soccer History Archives, updated February 17, 2008, http://homepages.sover.net/~spectrum/year/1962.html.

59. "History," CONCACAF, accessed January 19, 2019, http://www.concacaf.com/en/concacaf/history.

60. "Soccer Guide: The CONCACAF Champions League," U.S. Soccer Players Association, March 11, 2014, https://ussoccerplayers.com/2014/03/soccer-guide-the-concacaf-champions-league.html.

61. William Leggett, "The 28-Million-Dollar Deal," *Sports Illustrated*, February 3, 1964, https://www.si.com/vault/1964/02/03/607926/the-28milliondollar-deal.

62. Steve Holroyd and David Litterer, "The Year in American Soccer—1965," American Soccer History Archives, updated February 17, 2008, http://homepages.sover.net/~spectrum/year/1965.html.

63. Dure, "The Trailblazing Trophy That Started a Soccer Trend."

64. Steve Holroyd, "Another Soccer War?" Society for American Soccer History, September 4, 2015, http://www.ussoccerhistory.org/another-soccer-war/.

65. David Keyes, "Making the Mainstream: The Domestication of American Soccer," in *Soccer Culture in America: Essays on the World's Sport in Red, White and Blue*, edited by Yuya Kiuchi (Jefferson, NC: McFarland, 2014), chapter 1.

66. "Average and Total Attendance at FIFA Football World Cup Games from 1930 to 2018," Statista, accessed January 19, 2019, https://www.statista.com/statistics/264441/number-of-spectators-at-football-world-cups-since-1930/.

67. Bohdan Kolinsky, "Youth Soccer Booming," *Hartford Courant*, May 11, 1974, accessed at https://www.newspapers.com/image/236933575/?terms=us%2Byouth%2Bsoccer.

68. "Super Bowl Ratings History (1967–present)," Sports Media Watch, accessed January 19, 2019, http://www.sportsmediawatch.com/super-bowl-ratings-historical-viewership-chart-cbs-nbc-fox-abc/.

69. Kenn Tomasch, "Attendance Project: NASL," *Kenn.com* (blog), accessed January 19, 2019, http://www.kenn.com/the_blog/?page_id=496.

70. Kenn Tomasch, "Attendance Project: MISL I," *Kenn.com*, accessed January 19, 2019, http://www.kenn.com/the_blog/?page_id=4386.

71. Keir Radnedge, "Skulduggery That Led to US Losing 1986 World Cup Finals to Mexico," *World Soccer*, April 19, 2016, https://www.worldsoccer.com/features/skulduggery-that-led-to-us-losing-1986-world-cup-finals-to-mexico-370181.

72. Marc Appleman, "Wichita Midfielder Borja Is Surprising the League," *Los Angeles Times*, January 3, 1986, http://articles.latimes.com/1986-01-03/sports/sp-23968_1_chico-borja.

73. Steven Goff, "U.S. Team Has Shot at Wegerle," *Washington Post*, January 27, 1991, https://www.washingtonpost.com/archive/sports/1991/01/27/us-team-has-shot-at-wegerle/95911083-9c22-42e2-9b0d-e9dd235a5e51/.

74. Mario R. Sarmento, "The NBA on Network Television: A Historical Analysis," master's thesis (University of Florida, 1998), available at http://citeseerx.ist.psu.edu/viewdoc/download?doi=10.1.1.26.1281&rep=rep1&type=pdf.

75. Alex Yannis, "Chico Borja Quitting Cosmos," *New York Times*, October 8, 1984, https://www.nytimes.com/1984/10/08/sports/chico-borja-quitting-cosmos.html.

76. Associated Press, "M.I.S.L. Going on without Cosmos," *New York Times*, February 24, 1985, https://www.nytimes.com/1985/02/24/sports/misl-going-on-without-cosmos.html.

77. Alex Yannis, "Cosmos Abandon Schedule, Plans," *New York Times*, June 22, 1985, https://www.nytimes.com/1985/06/22/sports/cosmos-abandon-schedule-plans.html.

78. Beau Dure, "USMNT Qualifying Failures, Then and Now: How 1985 Compared to 2017," FourFourTwo, https://www.fourfourtwo.com/us/features/usmnt-qualifying-failures-then-and-now-how-1985-compared-2017.

79. Daniel Gross, "The Capitalism of Soccer," *Slate*, June 30, 2004, http://www.slate.com/articles/business/moneybox/2004/06/the_capitalism_of_soccer.html.

80. Alessandrea C. Handley, Cathy J. Handley, Hope E. Handley, Lawrence M. Handley, Lawrence R. Handley, Nathanial S. Handley, "Youth Soccer in the United States," *Gamma Theta Upsilon: The Geographical Bulletin* 36, no. 1 (May 1994), https://gammathetaupsilon.org/the-geographical-bulletin/1990s/volume36-1/article1.pdf.

81. "Participation Statistics," National Federation of State High School Associations, accessed January 19, 2019, http://www.nfhs.org/ParticipationStatics/ParticipationStatics.aspx/.

82. Michael Lewis, "How USA Was Chosen to Host World Cup 94: The Inside Story of a Historic Day," *Guardian*, July 4, 2015, https://www.theguardian.com/football/2015/jul/04/usa-world-cup-94-inside-story.

83. Paul Kennedy, "U.S. Soccer Presidential Race: 1990 Election in Trivia," *Soccer America*, February 4, 2018, https://www.socceramerica.com/publications/article/76657/us-soccer-presidential-race-1990-election-in-tr.html.

84. Sarmento, "The NBA on Network Television."

85. Tim Froh, "Legacy of 1991: How the United States Shocked CONCACAF and Won First-Ever Gold Cup," MLSSoccer.com, July 17, 2015, https://www.mlssoccer.com/post/2015/07/17/legacy-1991-how-united-states-shocked-concacaf-won-first-ever-gold-cup-word.

86. Kenn Tomasch, "Attendance Project: MISL I."

87. Jack Williams, "Three Points for a Goal? League 1 America: the Soccer Revolution That Never Was," *Guardian*, March 2, 2016, https://www.

theguardian.com/football/blog/2016/mar/02/league-1-america-soccer-revolution-never-was.

88. Sources diverge here—Statista says 68,626 ("Average and Total Attendance at FIFA Football World Cup Games from 1930 to 2018," Statista, accessed January 19, 2019, https://www.statista.com/statistics/264441/number-of-spectators-at-football-world-cups-since-1930/) while U.S. Soccer claims 68,991 ("World Cup USA 1994 Was the Most Successful Event in FIFA History," U.S. Soccer Federation, accessed January 19, 2019, https://www.ussoccer.com/about/history/us-soccer-as-host/1994-fifa-world-cup).

89. Alexander Abnos, "Lost in the Moment," *Sports Illustrated,* accessed January 19, 2019, https://www.si.com/longform/soccer-goals/goal5.html.

90. Sarmento, "The NBA on Network Television."

91. "Average Number of Spectators at Games of the FIFA Women's World Championships from 1991 to 2015," Statista, accessed January 19, 2019, https://www.statista.com/statistics/272800/average-number-of-spectatators-at-the-fifa-womens-world-cup/.

92. Kenn Tomasch, "A Brief History of Promotion and Relegation in American Soccer," *Kenn.com* (blog), February 2, 2012, http://www.kenn.com/the_blog/?p=4440.

93. Jonathan Tannenwald, "The Most-Watched Soccer Games in U.S. Television and Online Streaming History," *Philadelphia Inquirer*, June 4, 2015, http://www.philly.com/philly/blogs/thegoalkeeper/most-watched-soccer-games-united-states-world-cup-copa-america.html.

94. Kenn Tomasch, "USSF Professional Standards," *Kenn.com* (blog), accessed February 20, 2019, http://www.kenn.com/the_blog/?page_id=5449.

95. Neil Morris, "NASL League and Club Officials, Including Aaron Davidson, Shed Revealing Light on D1 Aspirations," WRALSportsFan, September 16, 2015, https://www.wralsportsfan.com/nasl-league-and-club-officials-including-aaron-davidson-shed-revealing-light-on-d1-aspirations/14903504/.

96. Jeré Longman and Doreen Carvajal, "FIFA Power Broker Is Out after Years of Whispers," *New York Times*, June 20, 2011, https://www.nytimes.com/2011/06/21/sports/soccer/jack-warner-fifa-and-concacaf-power-broker-resigns.html.

97. Owen Gibson and Paul Lewis, "FIFA Informant Chuck Blazer: I Took Bribes over 1998 and 2010 World Cups," *Guardian*, June 3, 2015, https://www.theguardian.com/football/2015/jun/03/fifa-chuck-blazer-bribes-world-cup.

98. Kurt Badenhausen, "The NFL Signs TV Deals Worth $27 Billion," *Forbes*, December 14, 2011, https://www.forbes.com/sites/kurtbadenhausen/2011/12/14/the-nfl-signs-tv-deals-worth-26-billion/#346c033d22b4.

99. "Statistics," National Federation of State High School Associations.

100. Alex Ben Block, "Major League Baseball's $12.4 Billion Bonanza Is Official," *Hollywood Reporter*, October 2, 2012, https://www.hollywoodreporter.com/news/mlb-fox-turner-deal-375739.

101. Jonathan Tannenwald, "MLS, U.S. Soccer Officially Announce New TV Deal with ESPN, Fox, Univision," *Philadelphia Inquirer*, May 11, 2014, updated January 29, 2015, http://www.philly.com/philly/blogs/thegoalkeeper/Live-MLS-US-Soccer-officially-announce-new-TV-deal-with-ESPN-Fox-Univision.html.

102. Jimmy Traina, "Here's What ESPN Pays for Most of its Sports Rights," *Sports Illustrated*, June 26, 2017, https://www.si.com/extra-mustard/2017/06/26/espn-sports-rights-cost.

103. "Average Per Game Attendance of the Biggest European Soccer Leagues from 1996/97 to 2017/18 (in 1,000s)," Statista, accessed January 19, 2019, https://www.statista.com/statistics/261213/european-soccer-leagues-average-attendance/.

104. Dan Burke, "Top 10 Best Attended Leagues in the World Revealed," Onefootball, October 24, 2017, https://en.onefootball.com/top-10-best-attended-leagues-world-revealed/.

105. "Global Club Soccer Rankings," FiveThirtyEight, accessed January 19, 2019, https://projects.fivethirtyeight.com/global-club-soccer-rankings/. For a deeper analysis of ratings from the summer of 2018, see Beau Dure, "Fun with International Club Rankings," *Ranting Soccer Dad* (blog), July 29, 2018, https://rantingsoccerdad.com/2018/07/29/fun-with-international-club-rankings/.

106. "World Football Elo Ratings: United States," EloRatings.net, accessed January 19, 2019, https://www.eloratings.net/United_States.

7. WE'RE OBSESSED WITH THE QUICK FIX

1. David Hellier and Jonathan Browning, "European Sports Hit by Collapse of Agency Once Worth $1 Billion," *Bloomberg*, October 19, 2018, https://www.bloomberg.com/news/articles/2018-10-19/european-sport-hit-by-collapse-of-agency-once-worth-1-billion.

2. Graham Parker, "Why MLS' $4 billion Headline is about Forcing Uncomfortable Conversations," FourFourTwo, July 26, 2017, https://www.fourfourtwo.com/us/features/riccardo-silva-mls-4-billion-tv-rights-about-forcing-uncomfortable-conversations.

3. Michael Long, "The Long Read: Riccardo Silva's American Soccer Power Play," *Sports Pro Media,* July 25, 2017, http://www.sportspromedia.com/opinion/the-long-read-riccardo-silvas-american-soccer-power-play.

4. Gabriele Marcotti, "Promotion and Relegation Could Unlock U.S. Soccer's Potential—Riccardo Silva," ESPN, October 16, 2017, http://www.espn.

com/soccer/club/united-states/660/blog/post/3228135/promotion-relegation-system-could-unlock-usa-soccer-potential-riccardo-silva.

5. Chris Hummer, "Hummer: U.S. World Cup Miss Makes Best Case Yet for Promotion-Relegation Need in Major League Soccer," *SoccerWire*, October 11, 2017, https://www.soccerwire.com/blog-posts/u-s-world-cup-miss-makes-best-case-yet-for-promotion-relegation-need-in-major-league-soccer/.

6. Ibid.

7. "Ellis Short: Outgoing Sunderland Owner Gives Club 'Clean Sheet'—His Tenure in Numbers," BBC, April 30, 2018, https://www.bbc.com/sport/football/43950121.

8. Bill Shea, "Rochester's Andy Appleby Sells English Soccer Team to Candy Crush Mogul," *Crain's Detroit Business*, September 3, 2015, https://www.crainsdetroit.com/article/20150903/NEWS/150909950/rochesters-andy-appleby-sells-english-soccer-team-to-candy-crush.

9. Brian Kay, "Beyond the Prem: 9 Lesser-Known Clubs with American Owners," FourFourTwo, April 25, 2017, https://www.fourfourtwo.com/us/features/american-owners-world-soccer-clubs-football-beyond-premier-league.

10. David Conn, Randy Lerner Profile, *Guardian*, March 6, 2008, https://www.theguardian.com/football/2008/mar/07/newsstory.astonvilla.

11. Sandy Macaskill, "Aston Villa Still Living the American Dream under Randy Lerner," *Telegraph*, January 20, 2010, https://www.telegraph.co.uk/sport/football/teams/aston-villa/7029753/Aston-Villa-still-living-the-American-dream-under-Randy-Lerner.html.

12. "Aston Villa: Owner Randy Lerner puts club up for sale," BBC, May 12, 2014, https://www.bbc.com/sport/football/27372342.

13. Andrew Raeburn, "Aston Villa Sold: Six Things Randy Lerner Got Right at Villa Park," *Metro,* May 19, 2016, https://metro.co.uk/2016/05/19/aston-villa-sold-six-things-randy-lerner-got-right-at-villa-park-5891144/.

14. Gregg Evans, "Aston Villa: One Year On So Did Randy Lerner Get His Parting Wish?" *Birmingham Mail,* June 14, 2017, https://www.birminghammail.co.uk/sport/football/football-news/aston-villa-one-year-randy-13186368.

15. Mike Ozanian, "Randy Lerner Will Suffer $400 Million Loss with Sale of Aston Villa," *Forbes,* May 18, 2016, https://www.forbes.com/sites/mikeozanian/2016/05/18/randy-lerner-suffers-400-million-loss-with-sale-of-aston-villa/.

16. Joshua Robinson and Jonathan Clegg, "The American Billionaire Who Got Chewed Up by English Soccer," *Wall Street Journal*, November 30, 2018, https://www.wsj.com/articles/the-nfl-owner-who-got-chewed-up-by-english-soccer-1543587247.

17. "Documents Show Secret Plans for Elite League of Top Clubs," *Der Spiegel,* November 2, 2018, http://www.spiegel.de/international/world/football-documents-show-secret-plans-for-elite-league-of-top-clubs-a-1236447.html.

18. Jonathan Clegg and Joshua Robinson, *The Club: How the English Premier League Became the Wildest, Richest, Most Disruptive Force in Sports* (Boston and New York: Houghton Mifflin Harcourt, 2018), 280.

19. Jonathan Clegg and Joshua Robinson, "How a Deluge of Money Nearly Broke the Premier League," *Guardian*, January 17, 2019, https://www.theguardian.com/news/2019/jan/17/how-a-deluge-of-money-nearly-broke-the-premier-league.

20. Jarvis Greer, "Tim Howard Excited to Launch Pro Soccer in Memphis," WMC News, August 29, 2018, http://www.wmcactionnews5.com/story/38982470/tim-howard-excited-to-launch-pro-soccer-in-memphis/.

21. Nipun Chopra, "USL Franchise Fees: Shepard Tone or Sign of Progress?" SocTakes, July 30, 2018, https://www.soctakes.com/2018/07/30/usl-franchise-fees-shepard-tone-or-progress/.

22. Details and additional sources at Beau Dure, "The Myth of Promotion/Relegation and Youth Development (continued)," *Ranting Soccer Dad* (blog), November 9, 2017, https://rantingsoccerdad.com/2017/11/09/the-myth-of-promotion-relegation-and-youth-development-continued/.

23. Raphael Honigstein, "How German Football Rose from the Ashes of 1998 to Become the Best in the World" (excerpt from Honigstein's 2015 book, *Das Reboot: How German Soccer Reinvented Itself and Conquered the World*), *Guardian*, September 5, 2015, https://www.theguardian.com/football/2015/sep/05/germany-football-team-youth-development-to-world-cup-win-2014.

24. Charles Boehm, "Proving Ground: 5 Years In, USL-MLS Partnership Offers Rich Opportunities," MLSSoccer.com, November 13, 2017, https://www.mlssoccer.com/post/2017/11/13/proving-ground-5-years-usl-mls-partnership-offers-rich-opportunities.

25. Frank Dell'Apa and Michael Lewis, "The State of the Game: Former U.S. Internationals and Coaches and Administrators Address the Good, Bad and Ugly of American Men's Soccer," Front Row Soccer, June 12, 2018, https://www.frontrowsoccer.com/2018/06/12/the-state-of-the-game-former-u-s-internationals-and-coaches-and-administrators-address-the-good-bad-and-ugly-of-american-mens-soccer/.

26. Ibid.

27. Download the Deloitte executive summary for "Professional Club Soccer in the USA: An Analysis of Promotion and Relegation" at https://www2.deloitte.com/uk/en/pages/sports-business-group/articles/professional-club-soccer-in-the-usa.html.

28. Ibid.

29. Paul Gardner, "Enough Already with the Court Cases," *Soccer America*, December 25, 2000, accessed at https://digital.la84.org/digital/collection/p17103coll2/id/18411/rec/1.

30. Stefan Szymanski, "So What Is the MLS Business Model?" Soccernomics, April 23, 2015, http://www.soccernomics-agency.com/?p=692. For a rebuttal, see Kim McCauley, "'Soccernomics' Author Says MLS' Collapse Is Imminent. His Argument Is Awful," SB Nation, April 23, 2015, https://www.sbnation.com/soccer/2015/4/23/8482407/soccernomics-mls-collapse-stefan-szymanski.

31. Stefan Szymanski and Andrew Zimbalist, *National Pastime: How Americans Play Baseball and the Rest of the World Plays Soccer* (Washington, DC: Brookings Institution, 2005), Kindle edition, chapter 1.

32. Ibid.

33. Dan Orlowitz, "Aspiring J-League First-Division Clubs Face Licensing Obstacles," *Japan Times*, October 8, 2018, https://www.japantimes.co.jp/sports/2018/10/08/soccer/j-league/aspiring-j-league-first-division-clubs-face-licensing-obstacles/#.XB0aUFxKjIU.

34. Szymanski and Zimbalist, *National Pastime*, chapter 1.

35. Nicholas Murray, "New Brand, New Era as USL's Growth Continues," United Soccer League, December 27, 2018, https://www.uslchampionship.com/news_article/show/980103.

36. Deloitte, "Professional Club Soccer in the USA."

37. Steve Holroyd, "Pro/Rel and the Fricker Plan: Killed or Never Was?" *Philly Soccer Page*, September 10, 2015, http://phillysoccerpage.net/2015/09/10/prorel-and-the-fricker-plan-killed-or-never-was/.

38. Paul Kennedy, "Bondy and the French Grassroots System," *Soccer America*, July 24, 2018, https://www.socceramerica.com/publications/article/78916/bondy-and-the-french-grassroots-system.html.

39. "Club Cashback," Victoria Dock Rangers, accessed December 14, 2018, https://www.clubwebsite.com/victoriadockrangers/Cashback.

8. WE'RE TOO SERIOUS TO SUCCEED AT A SPORT BUILT ON JOY

1. Neil Humphreys, "Football Never Bigger Than Life and Death," FourFourTwo, October 19, 2017, https://www.fourfourtwo.com/my/features/football-never-bigger-life-and-death.

2. Daryl Grove, "30 Great Bill Shankly Quotes Every Liverpool FC Fan Should Read," *Paste*, March 3, 2015, https://www.pastemagazine.com/articles/2015/03/bill-shankly-quotes.html.

3. Cole Moreton, "Seriously, Sport Is Not a Matter of Life and Death," *Telegraph*, December 3, 2013, https://www.telegraph.co.uk/men/thinking-man/10489571/Seriously-sport-is-not-a-matter-of-life-and-death.html.

4. Gary Kleiban, "The American Soccer Culture Problem," *3four3* (blog), September 12, 2016, http://blog.3four3.com/2016/09/12/the-american-soccer-culture-problem/.

5. Ibid.

6. Alexi Lalas, "Seattle Sounders vs. Los Angeles Galaxy," aired September 10, 2017, on Fox Sports 1; excerpt posted on Twitter, September 10, 2017, https://twitter.com/FOXSoccer/status/907082469337317377.

7. Gary Kleiban, Twitter post, September 10, 2017, 10:47 p.m. ET, https://twitter.com/3four3/status/907073164118695936.

8. Mike Woitalla, "Galaxy Coach Brian Kleiban Has the American Messi's Back," *Soccer America*, July 21, 2017, https://www.socceramerica.com/publications/article/74231/galaxy-coach-brian-kleiban-has-the-american-messi.html.

9. Andrei S. Markovits and Adam I. Green, "FIFA, the Video Game: A Major Vehicle for Soccer's Popularization in the United States" (abstract), *Sport in Society* 20, nos. 5–6 (2016): 716–34, accessed at https://www.tandfonline.com/doi/figure/10.1080/17430437.2016.1158473?scroll=top&needAccess=true.

10. Stuart James, "How Germany Went from Bust to Boom on the Talent Production Line," *Guardian*, May 23, 2013, https://www.theguardian.com/football/2013/may/23/germany-bust-boom-talent.

11. Tryggvi Kristjánsson, "The Icelandic Roadmap to Success," *These Football Times*, January 1, 2015, http://thesefootballtimes.co/2015/01/15/the-icelandic-roadmap-to-success/.

12. Lalas, "Seattle Sounders vs. Los Angeles Galaxy."

13. Jon Townsend, "Superman Complex or Savior Syndrome: The Inconvenient Truth of American Soccer," *These Football Times*, June 26, 2016, https://thesefootballtimes.co/2016/06/26/superman-complex-or-savior-syndrome-the-inconvenient-truth-of-american-soccer/.

14. James Young, "Rocky Road to Brazil: Poverty—The Creator of Superstars," *Independent*, May 25, 2014, https://www.independent.co.uk/sport/football/international/rocky-road-to-brazil-poverty-the-creator-of-superstars-9432245.html.

15. Simon Kuper and Stefan Szymanski, *Soccernomics* (New York: Nation Books, 2009), 306.

16. Ibid., 164.

17. James, "How Germany Went from Bust to Boom."

18. "Report on Youth Academies in Europe," European Club Association, August 2012, https://www.ecaeurope.com/media/2730/eca-report-on-youth-academies.pdf.

19. Andrew M. Guest, "Individualism vs. Community: The Globally Strange Relationship Between the U.S. Soccer System and the U.S. School System," in

Soccer Culture in America: Essays on the World's Sport in Red, White and Blue, ed. Yuya Kiuchi (Jefferson, NC: McFarland, 2014), 26.

20. Ibid.

21. Mike Woitalla, "Steve Gans on the Development Academy's Flaws, the Alienating Turf Wars, and What U.S. Soccer Should Do," *Soccer America*, May 8, 2018, https://www.socceramerica.com/publications/article/77821/steve-gans-on-the-development-academys-flaws-the.html.

22. Todd Beane, "Honor the Innate Desire of Children to Learn Through Play," *Soccer America*, December 28, 2017, https://www.socceramerica.com/publications/article/76225/honor-the-innate-desire-of-children-to-learn-throu.html.

23. "Industry Statistics: April 2015 to March 2018," Gambling Commission (UK), November 2018, https://www.gamblingcommission.gov.uk/PDF/survey-data/Gambling-industry-statistics.pdf.

24. "New Research Shows Almost Half of People in Britain Gamble," Gambling Commission (UK), February 28, 2017, https://www.gamblingcommission.gov.uk/news-action-and-statistics/news/2017/New-research-shows-almost-half-of-people-in-Britain-gamble.aspx.

25. Drew DeSilver, "U.S. Students' Academic Achievement Still Lags That of Their Peers in Many Other Countries," Pew Research Center, February 15, 2017, http://www.pewresearch.org/fact-tank/2017/02/15/u-s-students-internationally-math-science/.

9. BUT WILL THE WOMEN KEEP WINNING?

1. "Dominant USA Falls to Sweden 4–3 in Penalty Shootout after 1–1 Draw in 2016 Olympic Quarterfinals," U.S. Soccer Federation, August 12, 2016, https://www.ussoccer.com/stories/2016/08/12/19/37/160812-wnt-falls-to-sweden-4-3-in-penalty-shootout-after-1-1-draw-in-2016-olympic-quarterfinals.

2. "USA Opens 2016 Olympic Games with 2–0 Group G Win against New Zealand," U.S. Soccer Federation, August 3, 2016, https://www.ussoccer.com/stories/2016/08/04/00/21/160803-wnt-160803-wnt-usa-opens-2016-olympic-games-with-2-0-group-g-win-against-new-zealand.

3. Kate Markgraf, video clip, *ESPN FC*, accessed December 16, 2018, http://www.espn.com/video/clip?id=3727794.

4. Jenna Pel, "German Pro League Brings Success," *ESPNW*, June 18, 2011, http://www.espn.com/espnw/news/article/6670374/women-world-cup-german-pro-league-brings-success.

5. Nick Harris, "Oklahoma City Thunder No. 1 Earners in Sport as Gender Gulf Endures," Sporting Intelligence, November 26, 2017, https://www.

sportingintelligence.com/2017/11/26/oklahoma-city-thunder-no1-earners-in-sport-as-gender-gulf-endures-261101/. The full survey can be accessed at https://www.globalsportssalaries.com/GSSS%202017.pdf.

6. "Liga MX Femenil Reveals Impressive Attendance Numbers," CONCA-CAF, November 25, 2017, https://www.concacaf.com/article/liga-mx-femenil-reveals-impressive-attendance-numbers.

7. "Canada 2015 Technical Report Published, All-Star Squad Announced," FIFA, August 17, 2015, https://www.fifa.com/womens-football/news/canada-2015-technical-report-published-all-star-squad-announced-2671299.

8. Rich Laverty, "The 100 Best Female Footballers in the World 2018," *Guardian*, December 7, 2018, https://www.theguardian.com/football/ng-interactive/2018/dec/04/the-100-best-female-footballers-in-the-world-2018.

9. "Senior" does not mean "old." The "senior" team is the full national team, the one that plays in World Cups and the women's Olympic tournament.

10. Neil Paine, "Should the U.S. Be Worried about the Next Generation of Women's Soccer?" FiveThirtyEight, December 7, 2018, https://fivethirtyeight.com/features/should-the-u-s-be-worried-about-the-next-generation-of-womens-soccer/.

11. Mike Woitalla, "Albertin Montoya: 'At the Younger Age Groups, Train Everyone to Be a Midfielder,'" *Soccer America*, December 11, 2018, https://www.socceramerica.com/publications/article/80679/albertin-montoya-at-the-younger-age-groups-trai.html.

12. Anthony DiCicco, Twitter post, April 18, 2018, 9:38 a.m. ET, https://twitter.com/DiCiccoMethod/status/986599783296053248.

13. Julie Foudy, "Q&A with Brandi Chastain about U.S. Soccer's New Girls' Development Academy," ESPNW, August 30, 2017, http://www.espn.com/espnw/sports/article/20509307/qa-brandi-chastain-us-soccer-new-girls-development-academy.

CONCLUSION

1. Gerry Callahan, "Can the Cup—Hub and Soccer Just Don't Mix," *Boston Herald*, March 25, 1992, accessed via Newsbank.com, November 23, 2018.

2. Gerry Callahan, "Callahan: Once U.S. Cup Run Ends, So Does Interest in Soccer," *Boston Herald*, July 1, 2014, http://www.bostonherald.com/sports/columnists/gerry_callahan/2014/06/callahan_once_us_cup_run_ends_so_does_interest_in_soccer.

3. "The Mut and Callahan Show," WEEI (radio), June 13, 2018, https://weei.radio.com/media/audio-channel/kc-gerry-cant-believe-sports-illustrated-put-egyptian-soccer-star-its-cover-kirk.

4. Simon Kuper, *Soccer against the Enemy* (New York: Nation Books, 2006), 204.

BIBLIOGRAPHY

To be kind to every person and every organization listed below—no one has endorsed this book, or the premise of its title. But I couldn't have written this book without them.

BOOKS

The following books either directly or indirectly influenced this book:

Allaway, Roger. *Corner Offices & Corner Kicks*. Haworth, NJ: St. Johann Press, 2009.

Arena, Bruce, and Steve Kettmann. *What's Wrong with Us?: A Coach's Blunt Take on the State of American Soccer after a Lifetime on the Touchline*. New York: HarperCollins, 2018.

Calvin, Michael. *No Hunger in Paradise: The Players. The Journey. The Dream.* London: Century, 2017.

Clegg, Jonathan, and Joshua Robinson. *The Club: How the English Premier League Became the Wildest, Richest, Most Disruptive Business in Sports*. Boston and New York: Houghton Mifflin Harcourt, 2018.

Dure, Beau. *Long-Range Goals: The Success Story of Major League Soccer*. Washington, DC: Potomac Books, 2010.

Foer, Franklin. *How Soccer Explains the World*. New York: HarperCollins, 2004.

Harkes, John, with Denise Kiernan. *Captain for Life and Other Temporary Assignments*. Chelsea, MI: Sleeping Bear Press, 1999.

Honigstein, Raphael. *Das Reboot: How German Soccer Reinvented Itself and Conquered the World*. New York: Nation Books, 2015.

Kiuchi, Yuya, ed. *Soccer Culture in America: Essays on the World's Sport in Red, White and Blue*. Jefferson, NC: McFarland, 2014.

Krishnaiyer, Kartik. *SoccerWarz: Inside America's Soccer Feud between MLS, NASL and USL*. World Soccer Talk, 2016.

Kuper, Simon. *Soccer against the Enemy*. New York: Nation Books, 1994.

Kuper, Simon, and Stefan Szymanski. *Soccernomics*. New York: Nation Books, 2009.

Lisi, Clemente A. *A History of the U.S. Men's National Soccer Team*. Lanham, MD: Rowman & Littlefield, 2017.

Lisi, Clemente A. *A History of the World Cup: 1930–2014*. Lanham, MD: Rowman & Little-field, 2015.
Markovits, Andrei S., and Steven L. Hellerman. *Offside: Soccer and American Exceptionalism*. Princeton, NJ: Princeton University Press, 2001.
Oxenham, Gwendolyn. *Finding the Game: Three Years, Twenty-Five Countries, and the Search for Pickup Soccer*. New York: St. Martin's Press, 2012.
Philipakos, Ted. *On Level Terms: 10 Legal Battles That Tested and Shaped Soccer in the Modern Era*. Chicago: American Bar Association, 2015.
Szymanski, Stefan, and Andrew Zimbalist. *National Pastime: How Americans Play Baseball and the Rest of the World Plays Soccer*. Washington, DC: Brookings Institution, 2005.
Wahl, Grant. *The Beckham Experiment: How the World's Most Famous Athlete Tried to Conquer America*. New York: Crown Books, 2009.
Wangerin, David. *Soccer in a Football World*. London: When Saturday Comes Books, 2006.
Wong, Glenn M. *Essentials of Sports Law*, 4th ed. Santa Barbara, CA: Praeger: Imprint of ABC-CLIO, 2010.

WEBSITES

The following news organizations and independent websites have been essential to this book, providing either historical overviews or the proverbial first draft of history: American Soccer History Archives, *Der Spiegel*, ESPN, ESPNW, FourFourTwo, Rec.Sport.Soccer Statistics Foundation, Society for American Soccer History, *Soccer America*, *Guardian* (UK), *New York Times*, *Philadelphia Inquirer*, and the *Philly Soccer Page*.

The following online sources are also cited at least once: *3four3*, AdAge, *Akron Beacon-Journal*, Baseball Reference, BBC, *Belfast News-Letter*, BethlehemSteelSoccer.org, BigSoccer (information compiled from listed sources), *Birmingham Mail*, the *Blizzard*, *Bloomberg*, *Boston Herald*, Cayman News Service, City AM, Cornell University's Legal Information Institute, *Crain's Detroit Business*, *Daily News* (New York), *Dallas Morning News*, the *Day*, Deadspin, Digital Spy, EloRatings.net, FiveThirtyEight, *Forbes*, Front Row Soccer, *Fun while It Lasted*, Gilt Edge Soccer, Guinness World Records, *Hartford Courant*, History Extra, HockeyDB.com, *Hollywood Reporter*, *Independent* (UK), *Irish Times*, *Japan Times*, *Kenn.com*, Law School Case Briefs, *Los Angeles Times*, *MarketWatch*, *Medium*, *Metro*, *Miami Herald*, MostPopularSports, Multichannel News, Onefootball, the *Onion*, *Paste*, *Pittsburgh Press*, *Ranting Soccer Dad*, *San Francisco Call*, SB Nation, ShowBuzzDaily, *Slate*, SoccerESQ, Soccernomics, *Soccer Stadium Digest*, *SoccerWire*, SocTakes, Sporting Intelligence, *SportsBusiness Daily*, *Sports Illustrated*, Sports Media Watch, *SportsMyriad* (defunct, archived at Duresport.com),

Sports Pro Media, Statista, *Telegraph, These Football Times, The Week*, Top Drawer Soccer, Twitter, *USA TODAY, Variety, Vice, Wall Street Journal, Washington Post*, WEEI (radio), *When Saturday Comes*, Wikipedia (information compiled from listed sources), WMC (TV), worldfootball.net, *World Soccer*, World Soccer Talk, WRALSportsFan.

The following organizations' online content is cited at least once: Borough of East Newark, Broadcasters' Audience Research Board, CONCACAF, Corinthian-Casuals Football Club, Deloitte, Ernst and Young, European Club Association, FC Dallas, FIFA, FIFPro, Football Association (UK), Gallup, Gambling Commission (UK), MLS Players Association, MLS Soccer, National Federation of State High School Associations, National Soccer Hall of Fame, NBA, NBC Sports Group, NFL, NHL, Nielsen, Nippon Professional Baseball, Pew Research Center, Scottish FA, Union of European Football Associations (UEFA), United Soccer League (USL), U.S. National Soccer Team Players Association, U.S. Soccer Federation, U.S. Soccer Players Association, U.S. Youth Soccer, Victoria Dock Rangers, Virginia Premier League.

LAWSUITS

You can't write a book on U.S. soccer without citing various legal actions. Here are the suits cited in this book:

Championsworld LLC. v. United States Soccer Federation, Inc. et al., No. 1:2006cv05724 - Document 184 (Northern District of Illinois, 2010)

Fraser v. Major League Soccer, LLC, No. 97-10342-GAO (Massachusetts District Court, 2000)

Morio v. North American Soccer League, 501 F. Supp. 633 (Southern District of New York, 1980)

North American Soccer League v. National Labor Relations Board, No. 79-2069 (United States Court of Appeals, Fifth Circuit, 1980)

North American Soccer League v. United States Soccer Federation, Inc., No. 1:17-cv-05495 (Eastern District of New York, 2017)

Piterman v. USISL, Inc., No. 8:12-cv-00208, PACER (Middle District of Florida, 2012)

Rough Riders Soccer LLC v. USISL, Inc., No. 2:07-cv-00915 (Eastern District of New York, 2007)

United States Soccer Fed'n Inc. v. United States Nat'l Soccer Ass'n,
    No. 15-3402 (US Court of Appeals for the Seventh Circuit, 2016)
United States Soccer Federation, Inc. v. United States Women's National Soccer Team Players Association, No. 1:16-cv-01923
    (Northern District of Illinois, Eastern Division, 2016)
*United States Soccer Federation Foundation, Inc. v. United States
    Soccer Federation, Inc.,* No. 1:18-cv-02856 (D.C. District Court,
    2018)

JOURNALS AND ACADEMIC SITES

I have cited *Emory International Law Review, Gamma Theta Upsilon: The Geographical Bulletin, JETlaw (Vanderbilt Journal of Entertainment and Technology Law), Journal of Legal Aspects of Sport, Soccer & Society,* and *Sport in Society.*

FILMS AND TV

I've cited an online clip from the show *ESPN FC,* an MLS broadcast from Fox Sports 1, and *The Late Show with Stephen Colbert.* I've also cited the documentary film *Once in a Lifetime: The Extraordinary Story of the New York Cosmos.*

Last, and I'm sure they'd say least, I've cited *Monty Python and the Holy Grail.*

INDEX

ABOUT THE AUTHOR

Beau Dure has written for *USA TODAY*, the *Guardian*, ESPN, *Soccer America*, FourFourTwo, *SoccerWire*, OZY, Fox Soccer, Knight Ridder/ Tribune, the *News & Record* (Greensboro, North Carolina), the *Star-News* (Wilmington, North Carolina), Popdose, the Huffington Post, Bloody Elbow, and most importantly, the *Chronicle* (Duke University, from which he holds a BA in philosophy and music, and an MA in liberal studies). He's the author of three books on soccer: *Long-Range Goals: The Success Story of Major League Soccer* (2010), *Enduring Spirit: Restoring Professional Women's Soccer to Washington* (2013), and *Single-Digit Soccer: Keeping Sanity in the Earliest Ages of the Beautiful Game* (2015). He has a blog and podcast called *Ranting Soccer Dad*, and he once ran a blog titled *SportsMyriad* that is archived, along with clips of his work from all news organizations, at Duresport.com. He has covered four Olympic Games and one Women's World Cup, along with several MLS Cups and UFC events.

He really wants to cover curling.

Dure lives in Vienna, Virginia, with his wife, two kids, a dog, and hundreds of those little artificial-turf pellets that cling to shoes, soccer balls, and anything else that touches a soccer field.